THE MAYORS' COOKBOOK

What's Cooking at City Hall?

The Favorite Recipes of over 300 Mayors Across the U.S.A.

THE MAYORS' COOKBOOK

by the
United States Conference of Mayors

Editor:
Thomas L. McClimon

Associate Editors:
Danielle D. Dietz
Julie Morgan

ACROPOLIS BOOKS LTD.
WASHINGTON, D.C.

ACROPOLIS BOOKS, LTD.
Alphons J. Hackl, Publisher
Colortone Building, 2400 17th St., N.W.
Washington, D.C. 20009

Printed in the United States of America by
COLORTONE PRESS
Creative Graphics, Inc.
Washington, D.C. 20009

Attention: Schools and Corporations
ACROPOLIS books are available at quantity discounts with bulk
purchase for educational, business, or sales promotional use. For
information, please write to:
SPECIAL SALES DEPARTMENT, ACROPOLIS BOOKS LTD.
2400 17th ST., N.W., WASHINGTON, D.C. 20009

**Are there Acropolis Books you want but cannot find in your
local stores?**
You can get any Acropolis book title in print. Simply send title
and retail price, plus $1.00 per copy to cover mailing and handl-
ing costs for each book desired. District of Columbia residents
add applicable sales tax. Enclose check or money order only, no
cash please, to:
ACROPOLIS BOOKS, LTD.
2400 17th ST., N.W.,
WASHINGTON, D.C. 20009.

4

Dedication

To Jeanne-Marie Allison Doane
whose good nature and enthusiasm
will long be remembered
by her colleagues.

CONTENTS

PLAINS 147

(Kansas, Nebraska, North Dakota,
Oklahoma, Texas)

MOUNTAIN 167

(Arizona, Colorado, Idaho, Montana,
Nevada, New Mexico, Utah, Wyoming)

WEST COAST 182

(Alaska, California, Hawaii, Oregon,
Washington)

Foreword

The United States Conference of Mayors, well into its second half century of service to cities, developed *The Mayor's Cookbook* to bring to the nation's attention the favorite dishes of America's leading local elected officials — mayors. The book also provides information, facts and figures on over 300 communities.

The United States Conference of Mayors published this book as part of its Mayors Leadership Institute program, our continuing education program for mayors and their staffs. This book is intended not only to help support this program, but to also help publicize its efforts to assist mayors become better informed and more effective leaders.

We hope that you will enjoy using this book as much as we enjoyed preparing it.

John J. Gunther
Executive Director
United States Conference of Mayors

Acknowledgements

This cookbook would not have been possible without the support and involvement of a number of people, first and foremost the mayors of this country. We want to thank all who contributed for their interest and support. We know that for many it meant taking time out of their often hectic official and personal lives to participate in this project. Our sincere thanks also goes to many mayors' spouses who took the time to rummage through family recipe cards, leaf through well used cookbooks, and, in some circumstances, contrived new recipes especially for this cookbook.

A special thanks is extended to all those key individuals in the mayors' offices who made certain their recipes reached our hands. We very much appreciate their help in compiling and verifying recipe and city information, and generally helping us to meet our production deadlines. Heartfelt thanks also goes out to the staff of the National Center for Municipal Development and all the other city representatives who encouraged their mayors' participation.

Very special acknowledgements are of course due to the United States Conference of Mayors, Mayor Joseph P. Riley, Jr., President, John J. Gunther, Executive Director, and J. Thomas Cochran, Deputy Executive Director, for their support and encouragement in this project. Thanks also goes to all the Conference staff whose input added to our ideas, endured our demands and helped to make the book a success.

Finally, our thanks go to a number of people who helped to make our ideas a reality: Len and Roberta Biegel, Connie McDermott Slater, Celeste and Leonard McClimon, Tom and Cecile Shea, Daniel Malachuk, Jr., all the people at Acropolis Books and above all to our families and friends.

The Editors

United States Conference of Mayors

The United States Conference of Mayors is the official nonpartisan organization of cities with populations of 30,000 or more. There are well over 800 such cities in the country today. Each city is represented in the Conference by its chief elected official, the Mayor.

Established in 1932, the Conference of Mayors principal role is to provide for the development of effective national urban policy, to serve as a legislative action force in federal-city relationships, to ensure that federal policy meets urban needs, and to provide mayors with leadership and management tools of value in their cities.

Collectively, Conference of Mayors members speak with a united voice on matters pertaining to organizational policies and goals. Individually, each mayor contributes to development of national urban policy through service on standing committees and task forces. Current committees are concerned with urban economic policy, community development and housing, human development, transportation, communications, energy, environment, arts, and international trade.

Conference policies are adopted yearly at the Annual Conference held each summer. A midwinter leadership meeting is convened each January so that mayors can be briefed on relevant issues by Senate and House leaders, Cabinet members and other top Administration officials.

The history of the Conference of Mayors is one of legislative accomplishments for the nation's cities. During its earlier years, the Conference worked with Presidents Hoover and Roosevelt to help victims of the Great Depression. During the 1940s and '50s, the organization concentrated on housing, transportation and civil rights protection for all citizens. In the 1960s the Conference contributed directly to several legislative successes for cities among them the Economic Opportunity Act, General Revenue Sharing, and the Community Development Block Grant Program. Recent efforts in the 1980s have included legislation governing surface transportation, employment, communications, and community development.

The growth of federal-state-local relationships over the years has created increasingly complex problems for mayors and their staffs. In response, the Conference has developed a number of programs to provide mayors and their local officials with timely problem-solving tools. These include its Mayors Leadership Institute program, Labor-Management Relations Service, economic development programs, public health activities, city livability awards, and an allied membership program through which private companies can participate in Conference activities.

Mayors Leadership Institute Program

The Mayors Leadership Institute (MLI) program is the only activity of its kind in the country devoted exclusively to the continuing education of today's mayors. In operation for over 10 years, the program has assisted more than 750 mayors and its hands-on publications and meetings are widely utilized by mayors and their staffs.

The cornerstone of mayoral training are the Mayors Leadership Institutes. Held periodically throughout the year, the MLIs provide mayors with important information on municipal issues as economic development, financial management, communications and labor relations. Discussion leaders for each of the MLIs are senior executives from the public and private sectors such as the Department of Housing and Urban Development, Arthur Young and Company, Control Data Corporation, Real Estate Research Corporation and Burson-Marsteller. Special MLIs are held for newly-elected mayors and Executive Staff Institutes provide similar information and instruction for those who assist the mayors.

Other Mayor Leadership Institute activities include *The Mayor's Role,* a handbook for mayors on a wide range of urban subjects and leadership building techniques; Mayors Leadership videotapes, an educational video series for use by mayors and their staffs; and technical assistance activities designed to assist mayors, especially new mayors, in identifying problem areas and developing solutions.

The Mayors Leadership Institute program and its different components, are all designed to help mayors become better informed and more effective leaders; important ingredients to the success of any community.

Introduction

"Mayors don't cook; they make reservations" was a phrase that we heard often in soliciting recipes for this cookbook. This reflects mayors' busy schedules ranging from dealing with a neighborhood's potholes to groundbreakings at downtown development projects to overseeing the management of multimillion dollar municipal corporations. In addition, mayors must take time out of their personal and family lives to attend neighborhoods' associations meetings, officiate at civic ceremonies and listen to residents complaints and suggestions. Hubert Humphrey, who served one term as mayor of Minneapolis once said "It takes a contortionist to be a central city mayor. For one foot dances to the tune of lower taxes with the mayor's leg in the bearpit of inflation; while the other foot walks the tightrope of demands for services. All of this happens with the local newspaper chewing away at his rear end."

No matter what the circumstance or problem, mayors are always extremely proud of their job, its responsibilities, and the community in which they live. Mayors are often the city's chief booster and will do many things to promote their community locally, nationally, and internationally, which brings us to this book, *The Mayors' Cookbook*.

The idea for the cookbook originated from a discussion with mayors about their varying duties and responsibilities, one of which is often to enter or judge local cooking contests. In some instances, not only were mayors asked to enter the contests, but they ended up winning the contests, something mayors as good politicians would prefer not to have happen. Some of the winning recipes can be found in this cookbook, (i.e. Birmingham, Alabama's Mayor Richard Arrington's Snappy Salmon, and Stamford, Connecticut's Mayor Thom Serrani's Clams Casino).

The cookbook idea was first tried out at the Conference of Mayors' Mid-Winter Meeting in January, 1986, where it was met with a great deal of enthusiasm and some skepticism — skepticism that we would be able to get over 300 mayors to submit their favorite recipes to us on a strict schedule. Many of the mayors left the meeting not only pondering ways to deal with their urban problems, but also having to decide what recipe to submit for the cookbook. Some went looking to the community for assistance, such as Mayor Barbara Fass of Stockton, California, who used a local contest to pick the recipes to submit. In Alameda, California, Mayor Anne Diament shared the task of deciding which recipe to submit by making the choice a project for all at city hall.

As the recipes began to filter in, we noticed a regional flavor to them with each being distinctive and reflective of the heterogeneous body of mayors and the diverse communities they represent. We have divided the cookbook into seven sections of the country in order to highlight this regional diversity. We have also attempted to maintain much of the local flavor and colloquialism in each recipe and city description.

The recipes do not attempt to represent the "best" gourmet or winning dishes from a community, but rather mirror the dishes prepared by mayors and their families in their homes. While we did not test every recipe, each was reviewed by our committee; all of whom are experienced cooks.

The idea of incorporating a small paragraph about each city was added to provide you with a little information about the participating cities. The city trivia questions, found scattered throughout the book, are taken from these city descriptions and hopefully will provide some fun as you stand over a hot stove or oven while preparing the recipes.

Unfortunately or fortunately, mayors do change jobs. We have tried our best to reflect the current mayors at the time the book went to print. However, while some mayors may have changed, the book still reflects the regional flavors and contemporary dishes that are being made in kitchens across the country.

Proceeds from the cookbook will be used to help support the Mayors Leadership Institute program, the Conference's program to provide for the continuing education of mayors by bringing to their attention the best and most successful ways to deal with urban problems. Having better informed mayors will help to ensure that our nation's communities remain vibrant places of learning, laboratories for finding solutions to economic and social problems, and exciting places to raise our families and to work.

We hope that you will enjoy not only the cooking and tasting of these recipes, but that you will have some fun in learning about the most exciting and interesting places to live in this country — our nation's cities.

Thomas L. McClimon
Danielle D. Dietz
Julie Morgan

NEW ENGLAND

"Someone's in the kitchen
with Dinah"
Mayor Thom Serrani
Stamford, CT

"Just like Momma
used to make"
Mayor Biagio "Ben" DiLieto
New Haven, CT

"To market, to market..."
Mayor Carmelina Kanzler
New London, CT

"Waiting for the Great Pumpkin"
Mayor Richard Neal
Springfield, MA

STARTERS

Chicken Wings

Mayor Francis X. Flaherty
Warwick, Rhode Island

3 lb. chicken wings
2 tbsp. salad oil
½ cup soy sauce
⅔ cup medium or dry sherry
¼ cup ketchup
2 tbsp. sugar
½ tsp. ground ginger

4-6 servings

In 5 qt. Dutch oven, cook chicken wings over high heat in hot salad oil, stirring constantly, for about 7 minutes. Reduce heat to medium and add soy sauce and remaining ingredients, stirring to blend well. Cover and cook about 25 minutes, stirring occasionally. Uncover and cook 10 minutes longer, stirring frequently, until all liquid is absorbed and chicken wings are tender. Serve warm.

Warwick, Rhode Island, is the state's second largest and fastest-growing city, with over 90,000 residents and an ever-expanding business base.

With 39 miles of attractive shoreline on Narragansett Bay, Warwick offers unique opportunities for seaside recreation, relaxation, and industry. Our shellfishing fleet is among the largest in New England.

Warwick is also a city that celebrates its past, especially its Revolutionary past. Each year, the people of Warwick launch the American Revolution all over again, sinking the British revenue cutter *Gaspee*...just as they did in 1772, well before Bunker Hill.

Clams Casino

Mayor Thom Serrani
Stamford, Connecticut

12 littleneck clams on half shell
2 tbsp. soft butter
5 drops Tabasco sauce
3 scallion stalks (finely minced)
1 tbsp. garlic (finely minced)
1 tbsp. shallots
½ tsp. cayenne pepper
2 tbsp. lemon juice
¼ cup red and green peppers (finely diced)
1 tbsp. Dijon mustard
2 oz. brandy
salt and pepper to taste
4 pieces blanched bacon
½ cup Ritz cracker crumbs
4 oz. melted butter

4 servings

Mix all ingredients except for melted butter, Ritz crackers, bacon, and clams. Place buttered mixture on top of clams. Put bacon on top and sprinkle with Ritz crackers and melted butter. Bake at 375⁰ for 8 minutes.

This recipe was awarded Best Regional American Recipe at a March of Dimes benefit. "It's the best clams casino I've ever had in my life," said Craig Claiborne, food editor for The New York Times.

Settled in 1641, **Stamford**, Connecticut, is located on Long Island Sound. Stamford today is a dynamic, diversified community with a population of 103,360. It is a center for major international corporate headquarters and the major retail trade center of Fairchild County, yet it maintains its suburban character, with quiet wooded hills, fine beaches, and marinas on Long Island Sound.

Dill Dip
in Pumpernickel Bread

Mayor Kevin J. Sullivan
Lawrence, Massachusetts

1 large round pumpernickel bread (unsliced)
1 cup sour cream
½ cup mayonnaise
1 tsp. chopped onion
2 tsp. dill weed
2 tsp. parsley
1 tsp. seasoned salt

20 servings

Mix all ingredients (except bread) together and set aside.

Cut center out of the bread, leaving a ½"-1" margin on the sides. Do not cut through to the bottom of the bread. Cut the removed section of bread into cubes, or tear into medium-small pieces. Fill the bread "bowl" with the dip. Arrange bread for dipping around the bowl on a platter.

Dip is best when prepared 12 hours before serving.

Lawrence is an historic city with approximately 60,000 residents. It was once the leading city of textile manufacturing in the world; today these mills are being renovated and used for housing, office, and research and development space. By 1989, Lawrence should be known as a college town rather than a mill town, as Emerson College is building a new campus in the city.

Hot Crabmeat Cocktail Dip

Mayor George A. Varelas
Westfield, Massachusetts

1 7 oz. can crab meat (drained well)
2 3 oz. pkgs. cream cheese with chives
½ cup mayonnaise
dash of tabasco sauce
1 tsp. Worcestershire sauce

10-12 servings

Combine all ingredients, and bake for 20 minutes at 350⁰. Serve warm with fancy dark or light rye rounds or crackers.

Westfield, located in central Massachusetts, has historically been known for the manufacturer of buggy whips. Remnants of the trade are still visible in this historic community, and Columbia bicycles are manufactured here today. The city has a number of historic homes and beautiful parks.

New England Fish Chowder

Mayor James E. Milano
Melrose, Massachusetts

3 lb. fresh haddock fillets (skin removed)
8 medium-sized onions (peeled and left whole)
2 or 3 sticks of butter
3 pts. light cream
½ lb. salt pork
3 or 4 potatoes (small)
Salt and pepper to taste

8-10 servings

Boil onions (pressure cooker speeds cooking) until fairly soft. (Do not break them.) Save some of the water.

continued

Simmer fish and salt pork over low heat in large fry pan 12 to 15 minutes while keeping well buttered. Save this liquid also.

Place fish and salt pork in medium saucepan and add part of cream; cook over very low heat and stir occasionally with wooden spoon. Add onion, salt and pepper to fish.

Boil potatoes separately until almost cooked and add to fish and cream. Add rest of cream, butter drippings from simmered fish, and a small amount of water from the onions. Serve hot.

If this chowder is made a day ahead and then reheated for use the taste is improved a great deal.

Melrose is a city of about 30,000 people in the metropolitan Boston area. Most of our people work either in Boston or in the Rte 128 area (Hi-Tech Industry Location). Melrose was the home of the great Marathoner Runner Clarence DeMar, who won the Boston Marathon more than any other man in history, and was also the home of opera singer Geraldine Ferrar. It has an excellent school system that has attracted many young homeowners.

Salmon With Dill Sauce

Mayor James E. Dyer
Danbury, Connecticut

2½ lb. salmon cleaned
2 tbsp. sugar
1 tbsp. pepper
1 tbsp. vegetable oil
1 large bunch fresh dill
1 tbsp. brandy
DILL SAUCE:
3 tbsp. Dijon mustard
1 tbsp. sugar
2 tbsp. white vinegar
½ cup vegetable oil
½ cup fresh dill, chopped
salt and pepper

6-8 servings

Cut the salmon in half lengthwise. Bone, pat dry and reserve.

In a small bowl, combine sugar and pepper. Rub both sides of the salmon with oil and brandy, then season with half the sugar and pepper mixture.

Spread ⅓ of the dill in a shallow baking dish. Place 1 piece of fish (skin side down) on top. Sprinkle on half the remaining dill. Cover the second piece of fish (skin side up), then sprinkle on the remaining dill. Cover with a double thickness of aluminum foil, place a plate on top and weight. Refrigerate for 2 to 7 days, turning and basting the fish every 12 hours.

Prepare sauce: Combine mustard, sugar, and vinegar in small bowl. Using a wire whisk, beat in the oil, then add the dill, salt, and pepper.

Slice the cured salmon in long, thin strips and serve with the dill sauce, lemon wedges, and black bread or toast.

Danbury, Connecticut, a progressive city in the southwestern part of the state, serves as the regional provider of goods, employment, and services to a population of over 300,000. Known as the "hat capital" of the world early in the twentieth century, Danbury has become a corporate center with a comfortable standard of living for its citizens. Only "75 minutes from Broadway," Danbury is the gateway to New England.

CITY TRIVIA QUESTION #1

This city is home to the United States Naval Academy.

Answer on page 39.

Seafood Dip

Mayor William H. Ryan
Haverhill, Massachusetts

4 8 oz. pkgs. cream cheese
4 tsp. horseradish
1/8 tsp. tabasco
2 cans (4½ oz.) small shrimp
12 oz. frozen langostinos
¼ tsp. garlic salt
8 seafood sticks (chopped)
1 tbsp. cooking sherry
7 tbsp. butter
2 tubes Ritz crackers
salt and pepper

24 servings

Soften cream cheese and add 1/8 tsp. garlic salt. Squeeze juice from the langostinos and use with the juice from 1 can of shrimp. Add sherry, horseradish, and tabasco. (Use beater until soft.) Add shrimp, langostinos, and seafood sticks. Place mixture in a standard size quiche dish and sprinkle paprika on top.

In a separate pan, melt 7 tbsp. of butter. Set aside. Crumble 1½ to 2 tubes of Ritz crackers in a plastic bag. Add 1/8 tsp. of garlic salt, salt and pepper to crackers. Stir this mixture into melted butter. Mixture should be moist enough to spread; if not, add cooking sherry accordingly.

Spread cracker mixture over ingredients already in quiche dish. Bake at 350⁰ for 15 minutes. When using a microwave oven, heat until bottom of dish is hot. Best served with Town House crackers.

A traditional New England dip with a touch of the sea.

Haverhill is a historic, 350 year old city of 50,000 with small town flavor, in northeastern Massachusetts only ten miles from the Atlantic ocean. Birthplace of poet John Greenleaf Whittier and the city where R. H. Macy and Louis B. Mayer got their start, Haverhill is a thriving community in one of nation's fastest growing areas. Known for its growing economy, residential areas, and recreational sites and its closeness to Boston, the seashore, and mountains.

Tiropita

Mayor Albert V. Di Virgilio
Lynn, Massachusetts

4 eggs (well beaten)
1 lb. feta cheese (crumbled)
1 8 oz. container cottage cheese
1 4 oz. cream cheese (softened)
Dash of pepper
Fresh chopped parsley (dry parsley may be used)
1 box filo dough
½ stick melted butter

6-8 servings

Blend eggs, cheese, parsley and pepper in bowl.

Melt butter. Unroll filo dough and butter one sheet at a time. Place 4 or 5 buttered sheets on top of each other, then cut into 4 or 5 long strips. Place 1 tbsp. of cheese mixture on bottom of strip and fold into triangles. Repeat until mixture is gone.

Place triangles on cookie sheet. Brush tops with melted butter. Bake in oven at 350⁰ for about 10-15 minutes or until golden brown. Serve warm.

Triangles can be frozen and baked when needed.

Excellent hors d'oeuvre. Can be made ahead of time and baked when needed.

The city of **Lynn** has a population of about 80,000 and is located 15 minutes from Boston. It was once the shoe capital of the world. Lynn has beautiful beaches and is the birthplace of the jet engine.

MAIN DISHES

Boneless Chicken Cacciatore

Mayor Marilyn Catino Porreca
Medford, Massachusetts

4-6 lb. boneless chicken breasts
¼ cup of oil
4 cloves of garlic (finely diced)
2 28 oz. cans crushed Italian tomatoes
Salt, pepper
½ tsp. basil
4 green peppers (sliced lengthwise)
½ lb. fresh mushrooms
2 lb. spaghetti

6-8 servings

Cut boneless chicken breasts in quarters and cook until slightly brown. Cover bottom of a large pan with oil, add garlic, and simmer until it starts to turn golden; then remove. Add tomatoes and one can water. Add salt and pepper and small amount of basil to taste. Add green peppers and mushrooms. Simmer on low heat and add chicken. Continue cooking until peppers and mushrooms are soft. Serve with hot Italian bread or over spaghetti.

Medford, Massachusetts, was founded in 1630 and incorporated as a city in 1892. Famous for ship-building and Medford rum, the city today is the center of a number of light manufacturing industries.

Boston Baked Beans Burgundy

Mayor Raymond L. Flynn
Boston, Massachusetts

6 large green peppers (chopped)
6 medium onions (sliced)
1 3 oz. can tomato paste
1 tsp. dry mustard
3 tbsp. dark molasses
2 medium size cans of baked beans
1 lb. bacon
1 lb. sweet Italian sausage
2 cups Burgundy wine

8-10 servings

In a large frying pan, fry bacon until crisp. Remove from pan, blot on paper towels, and break into pieces. Brown sausages on all sides, remove from pan, blot on paper towels, and cut into bite-size pieces. Add onions and peppers and saute for 3 to 5 minutes. Remove from pan and blot on paper towels.

In a large bean pot or Dutch oven, combine bacon, sausage, peppers, onions, tomato paste, dry mustard, molasses, baked beans, and wine.

Cook uncovered at 350⁰ for 1 hour. To reheat, add ½ cup more wine.

Boston is the center of a dynamic urban environment, where the roots of American government, industry, and culture first began to flourish.

Today, our city generates a spirit of energy and optimism. Located here are world renowned academic, financial, and medical institutions. Historic landmarks (i.e. such as where the Boston "Tea Party" was held and is re-enacted every December 16) and architectural wonders grace our neighborhoods, which are as diverse as the people of our city. Boston is also home to the 1986 NBA Champions— the Boston Celtics. Here in Boston, the old and the new exist together in harmony, producing opportunities for growth for the city's people and the millions who visit Boston each year.

Calamari and Peas

Mayor Azelio M. Guerra
West Haven, Connecticut

3 lb. cleaned calamari (cut into ¼" circles)
1 lb. frozen peas
½ cup pure olive oil
1 small onion (diced)
2 cloves garlic (minced)
1 small can Italian tomatoes
1 tsp. black pepper
1 tbsp. salt
½ tsp. red pepper seed

5-6 servings

Saute onion in oil until soft. Add minced garlic and calamari and saute for 20 minutes. Add tomatoes, pepper seed, salt, and pepper. Cook gently for an additional 45-60 minutes. Rinse peas with cold water and add to ingredients 5 minutes before serving.

West Haven, first permanently settled in 1648, has grown from a small collection of fishermen, oystermen, and herder's huts to a full-fledged city of 53,000 residents. Blessed with the longest municipality-owned beach in Connecticut and a quaint green, West Haven is well known for tightly knit neighborhoods where traditional values and hospitality still thrive. West Haven recently celebrated its Silver Anniversary as a city.

Chicken Breasts With Mushrooms

Mayor Richard E. Neal
Springfield, Massachusetts

4 whole boneless, skinless chicken breasts
2 well-beaten eggs
1 cup seasoned bread crumbs (more if needed)
Accent meat tenderizer
6-8 slices meunster cheese
Fresh or canned mushrooms (as many or as few as you prefer)
½ cup chicken broth or 1 bouillon cube
lemon juice (optional)

4 servings

Cut chicken in 1"-2" strips and sprinkle with Accent. Marinate for one hour in well-beaten eggs. Roll in bread crumbs and brown chicken in butter until golden brown.

Place in a 9"x13" pan in one layer, then add a layer of mushrooms and then a layer of cheese. Pour chicken broth over everything. Bake at 350⁰ for 30 minutes, marinating with broth often. Remove from oven and sprinkle with lemon juice.

Springfield, a 350-year-old city, is the financial and cultural center of western Massachusetts. Strategically located on the banks of the Connecticut River, Springfield combines a totally revitalized downtown business district with strong neighborhoods, a park system second to none, and many open spaces. This "City In The Country" launches the NBA and collegiate basketball seasons at its NBA Hall Of Fame Game and NCAA Division I Tip-Off Classic, and is proud to be the birthplace of basketball and home to the National Basketball Hall Of Fame.

Chicken Francaise and Rice Pilaf

Mayor Michael Traficante
Cranston, Rhode Island

2 lb. chicken cutlets
1 stick butter
¼ cup oil
6 cloves garlic
1 cup dry white wine
1-2 tbsp. flour
basil, parsley, salt, and pepper to taste
RICE:
1 cup rice (raw)
1 can mushrooms
3 tbsp. oil
2 cups chicken broth
1 cup Pennsylvania Dutch noodles (raw)

4 servings

Cut up chicken cutlets. In frying pan, add ½ stick of butter, oil, and garlic and cook over medium to medium-low heat until chicken turns white. Add white wine, basil, parsley, salt, and pepper to taste. Cover pan and simmer for ½ hour. Remove garlic. Melt remaining butter, add 1-2 tablespoons flour and add to chicken mixture.

RICE: Cover bottom of pan with oil. Brown 1 cup of Pennsylvania Dutch noodles. Add rice, chicken broth, and mushrooms; stir well and cover. Simmer 30 minutes until liquid is absorbed and rice and noodles are tender.

Serve chicken on the Rice Pilaf.

Cranston, Rhode Island's third largest city, is home to one of Rhode Island's earliest ports, Pawtuxet Village; and is the birthplace of the state's May breakfast tradition, as well as several outstanding Governors.

Eggs McChicopee

Mayor Richard S. Lak
Chicopee, Massachusetts

30 eggs
30 slices American cheese
1 large ring Kielbasa
15 English muffins (toasted)
Barbeque sauce (optional)

15-20 servings

Cover Keilbasa with water and parboil. Baste with barbecue sauce and cover with aluminum foil. Place in preheated 350° oven for 20 minutes.

Slice Kielbasa at a slight angle in ¼-½ inch slices. Fry the eggs. Place one slice of cheese on each egg just before egg is completely cooked and allow cheese to melt on egg. Place two slices of Kielbasa on each muffin half. Top with egg/cheese. Keep warm in chafing dish or sterno.

May be served with horseradish or mustard.

Eggs McChicopee is used as an entree for brunches. Serve with a fruit cup and assorted pastries. Chicopee has a large Polish population and several Kielbasa-producing industries. This combination has been used for political brunches as representative of the city's heritage and industry.

Chicopee, an Indian name believed to mean "Place of the White Birch," is a western Massachusetts community rich in the cultural heritage and ethnicity of its people. Home to those of French, Portuguese, Irish, Greek, and Polish descent, Chicopee hosts a variety of traditional celebrations and festivities. One such event is the

Annual World's Kielbasa Festival, which boasts the "King Kielbasa," a Polish ring sausage with an ever-increasing yearly size — the 1985 weight being 306 pounds.

Election Day Beef Stew

Mayor Francis X. McCauley
Quincy, Massachusetts

1½ lb. stew beef (cut up)
3 qts. water
2 stalks celery (cut up)
3 carrots (cut up)
3 large potatoes (cut up)
1 lb. can tomatoes
3 beef bouillon cubes or packets
¼ cup barley (optional)
2 tbsp. oil
flour to coat
salt and pepper to taste
1 large onion

6 servings

Heat oil in heavy 4 qt. pot, brown cut-up stew meat, which has been coated with flour, add water, tomatoes, cut-up celery, and onion. Bring to a boil and add bouillon. Simmer 1½ hours and add barley (if desired), simmer another ½ hour and add cut-up carrots, ¼ hour more, then add cut-up potatoes. Simmer about 15 minutes more or until carrots and potatoes are tender.

We have been serving this beef stew every election day for the past 22 years. Personally it has been "lucky" for us for 10 out of 12 elections. We double, triple, etc. the recipe as needed. In our mayoral campaigns we serve it at our campaign headquarters on election day to one and all. It can be stretched and stretched, and since our weather on election days is usually cold and/or nasty, it keeps our workers "going"!

Quincy is known as the "City of Presidents." Quincy is the birthplace of two former Presidents of the United States: John Adams, second President and John Quincy Adams, sixth President.

Both former Presidents, along with their wives, are entombed at the First Parish Church on Hancock Street in Quincy. This landmark is one of many of the historic sites included in the Historic Walking Trail in Quincy.

CITY TRIVIA QUESTION #2

Match city slogan with city:

____Airplane Capital of the World	A. Reno, NV
____Salt City	B. Syracuse, NY
____Glass Capital of the World	C. Scottsdale, AZ
____City of Roses	D. Suffolk, VA
____Birthplace of Aviation	E. Dayton, OH
____City of Presidents	F. Elkhart, IN
____Peanut Capital of the World	G. Quincy, MA
____Biggest Little City in the World	H. Toledo, OH
____Circus City	I. Portland, OR
____City with a Heart	J. Sarasota, FL
____The West's Most Western Town	K. Wichita, KS

Answers on pages 152, 52, 111, 196, 107, 21, 100, 168, 61, 108, 174.

Lovable Liver and Onions

Mayor William J. McNamara
New Britain, Connecticut

1 large or 2 medium onions
2 lb. of calves' liver
½ lb. bacon (sliced)
flour

6 servings

Cover bottom of casserole with sliced onions. Dredge 2 lb. calves' liver with flour and place on top of onions. Cover with ½ lb. bacon slices.

Bake at 350⁰ for 1 hour. You can brown bacon under broiler if it doesn't get crisp.

Located midway between New York and Boston, **New Britain** is at the heart of the fast growing central Connecticut region. This small city has a diversity of cultural offerings including the world famous New Britain Museum of American Art. The city also boasts of a symphony orchestra, an opera association, two theaters, Main Street U.S.A. (all-city festival), The New Britain Red Sox (a Double AA minor league baseball team, affiliated with the Boston Red Sox), and celestial exploration by Central Connecticut State University. Truly a city of parks, New Britain devotes more than 13% of its area to 32 municipal parks which offer a unique array of scenic delights and leisure time activities.

Macaroni and Cheese

Mayor Thirman L. Milner, Hartford, Conn.

1 lb. of macaroni
1 lb. longhorn cheese (cut into small pieces)
¼ cup flour
½ stick of butter or margarine
1 cup evaporated milk
½ tsp. prepared mustard
½ tsp. salt
¼ tsp. black pepper
1-1½ cups warm water
1 cup cracker or potato chip crumbs

12 servings

Boil macaroni until done, but firm; drain and rinse with cold water. Melt butter/margarine in saucepan on low heat; stir in flour until smooth. Stir in milk gradually. Add water gradually, stirring constantly until desired thickness of sauce is reached. Gradually add half the cheese; continue to stir until melted. Add salt, pepper, and mustard.

Place half the macaroni in baking dish, cover with half the sauce, sprinkle with half the remaining cheese. Add remaining macaroni and sauce, sprinkle with remaining cheese. Sprinkle entire top with cracker or potato chip crumbs Bake in 350⁰ oven for 50 minutes.

Hartford, Connecticut's capital city, is the insurance capital of the world. Known as New England's gateway city, it lies halfway between Boston and New York City. Celebrating its 350th birthday, "Jubilee 350" (1636-1986), Hartford manages to preserve old New England traditions and blend them into a modern city of the future. The home of Harriet Beecher Stowe, Mark Twain, and a cross-section of this world's population, the city remains not a melting pot, but a gourmet mixture of ethnic delicacies that takes pride in sharing and maintaining individual cultures and traditions.

Sausage/Potato Casserole

Mayor Robert F. McNulty
East Hartford, Connecticut

1 lb. Italian sausage
4-5 good-sized potatoes (cut into eighths)
2 large onions (cut into eighths)
2 large green peppers (sliced in strips)
2 large cloves of garlic (minced or crushed)
1 16 oz. can sliced stewed tomatoes
1 tsp. oregano
1½ cups tomato sauce (homemade or ragu style)
salt and pepper to taste

4-5 servings

Slice uncooked sausage in half or thirds depending on size. Place sausage pieces on bottom of ungreased 9"x13" pan. Place cut-up potatoes over sausage and cut-up onions and peppers over potatoes. Sprinkle with minced garlic, cover with tomato sauce, and sprinkle with oregano. Pour stewed tomatoes over all of this.

Bake at 350⁰ until potatoes are tender. This takes a good hour and a half and sometimes more depending on the kind of potatoes used. VERY IMPORTANT! Stir this two or three times during cooking period to insure even cooking.

Although this recipe is a simple one, don't be deceived. It is absolutely delicious. Everyone who samples it is overwhelmed with the flavor.

East Hartford is a town of 52,000 located on the Connecticut River. Although it has the reputation of being a blue collar community, it actually is populated by a broad mix of people — from professional to the factory worker. It is a colorful, lively town with a long history of which it is justly proud.

Seafood Casserole

Mayor Carlton M. Viveiros
Fall River, Massachusetts

1½ lb. cut-up shrimp or langostinos
1 box Ritz crackers (crushed)
½ cup celery flakes
3 cans minced clams
¼ lb. butter
milk

6 servings

Drain the juice from the minced clams, and reserve adding enough milk so that there is 1 cup of liquid. Combine all the ingredients, including the liquid, and spread in a casserole dish. Bake 35 to 40 minutes at 325⁰.

Fall River, Massachusetts, first settled by members of the Plymouth Bay Colony in 1659, is a pristine coastal city located a short distance from Providence and Newport, Rhode Island, Boston and Cape Cod. The city was the country's leading textile center at the turn of the century. It's a city of opportunity — for shoppers, who'll find bargains and quality in over 60 factory outlet stores and quaint boutiques and shops; for tourists, who can visit the world-famous Battleship Cove, sample ethnic cuisine, and explore the city's colorful history; and for business and industry, who can tap the city's large, dedicated work force, its affordable and plentiful development space, and its excellent transportation system. In addition to these and other assets, the city is host to a world-class bicycle road race, which attracts competitors from around the globe, and numerous festivals and celebrations.

Shrimp Scampi

Mayor John J. Leone, Jr.
Bristol, Connecticut

1½ lb. uncooked large cocktail shrimp
1 tbsp. flour
2 sticks (½ lb.) lightly salted butter
1 tbsp. lemon juice
2 cloves garlic (crushed)
⅓ cup dry white wine
1 lb. fresh mushrooms, sliced
1 tsp. capers
4 cups cooked white rice
1 lb. fresh or frozen broccoli spears, cooked

4 servings

Split, shell, clean, and towel dry shrimp. Put in plastic baggy and add flour. Coat evenly by slightly shaking bag. In large skillet, over low heat, melt butter, and add lemon juice, garlic, and white wine. Let simmer 2 minutes.

Add coated shrimp—one at a time. Cook over low heat turning every 2 minutes. When shrimp are white and pink in color (about 10 minutes) add mushrooms and capers. Heat an additional 3 minutes, turning constantly.

Layer 4 individual au gratin dishes with cooked broccoli spears, flowerets on the outside, cooked rice, and shrimp, using all skillet juices.

Sandy and I hope you will enjoy this recipe as much as we do. It's fun to prepare, quick, and delicious.

Bristol, a city of 57,000 located in western Connecticut, has just celebrated it bicentennial. It is home to the Hersey/Lake Compounce Amusement Park, the oldest continuously operating amusement park in America. Started back in 1846, the park has the nation's oldest operating carousel and one of the few remaining wooden roller coasters in this country.

The city recently has undertaken a number of new initiatives in business development, education, and resource recovery—all designed to meet future needs as the city enters its next centennial.

Spaghetti Sauce and Meatballs

Mayor Charles C. Baldelli
Woonsocket, Rhode Island

SAUCE:
5 cups canned tomatoes
2 6 oz. cans tomato paste
1 tsp. salt
1 tsp. sugar
¼ tsp. oregano
½ tsp. crushed red pepper
2 tsp. onion powder
2 tbsp. pepper flakes
¼ cup parsley flakes
MEATBALLS:
2 lb. ground beef
1 cup bread crumbs
1 tsp. salt
½ tsp. oregano
¼ tsp. black pepper
1/8 tsp. garlic powder
1 egg (beaten)

8 servings

Combine all meatball ingredients. Shape into balls. Brown in 2 tbsp. melted shortening. Add sauce ingredients; simmer 2 hours; remove cover last hour. Serve with spaghetti and parmesan cheese.

This is one of the easiest spaghetti sauce recipes I have ever tried—and it's fun, too! (And delicious!)

continued

Woonsocket is known as the "Friendly City" and will be celebrating its centennial in 1988. It has the home of Napoleon "Nappy" Lajoie, the holder of the highest batting average (.422) in major league baseball. Cato Hill was the first working class neighborhood designated a historic district in the nation. Having been an old textile milling center, the city now has a diversified economy.

Veal in Lemon Sauce

Mayor James E. Dyer
Danbury, Connecticut

Veal Scallopini (Escalopes), 12 pieces
6 tbsp. butter
salt (to taste)
2 sprigs parsley, (finely chopped)
juice of 1 lemon
2½ tbsp. hot stock (dry white wine)
flour

6 servings

Beat the scallopini until thin and flat. Sprinkle with flour. Heat ⅔ of butter in large pan and brown meat quickly.

Remove meat to heated serving dish to keep hot. Add parsley, lemon juice, remaining butter, and hot stock to the pan. Stir well and as soon as the sauce is bubbling, pour it over the veal. Serve immediately.

Danbury is a progressive city in the southwestern part of the state that is the gateway to New England. Please see page 16 for additional information on Danbury.

White Seafood Sauce and Linguini

Mayor Ronald J. Dorler
Portland, Maine

2 sticks butter (not margarine)
2 large cloves garlic (chopped)
4 tbsp. flour
4 7 oz. cans minced clams (or 1 lb. whole)
1 lb. sea scallops (cut in half)
1 lb. Maine shrimp
1 lb. haddock (cut into large pieces)
1 lb. Maine lobster meat
2 small bottles or cans clam juice
8 tbsp. fresh parsley (chopped) or dried
3 tsp. fresh thyme (chopped) or dried
3 tsp. fresh basil (chopped) or dried
salt and pepper to taste
1 lb. linguini (cooked approximately 14-17 mins.)

4-8 servings

Heat butter and cook garlic about 1 minute. Stir in flour and juice from clams and 2 bottles clam juice. Bring to a full boil, stirring constantly. Add all the seafood, parsley, thyme, basil, and simmer 5 minutes, stirring. Season to taste with salt and pepper. Serve hot over linguini.

Portland, Maine, the beautiful "City By The Sea," and one of the most livable cities in the United States, has been experiencing a dramatic revitalization over the past ten years. What was once a blighted area now comprises rehabilitated historic buildings including the boyhood home of Henry Wadsworth Longfellow, and new construction that complements the older architecture. With this rebirth, Portland's amenities have grown to offer its citizens, young and old, many forms of cultural and recreational activities, from its own Portland Symphony Orchestra to rock concerts at the Cumberland County Civic Center, from its Art Museum to its beautiful ocean views. The City of Portland is truly a renaissance city that is bustling with activity.

Creamy Potato Puff

Mayor Carmelina Como Kanzler
New London, Connecticut

4 cups hot mashed potatoes
8 oz. cream cheese
⅓ cup finely chopped onion
1 tsp. salt
dash of pepper
1 egg, beaten
butter

6-8 servings

Combine softened cream cheese and potatoes and mix until well blended. Add onion, salt, pepper, and egg. Place in 1 qt. casserole. Dot with butter and bake at 350⁰ for 45 minutes.

New London, a major shipbuilding city, is also home to the U.S. Coast Guard Academy.

Grilled Eggplant

Mayor Carmelina Como Kanzler
New London, Connecticut

2 eggplants, 1½ lb. each, approximately 8″ long
⅔ cup olive oil
6 tbsp. lemon juice
2 tsp. lemon rind

6 servings

Wash and cut eggplant into slices one inch thick. Sprinkle the eggplant with salt and place in layers in a colander; place a weight on top and allow eggplant to drain for 2 hours. Wipe off salt and pat dry.

Marinate the eggplant in a mixture of olive oil, lemon juice and lemon rind for ½ hour. Grill the eggplant for about 2 minutes on each side. Serve hot as is or with your favorite sauce.

New London, Connecticut, was founded as Pequot Plantation by John Winthrop, Jr., in 1646. Soon renamed New London, the settlement took advantage of its deep natural harbor to become a major colonial seaport. Shipbuilding started in 1660 and continues to this day. Whaling, which started in 1819, was to become the economic lifeblood of the city for a half-century. By 1846, New London was the second largest whaling port in the world. With the decline of whaling, New Londoners turned to industry in the late 1800s. Silk mills and other industries soon located in the city. Today, New London thrives on the defense industry, light manufacturing, educational institutions such as the U.S. Coast Guard Academy and Connecticut College, and is rapidly becoming a major center for high technology firms.

Spinach Squares

Mayor Barbara B. Weinberg
Manchester, Connecticut

¼ lb. butter
3 eggs
1 cup flour
1 cup milk
1½ tsp. salt
1 tsp. baking powder
1 10 oz. pkg. frozen spinach
1 lb. cheddar cheese

6 servings

Melt butter in 9"x13" pan. Set aside.

Beat eggs, add flour and milk. Mix salt and baking powder. Grate cheddar cheese and add to above mixture. Squeeze excess water from thawed spinach and add to mixture.

Pour into pan (can be stored this way 3-4 days), and bake at 350⁰ for 35 minutes. Cool slightly. Cut into squares.

Manchester is traditionally described as a City of Village Charm. The community is located ten miles east of the City of Hartford and is considered part of the Greater Hartford Region. Much of the town's history centers around Cheney Brothers, which was at one time one of the largest manufacturers of silk in the world.

Today the community has grown to a population of 50,000 and is no longer dependent upon a single industry for employment and tax revenue. Working together, Manchester citizens have been able to retain the vibrant nature of the community and develop it into the focal point for a variety of services for individuals living east of the City of Hartford.

DESSERTS

Apple Cake

Mayor Theodore D. Mann
Newton, Massachusetts

5 or 6 apples (about 3 cups, peeled and sliced)
5 tbsp. sugar
3 cups sifted flour
5 tsp. cinnamon
2 cups sugar
1 tsp. salt
3 tsp. baking powder
4 eggs
1 cup salad oil
¼ cup orange juice
1 tsp. vanilla

Many servings

Combine apples with 5 tbsp. sugar and cinnamon and set aside. Mix flour, 2 cups sugar, baking powder, and salt in bowl. Make a well in the center. Pour in eggs, juice, oil, and vanilla. Beat until blended.

Spoon a third of the batter into a greased 9" or 10" springform pan. Make a layer of half of the apple mixture in the middle of the pan. Spoon another third of the batter, then the remaining apple mixture; top with remaining batter.

Bake in 350⁰ oven for 1¼ hours. Check after 45 minutes—if top is browning too fast, cover with foil.

Always a hit...

Newton, Massachusetts, the "Garden City," and namesake to the Fig Newton cookie, was founded in 1630, and has a well-deserved reputation for combining a cosmopolitan spirit with the special camaraderie of its 14 villages. Education, business, and industry abound in this area rich in history and tradition. The availability of art, music, culture, and easy access to the vacation lands of New England make the city's geography ideal.

CITY TRIVIA QUESTION #3

Match the cities with their automobile headquarters:

____Ford Motor Company   A. Highland Park, MI
____Chrysler Corporation   B. Dearborn, MI
____General Motors   C. Detroit, MI

Answers on pages 122, 111, 109.

Candied Fruit Cake

Mayor Carmelina Como Kanzler
New London, Connecticut

3 8 oz. packages pitted dates
1 lb. candied pineapple
1 lb. whole candied cherries plus some for garnish
2 cups sifted all-purpose flour
2 tsp. double-acting baking powder
½ tsp. salt
4 eggs
1 cup granulated sugar
2 lb. (8 cups) pecan halves, plus some for garnish
white corn syrup

12-16 servings

Use two 9"x5"x3" loaf pans, two 9" springform pans, *or* one of each. Grease pans well with butter or margarine and line bottoms and sides with brown paper cut to fit. Grease paper. Preheat oven to 275⁰.

Cut pitted dates and candied pineapple in coarse pieces. Add 1 lb. whole candied cherries. Sift, then lightly spoon flour into measuring cup and level top with a spatula. Put 2 cups sifted flour into sifter, add baking powder and salt, and sift onto fruit. Mix fruits and dry ingredients well with fingers, separating pieces of fruit so that all are well-coated with dry ingredients.

With electric mixer or rotary beater, beat eggs until frothy. Gradually beat in sugar, add to fruit mixture, and mix well with large spoon. Add pecan halves. Mix with hands until nuts are evenly distributed and coated with batter.

Pack into pans, pressing down with palms of hands. Decorate tops with rows of whole cherries and pecan halves. Let stand at room temperature for 1 hour. Bake springform cakes about 1¼ hours, loaf cakes 1½ hours at 275⁰. (Tops of cakes, where batter is visible should look dry but not brown. If in doubt, leave cakes in oven a few minutes longer, as a little extra baking does no harm.)

When cakes are done, remove from oven and put on cake racks. Let stand about 5 minutes. Peel off paper. Turn top side up, brush with corn syrup.

This is an easy recipe for what I think is the best fruit cake I have ever tasted. I have been using this recipe for 30 years. I have kept this cake in a crock in the back hall for upwards of two years.

New London, a major shipbuilding city, is also home to the U.S. Coast Guard Academy. For additional information on New London, please see page 26.

Carrot Cake

Mayor Joseph L. Santopietro
Waterbury, Connecticut

1¼ cup oil	2 tsp. baking soda
2 cups sugar	2 tsp. cinnamon
1 tsp. vanilla	½ tsp. salt
4 large eggs	3 cups grated carrots
3 cups flour	1 cup raisins
2 tsp. baking powder	½ cup nuts
FROSTING:	
2 cups confectioner's sugar	
3 oz. cream cheese	
2 tbsp. light corn syrup	
1 tsp. vanilla	

8 servings

Coat raisins and nuts with 2 tbsp. of flour. Beat sugar, oil, and vanilla. Add eggs; beat well. Stir in dry ingredients alternately with carrots. Add nuts and raisins. Pour into greased tube pan. Bake at 350⁰ for 1 hour 15 minutes.
FROSTING: Beat cream cheese, corn syrup, and vanilla. Gradually add sugar and beat until smooth.

Waterbury, Connecticut, is a thriving, industrious community located in central Connecticut. Mindful of its past, Waterbury has maintained and renovated many of its architectural treasures while benefiting from new development throughout the city. One of its treasures is Holyland, a collection of garden shedlike shrines and statues of scenes from the Bible. Waterbury retains an old world flavor with a diverse ethnic mix and downtown shops and stores reminiscent of another era.

Chief's Indian Pudding

Mayor Richard S. Lak
Chicopee, Massachusetts

⅓ cup yellow cornmeal
⅓ cup cold water
1 qt. whole milk
½ tsp. salt
½ tsp. cinnamon
¼ tsp. ginger
½ cup molasses (regular)

6 servings

Combine cornmeal and water. Scald milk, then add cornmeal mixture, stirring to prevent lumps. Simmer for 20 minutes or until mixture thickens, stirring frequently. Add salt, spices, and molasses. Pour into 1¼ qt. greased casserole. Bake in "slow" oven at 325⁰ for a minimum of 2 hours. Serve warm with vanilla ice cream.

A New England traditional hot dessert guaranteed to warm you from the inside out, especially on those cold winter days.

Chicopee, Massachusetts, hosts a variety of traditional celebrations and festivals, including the Annual World's Kielbasa Festival. See page 20 for additional information on Chicopee.

Lebanese Baklava

Mayor William A. Collins
Norwalk, Connecticut

½ cup plus 2 tbsp. butter
1½ cups nuts (unsalted pistachio or walnuts), chopped
¼ cup sugar
1 package "filo krousta" leaves
SYRUP:
1 cup sugar
½ cup water
2 tbsp. lemon juice, or to taste
1 tbsp. honey
¼ tsp. Lebanese rose water (optional)

36 servings

Preheat oven to 400°. Mix chopped nuts and sugar. Clarify butter if desired (melt). Butter the bottom of an 11"x17" pan.

Lay in two sheets of dough—fold edges over if dough doesn't fit. Paint sheets in pan with butter applied with a broad, soft basting brush. Lay in two more sheets of dough and brush with butter. Repeat layers of two sheets of dough buttered until half the dough is used up—about 14 or 16 sheets or 7 or 8 pairs. Do not butter the top layer.

Mix nuts and sugar and spread evenly over the dough. Repeat the dough and butter procedures until the rest of the dough is used up. Butter the top layer. Before cooking cut into squares or triangles. Put pan in the oven and immediately turn the heat down to 375°. Bake for 30 minutes or until brown and puffy.

SYRUP: Mix sugar and water in small saucepan while baklava is cooking. Boil for about 15 minutes on medium high heat. Do not overcook, or it will become too thick. Remove syrup from heat. Stir in lemon juice, honey and rose water. Cool syrup and pour over hot baklava.

NOTE: Filo dough may be frozen or refrigerated, but let stand at room temperature for two hours before using regardless. They are very delicate and tear easily. Keep them covered with a towel while you are assembling the baklawa, and don't be alarmed if they tear because it doesn't affect the looks or taste of the baklawa.

This is a quick, easy dessert for 36 which is fairly inexpensive. The lemon juice cuts the sweetness, which most people prefer.

Norwalk is a city of about 80,000 located on the Norwalk River on Long Island Sound. We enjoy great ethnic and economic diversity, beautiful beaches, fine schools, a revitalized historic district, a boom in corporate offices, and we're building a fabulous Maritime Center and Aquarium.

Peanut Butter Candy Cookies

Mayor Joseph R. Paolino, Jr.
Providence, Rhode Island

½ cup packed brown sugar
½ cup peanut butter
¼ cup evaporated milk
2½ cups Rice Krispies or granola

3 dozen cookies

In medium saucepan combine brown sugar, peanut butter, and evaporated milk. Bring to boil, stirring constantly until sugar is dissolved and peanut butter is melted. Remove from heat; stir in cereal or granola.

Drop by teaspoonfuls onto waxed paper.

Providence, the capital of Rhode Island, is celebrating the 350th anniversary of its founding by Roger Williams in 1636. Described by its founder as a "bold and lively experiment," Providence has lived up to that challenge and continues today to be a vibrant and progressive city proud of its rich ethnic, cultural, and architectural history. Providence is a special blend of old New England charm and modern urban life. Indeed, "Providence Harbors the Best."

roll is cooling, make frosting by beating all ingredients until smooth. Unroll, frost, re-roll and refrigerate.

Springfield is 350 years old and is the home of the NBA Basketball Hall of Fame. For additional information on Springfield, please see page 19.

Pumpkin Roll

Mayor Richard E. Neal
Springfield, Massachusetts

3 eggs
1 cup sugar
¾ cup pumpkin (canned)
1 tsp. lemon juice
¾ cup flour
1 tsp. baking powder
2 tsp. sugar
1 tsp. ginger
½ tsp. nutmeg
½ tsp. salt
½ cup crushed walnuts (optional)
FROSTING:
1 cup confectioner's sugar
2 3 oz. pkgs. cream cheese
4 tbsp. butter
½ tsp. vanilla

6 servings

Beat 3 eggs at high speed for 3 minutes. Gradually beat in 1 cup sugar, stir in pumpkin and lemon juice. In another bowl, mix ¾ cup flour, baking powder, 2 tsp. sugar, ginger, nutmeg, and salt. Fold two mixtures together, and spread onto a well- greased and floured cookie sheet. Top with walnuts (optional). Bake at 375⁰ for 15 minutes. Turn onto a towel powdered with confectioner's sugar. While pumpkin sheet is still warm, roll it in the towel, and let cool. While

Sour Cream Coffee Cake with Streusel Topping

Mayor Peter Torigian
Peabody, Massachusetts

½ cup margarine	
1 cup sugar	
2 eggs	
1 tsp. baking powder	
½ tsp. salt	
1 tsp. vanilla	
2 cups flour	
1 tsp. baking soda	
1 cup sour cream	
⅓ cup chopped nuts	
⅓ cup chocolate bits (optional)	
3 tbsp. each sugar and cinnamon combined	
STREUSEL TOPPING:	
5 tbsp. sugar	
2 tbsp. butter	2 tbsp. flour

12 servings

Cream margarine. Gradually add sugar. Add the eggs one at a time. Sift together flour, baking powder, baking soda, and salt. Add dry ingredients alternating with sour cream. Add vanilla. Stir in nuts and chocolate bits.

Preheat oven to 350⁰. Grease and flour 9" tube pan. Pour in half the batter and sprinkle with sugar and cinnamon mixture—half or less if you wish. Pour in remaining batter and sprinkle with sugar and cinnamon mixture. Blend streusel ingredients until crumbly. Sprinkle streusel topping over top of cake and press lightly. Bake 50-55 minutes. Let stand 3-5 minutes and remove. (Recipe may be doubled.)

Peabody is an ethnically diverse community and encourages participation by all groups in civic and social affairs. Downtown's historical architecture houses a variety of specialty retail and service businesses. Adjacent to downtown is the Washington Street historic district, the route local militia marched to the Battle of Lexington in 1776. Its wide streets and brick sidewalks are lined with historic homes rich in architectural detail built by early leather manufacturers. Our historic Peabody Institute Library is well stocked with current and historical literature and proudly displays mementos given by Queen Victoria to Peabody's famous son, George Peabody. The city-owned orchard, Brooksby Farm, provides year-round enjoyment with autumn apple picking, winter cross-country skiing, and summer strawberries.

CITY TRIVIA QUESTION #4

This city is America's choice to host the 1992 Winter Olympic Games.
Answer on page 197.

CITY TRIVIA QUESTION #5

Match the city slogan with the city:

____Shrimp Capital of the World	A. Denver, CO
____Presidential Resort City	B. Culver City, CA
____Buggy Whip Capital of the World	C. Manitowoc, WI
____Heart of Silicon Valley	D. Maui, HI
____Mile High City	E. Long Branch, NJ
____Insurance Capital of the World	F. Biloxi, MS
____Maui No Ka Oi	G. Sunnyvale, CA
____Aluminum Capital of the World	H. Hartford, CT
____Heart of Screenland	I. Danbury, CT
____Hat Capital	J. Fort Lauderdale, FL
____Venice of America	K. Westfield, MA

Answers on pages 68, 55, 15, 201, 170, 22, 202, 131, 189, 16, 78.

Spumoni

Mayor Carmelina Como Kanzler
New London, Connecticut

2 cups milk
¾ cup sugar
5 egg yolks
½ tsp. vanilla
FILLING:
2 cups heavy cream (beaten stiff)
½ cup sugar
16 maraschino cherries (cut into small pieces)
2 tbsp. candied orange peel (cut fine)
16 shelled, blanched almonds (cut into slivers)

10-12 servings

Combine milk, sugar, egg yolks, and vanilla in saucepan and cook over low heat, stirring constantly, until thick. Cool, place in refrigerator tray, and freeze medium hard (about 2 hours). It should be soft enough to spoon out easily.

FILLING: Mix all ingredients together gently, and chill thoroughly in refrigerator. Chill spumoni mold or 1 qt. jelly mold thoroughly. When first mixture is ready, remove from tray and line inside of mold, leaving a hollow center for second mixture. Fill the hollow with second mixture, cover top of mold with waxed paper, and freeze 2 hours. Dip mold briefly in warm water to unmold. Turn over onto serving tray and sprinkle with crushed nuts.

An elegant dessert to serve with an Italian meal.

New London, a major shipbuilding city, is also home to the U.S. Coast Guard Academy. For additional information on New London, please see page 26.

ETC.

Creamy Garlic Salad Dressing

Mayor Azelio M. Guerra
West Haven, Connecticut

1 cup mayonnaise
2 tbsp. minced fresh parsley
1 tbsp. white vinegar
1 tbsp. milk
1 clove minced garlic
½ tsp. sugar
¼ tsp. salt

Makes approximately 1¼ cups

Stir all ingredients together, cover, and chill, Toss with salad greens and serve immediately.

West Haven has grown from a small collection of fishermen, oystermen, and herder's huts to a full-fledged city. For more information on West Haven see page 19.

Whale of an Eggnog

Mayor John K. Bullard
New Bedford, Massachusetts

1 qt. milk
2 cups sugar
1 qt. whipping cream
6 eggs (separated)
Liquor of your preference (brandy, rum, bourbon, or a combination) to taste

Approximately 24 servings

Combine milk and sugar until sugar dissolves. Whip cream and set aside.

Separate eggs. Beat yolks well, using low speed. Liquor may be added here. Add egg yolk mixture to milk and sugar mixture, stirring while adding.

Beat egg whites until they hold peaks. Set aside. Fold whipped cream into mixture. Then gently fold egg whites into mixture. Chill. Serve with grated nutmeg.

New Bedford is famed as ''The Whaling City''—so what more fitting beverage than Mayor John K. Bullard's ''A Whale of an Eggnog.'' Even teetotalers love this thick, creamy eggnog made by the mayor for fund-raising events, parties, holiday gatherings, etc.

New Bedford, a city rich in culture and history, proudly blends its past and present linkage to the sea. The cobblestoned streets in the Historic District, the 19th century architecture, and the museums reflect the prosperous "whaling city" of yesterday. The hustle and bustle of an active commercial fishing fleet, the beaches, quaint shops, and restaurants along the waterfront represent the city today. Visitors and residents enjoy the many ethnic and street festivals and activities throughout the year.

MID-ATLANTIC

The apron says it all!
Mayor Arthur Holland
Trenton, NJ

*"An apple a day keeps the city
council away"*
Mayor Juanita Crabb
Binghamton, NY

*"Pastrami on rye—hold
the mayo(r)"*
Mayor Edward Koch
New York, NY

"Mmm Mmm Goode"
Mayor W. Wilson Goode
Philadelphia, PA

STARTERS

Cheddar Cheese Ball

Mayor Michael P. Lynch
Monroeville, Pennsylvania

2 8 oz. pkgs. cream cheese (softened)
10 oz. crock sharp cheddar spread
1 tsp. onion (minced)
1 tsp. seasoning salt
2 tsp. lemon juice
1 tsp. Worcestershire sauce

12 servings

Combine all ingredients. Form into ball. Roll in chopped nuts. Serve with crackers.

Wine and cheese parties are most successful fund raisers! Casual and fun. Great cheeseball!

Monroeville is a small, modern city of 35,000. It has extensive commercial, professional, and high technology development. A major health care center has attracted a medical economy to our city. Monroeville is located off the Pennsylvania Turnpike about 15 miles east of Pittsburgh.

Italian Smelts

Mayor Dale W. Yoho
New Castle, Pennsylvania

1 lb. smelts (cleaned and fileted if desired)
3 large eggs (beaten)
1 cup flour
¼ cup oil

4-6 servings

Preheat skillet with oil; dip smelts in flour, then in egg. Fry to a golden brown, turning to cook on both sides (about 3 minutes on each side). Remove from pan and drain smelts on paper towel to remove excess oil. Salt to taste. Serve warm with cocktail sauce if desired.

Smelts were first introduced in New Castle by Italian immigrants as part of their Christmas Eve Feast. Now it has become a specialty served in many of our fine Italian restaurants as an appetizer or main course.

New Castle, an industrial city in western Pennsylvania, is the seat of Lawrence County. Natural deposits of coal, limestone, iron ore, and clay, were responsible for New Castle at one time being one of the fastest growing cities in America, thus luring immigrants from many ethnic backgrounds to settle here. This fragrant blending of backgrounds is why we feel "New Castle, Pennsylvania is the Right Place—we love it."

CITY TRIVIA QUESTION #6

This northeastern city is the home port for the nation's oldest Navy floating ship, the "Constellation," and was also the home of Edgar Allan Poe and Babe Ruth.

Answer on page 46.

Italian Wedding Soup

Mayor Dale W. Yoho
New Castle, Pennsylvania

4 lb. stewing chicken
4 qts. cold water
1 tbsp. salt
12 peppercorns
2 large onions
2 garlic cloves
2 bay leaves
1 whole celery
parsley (fresh or flakes to taste)
2-3 bunches endive
Little Meatballs (see recipe below)

24 servings

Wash chicken and place in 8 qt. pot. Cover with cold water; add salt. Cover pot and bring to rapid boil. As water boils, it will foam (it can boil over here so be careful). Skim foam off until it no longer appears. Lower heat to simmer and add 1 onion (whole), garlic, peppercorns, bay leaves, parsley, and all the large outer stalks of celery with their leaves. Simmer slowly for 2 hours or until chicken is cooked. While soup cooks, wash endive and boil until tender; drain well and squeeze all liquid from greens, then cut into small pieces. Chop the other large onion and celery hearts and leaves; set aside. When soup is cooked, strain and discard cooked vegetables; set chicken aside to be deboned and cut into small pieces. Pour broth back into pot. Add chopped onions and celery. Boil until tender. Add cooked endive, Little Meatballs (see below), and chicken. Boil together for 20-25 minutes. Serve with grated Romano cheese.

Little Meatballs

1 lb. meatloaf mix (ground veal, beef, and pork)
½ cup unseasoned bread crumbs
¾ tsp. salt
pepper (to taste)
¼ tsp. sweet basil
2 eggs
1/8 tsp. garlic powder
2 tbsp. grated Romano cheese
1 tbsp. parsley flakes
¼ cup cold water

24 servings

Mix bread crumbs into meatloaf mix. Put all other ingredients in a bowl and beat well; pour over meat and mix very well with hands. Lightly grease cookie sheet with oil, adding some oil to hands. Roll meat mixture into meatballs (slightly smaller than a marble). Broil for several minutes under broiler. Remove from pan immediately and add to soup.

Italian Wedding Soup's name originated from a specialty served as the first course at Italian weddings. It has now become a favorite soup to New Castle diners served prior to any meal or as a meal in itself at many of our fine Italian restaurants and homes.

New Castle, is an industrial city in western Pennsylvania. For additional information, please see page 35.

CITY TRIVIA QUESTION #7

What city lays claim as the second oldest city in the United States and is also the capital city of the "Empire" state?

Answer on page 45.

Stuffed Fresh Mushrooms

Mayor Daniel S. Frawley
Wilmington, Delaware

1 lb. large Delaware mushrooms
1 qt. water
1 tsp. salt
1 tbsp. lemon juice
¼ cup butter
3-4 chopped green onions, tops and all
¾ cup beef bouillon
¼ lb. Delaware crabmeat
1 cup seasoned bread crumbs

10 servings

Wash and core mushrooms, reserving stems. Bring water, salt, and lemon juice to a boil. Add cored mushroom caps and boil for 2 minutes, then drain.

Saute onions and mushroom stems in butter until tender. Add bouillon and seasoned crumbs. Fill mushroom caps and top with crabmeat. Place in shallow baking pan and bake at 350⁰ for 15-20 minutes.

Delaware ranks fourth in the United States in the production of mushrooms. Production is centered around Wilmington. Top them off with local crabmeat and you have quite a treat.

Wilmington's rich cultural heritage and progressive spirit give this city small-town charm and urban sophistication. Located in the Brandywine Valley, home of the world famous Longwood Gardens and Winterthur Museum and gardens, the city offers something for everyone with great neighborhoods, wonderful parks, and a thriving business community.

MAIN DISHES

Braciola di Manza (Rolls of Beef)

Mayor Arthur J. Holland
Trenton, New Jersey

1 lb. roundsteak (thinly sliced)
2 cloves garlic (minced)
1/8 cup parmesan cheese
1 tbsp. parsley (minced)
½ tsp. salt
dash of pepper
¼ cup olive oil
1 small onion (sliced)
22 oz. can Italian tomatoes
½ tsp. salt
¼ tsp. pepper
1 bay leaf

4 servings

Mix garlic, cheese, parsley, salt, and pepper. Distribute by spoonfuls on one edge of each piece of steak. Roll steak like a crepe and tie with a string.

Brown onion lightly in oil. Add beef rolls and brown. Add tomatoes and seasonings (salt, pepper, bay leaf). Cover skillet and simmer about 1½ hours until tender. Can be seasoned to taste as well. Remove bay leaf and string before serving.

Recipe can easily be expanded for larger servings or more people.

Trenton is known for many firsts—including where the first professional basketball game was played and where the cables used in the construction of the Brooklyn and Golden Gate Bridges were manufactured.

The slogan, "Trenton Makes, the World Takes," was born as a result of Trenton's many varied industrial products. This slogan, however, can be applied equally well to the offerings of Trenton's restaurants. While Trenton, a miniature of America and thus of the world, offers many ethnic menus, our city is probably known best for its Italian cuisine. At almost every intersection of our "Little Italy," one will find a restaurant known for fine food and drink, nice atmosphere, and reasonable prices. People come from far and wide to sample and savor these products. Join them—tasting is believing!

Chicken Breasts Pecan

Mayor Anthony E. Russo
Union Township, New Jersey

2 whole chicken breasts (skinned, boned, and cut in half)
10 tbsp. butter
3 tbsp. Dijon mustard
5-6 oz. ground pecans
2 tbsp. safflower oil
⅔ cup sour cream
salt
freshly ground pepper

4 servings

Between 2 pieces of wax paper, lightly flatten the chicken breasts with a meat pounder. Season the chicken with salt and pepper. Melt 6 tbsp. butter in a small saucepan over medium heat. Remove from the heat and whisk in 2 tbsp. mustard. Dip each piece of chicken into the butter and mustard mixture and heavily coat each with the ground pecans by patting them on with your hands. Preheat the oven to 200⁰.

Melt 4 tbsp. butter in a 12"-14" skillet. Stir in oil. When hot, saute as many pieces of chicken at a time as you can without crowding them. Saute for about 3 minutes on each side. Remove to a baking dish and place in the oven to keep warm. Continue cooking the chicken pieces until all are done. (This, of course, can be done in half the time if you have 2 large skillets and use 4 tbsp. butter and 2 tbsp. of oil in each skillet.)

Discard the butter and oil. If you find that the pecans that are left in the skillet are too burnt, discard them; otherwise spoon them onto the chicken while it is being kept warm in the oven. Deglaze the pan with the sour cream, scraping up all the browned particles. Whisk the remaining tbsp. mustard, 1 tsp. salt and ¼ tsp. pepper into the sauce. The sauce should retain a strong mustardy flavor. Remove from the heat.

Place a spoonful of the sour cream sauce in the middle of warmed dinner plates and cover it completely with a portion of chicken. Only a small portion of sauce should accompany each piece so as not to overpower the chicken. It should not be visible on the plate and, thus, will be a surprise to the diner.

Union Township is a suburban community founded in 1808. One of the big strengths of Union is its location. It is minutes from Newark International Airport and the Garden State Parkway. In 1976, the Township of Union was one of nine cities in the nation to be awarded the title "All American City" for the years 1976-77. The town was cited for its cultural, recreational, and athletic programs as well as for its efforts regarding racial integration and the alleviation of poverty.

CITY TRIVIA QUESTION #8

This city is renown for its famed "Boardwalk," the game Monopoly uses the names of its streets and railroads, and it was where the first ferris wheel was built.

Answer on page 52.

Chicken Scampi

Mayor Carl Eilenberg
Rome, New York

1 3 lb. fryer (cut into 6 or 8 pieces)
1 tbsp. coarse salt
1 cup olive oil
1 lb. onions (chopped)
6 cloves garlic (minced)
1 heaping tbsp. oregano
1 tsp. dry sweet basil
1/8 tsp. red pepper
¾ cup chopped fresh parsley
6 heaping tbsp. bread crumbs (unseasoned)
½ cup chopped scallions
8 tbsp. grated parmesan cheese
1 lb. linguini (#17)

4 servings

Wash chicken well and dry. Sprinkle with coarse salt and let stand.

In a large heavy pot, saute onions in 3 tbsp. oil until translucent. Add garlic and saute another minute or so. DO NOT let onions or garlic brown! Remove to a small bowl.

Arrange chicken in same pot, placing large pieces on the bottom. Add remaining oil plus oregano, basil, pepper, salt, and ½ cup parsley. Cover and simmer gently for 25 minutes. Add sauteed onions and garlic; simmer another 15 minutes. Stir in bread crumbs.

Serve chicken and sauce over boiled linguini, cooked according to package directions. Garnish with scallions, remaining parsley, and cheese.

Messy but good! No need to brown chicken first.

The City of **Rome** and its environs provide visitors with a wide contrast of entertainment, activities, and vivid scenery. Rome is a safe community of approximately 50,000 inhabitants nestled in central New York State. In Rome you can relive great moments of American history by visiting a reconstructed revolutionary fort or stroll through a recreated 1840s canal village; or you can plunge into the future by viewing some of America's contemporary might and a showcase of tomorrow's ideas, at one of the largest military air installations in the Northeast.

Christmas Seafood Pot

Mayor Dennis Michael Callahan
Annapolis, Maryland

1 lb. shrimp (in shells)
2 doz. bay oysters (in shells)
2 doz. littleneck clams (in shells)
4 ears of corn
4 large potatoes
2 lb. Italian sausage

4 servings

Steam all ingredients in large crab pot for 1 hour with sausage on top. Serve with melted butter.

Annapolis, Maryland, "the sailing capital of the world," has three centuries of history kept alive in its historic buildings, including our State House, the oldest state capitol in the United States still in legislative use. Our City Dock area is the hub during good weather days with its yachting facilities, water tours, restaurants, hotel, summer theater, specialty shops, galleries, and waterfront strolling areas. It is also the scene of the United States Sailboat and Power Boat Shows (in-the-water) in October. We are especially proud of the U.S. Naval Academy housed here, with over 4000 midshipmen. It rests on the Severn River complex and visitors can tour the Naval Museum and John Paul Jones' crypt.

Cranberry Glazed Chicken

Mayor Stephen R. Reed
Harrisburg, Pennsylvania

½ cup flour

1 tsp. salt

1/8 tsp. pepper

1 cup brown sugar (firmly packed)

¾ cup water

1 tbsp. wine vinegar

3-3½ lb. fresh chicken pieces

2-3 tbsp. butter

1½ cups fresh cranberries

1 tbsp. flour

½ tsp. cinnamon

¼ tsp. cloves (ground)

¼ tsp. allspice

4-6 servings

Combine of flour, salt, and pepper. Roll chicken in this mixture to coat. Slowly brown chicken in butter for about 30 minutes. Remove chicken pieces from pan; add cranberries, brown sugar, and water to drippings in pan. Cook for 5 minutes or until the cranberry skins pop. Mix vinegar with flour and the cinnamon, cloves, and allspice. Add to cranberry mixture and cook, stirring constantly, until mixture thickens. Put chicken pieces into cranberry sauce and simmer for 30 minutes, turning constantly.

Harrisburg, the seat of Pennsylvania's state government since 1812, recently celebrated its 125th anniversary with the unveiling of a new slogan: "Rediscover Harrisburg." In 1985 the city was designated an All-American City and also was selected by *Money Guide* magazine as one of the three best cities in the nation in which to invest in a home. Nestled at the base of the Appalachian Mountains and on the banks of the serene Susquehanna River, Harrisburg offers a multitude of recreational, business, and cultural activities. Harrisburg is a special place to live, work, and eat.

Eggplant Parmigiana

Mayor Maria Barnaby Greenwald
Cherry Hill, New Jersey

2 medium eggplants

salt

½ small onion (chopped)

1 clove garlic

1 sliver green pepper (optional)

2 tbsp. oil

1 28 oz. can tomatoes

1 6 oz. can tomato paste and 1 can water

1 tsp. salt

1 tsp. sugar or small piece of beef for flavor

½-1 cup flour

2 eggs (well beaten with 3 tbsp. water)

¼ lb. Locatelli cheese (grated)

8 servings

Peel and cut eggplants in ⅓" slices; place on flat dish and sprinkle salt on each layer. Place another flat dish on top with weighted object to compress. Let stand 2 hours.

In a large pot, lightly brown chopped onion, garlic, and pepper in oil. Add large can tomatoes and cook for 10 minutes. Add small can tomato paste plus water and 1 tsp. salt and sugar or beef. Cook 1 hour.

Fill frying pan with ½" cooking oil. (Oil should completely cover eggplant at all times.) Heat oil to frying temperature. Dip eggplant slice in flour, then in egg mixture, then flour again. Fry until golden brown; drain on brown paper.

Cover bottom of baking dish with sauce, add layer of eggplant, more sauce and sprinkle with Locatelli cheese. Repeat until all ingredients are used. Bake at 350⁰ until sauce bubbles. Allow to bubble for 5 minutes.

Cherry Hill, a community of 70,000 residents across the Delaware River from Philadelphia, encompasses 24.5 square miles, and is the home of the world famous Garden State Park Racetrack and the Cherry Hill Mall.

Originally settled by Quakers, the township contains a 300-year-old cemetery and the Barclay Farmstead, a living history museum listed on the National Register of Historic Places.

Macaroni-Seafood Delight

Mayor John C. Hatcher, Jr.
East Orange, New Jersey

2 cups elbow macaroni
1 lb. shrimp (cut-up)
2 cans tuna (in oil)
12 eggs (hard-cooked, quartered, and chilled)
¾ lb. crabmeat
½ tsp. seasoned salt
4 stalks of celery (diced)
½ cup mayonnaise

15 servings

Cook macaroni; drain and rinse with cold water. Empty into a large bowl, add mayonnaise and tuna and mix together. Add flaked crabmeat, shrimp, diced celery, chilled eggs, and seasoned salt. Mix thoroughly, chill, and serve.

East Orange is a densely populated city that enjoys a strategic location within the northeastern industrial area of New Jersey. Because it is located where the Garden State Parkway intersects Interstate Route 280—which connects with the nearby New Jersey Turnpike—it is often considered the City at the Crossroads of New Jersey. Approximately 4 miles in size. the city has been renowned as a community of extravagantly luxurious apartment buildings, the "Fifth Avenue" of New Jersey.

Mid-Eastern Lamb-on-a-Rod

Mayor Dale W. Yoho
New Castle, Pennsylvania

6-7 lb. leg of lamb (boned and cubed)	
MARINADE:	
1½ cups oil	
¾ cup white wine	1½ tsp. thyme
3 tbsp. lemon juice	1½ tsp. oregano
3 cloves garlic (crushed)	1½ tsp. rosemary
salt and pepper to taste	1½ tsp. basil

10-12 servings

Marinate lamb for 3-4 hours or overnight. Put on skewers; cook over hot coals to desired doneness and serve immediately. Serve with hot pepper and raw onion mixture and fresh Syrian (unleavened) bread. Serve approximately ½ lb. per person.

This Mid-Eastern dish is a main entree to many residents of New Castle. Many Mid-Eastern countries claim its origin but New Castle claims it as a must when dining out or at home. This is just one of many ways it can be prepared.

New Castle became a thriving community rapidly, due to its natural deposits of coal, limestone, iron ore and clay. For further information on New Castle, turn to page 35.

CITY TRIVIA QUESTION #9

This southwestern city is a national leader in encouraging the use of safety belts in cities (Hint: It is also the oldest state capital city founded in 1610.)

Answer on page 176.

New York City Style Pasta Primavera

Mayor Edward Koch
New York City, New York

2 tbsp. butter
2 tbsp. olive oil
¼ lb. snow peas (trimmed)
¼ lb. mushrooms (washed and sliced)
8 asparagus tips
1 small zucchini (washed and sliced)
½ lb. angel hair pasta
2 cloves mashed garlic
½ cup good chicken stock
¼ cup white wine
parmesan cheese

4-6 servings

Melt 2 tbsp. butter and 2 tbsp. olive oil in a pan. Add mushrooms and zucchini, toss until coated. Add asparagus and snow peas. Toss over high heat but do not let brown. Add garlic and white wine. Cook pasta in boiling water when you add white wine to mixture. Cook for 30 seconds to reduce slightly. Add ½ cup of chicken stock and simmer for 1 minute. Season with salt and fresh pepper. Add parmesan cheese to taste. Add vegetable mixture to pasta. Toss over heat. Add more parmesan to taste. Serve very hot in a bowl that will hold pasta and sauce.

New York, the home of the "Big Apple" and the Statue of Liberty, a city of over 7 million people, is not only the international capital of the world, the home of high fashion salons of world reknown, and host to Broadway, it is also the restaurant capital of the world. It has more than 25,000 restaurants serving every known ethnic cuisine. New York is the place to feast be it Thai or tacos. Bon appetit.

Pasta Primavera

Mayor Karen B. Johnson
Schenectady, New York

1 lb. pasta
3 medium zucchini (sliced)
½ lb. broccoli (small pieces)
½ lb. fresh green beans or snow pea pods
1 roasted red pepper (sliced)
4 tbsp. olive oil
2-3 shallots
1 clove garlic (smashed)
¼ cup chopped parsley
2 tbsp. chopped, fresh basil or 2 tsp. dried
salt and pepper
¼ cup parmesan cheese

4-6 servings

Heat oil in large skillet, add green vegetables, shallots, and garlic, cover and steam for 5 minutes. Uncover, stir and add parsley, basil, red pepper. Cover and cook vegetables until crunchy. In the meantime, cook pasta, season the vegetables with salt and pepper, add to pasta, toss, sprinkle with cheese.

Schenectady's large Italian population makes Italian food (and our restaurants) special to us. Besides having General Electric as our major employer, we also have Union College and Proctor's, a restored vaudeville house drawing over 300,000 people a year to our city. On the banks of the beautiful Mohawk River, we celebrate our history where Mohawk Indians, Dutch, and later immigrants from all over the world enriched our city—and our cooking.

Pepperoni Pie

Mayor Joseph S. Daddona
Allentown, Pennsylvania

DOUGH:
3 cups flour
½ cup Crisco
1 cup water
1 egg
2 tsp. pepper
2 tbsp. cheese (grated)
FILLING:
2 lb. canned ham
12 eggs
2 sticks pepperoni
3 lb. Mozzarella cheese

3 pies

Slice pepperoni in thin slices. Cube ham. Grate cheese and set aside. Beat eggs. Add ⅓ cup grated cheese and 1 tbsp. pepper to eggs; mix well.

Mix dough ingredients as for pie dough. Roll dough to fit pie plates, leaving 1" to hang over pie plate. Layer ham, then cheese, then pepperoni. Take ½ cup egg mixture and pour over meat. Top with more pie dough, trim again ½" over pie plate. Pinch dough together and prick top with fork. Bake at 375⁰ for 45 minutes or until brown.

This pie is usually served around Easter, but whenever it is made it is a big hit with those who manage to get a slice.

Allentown is a dynamic community with an unmatched quality of life, boasting a thriving economy, 1700 acres of parks, recreation areas of all types, fine schools and colleges, and a unique downtown shopping mall. Arts, culture, festivals, and ethnic celebrations abound, from the Art Museum to our Stage Company, from the Allentown Fair to Mayfair to Super Sunday. It is also the hometown of Lee Iacocca.

Pierogi

Mayor Dale W. Yoho
New Castle, Pennsylvania

DOUGH:
1½ cups all purpose flour
½ tsp. salt
1 egg
5-6 tbsp. cold water
FILLINGS (see below)

6 servings

In a bowl sift together flour and salt; make a well in center and add egg and 5-6 tbsp. of cold water. Mix thoroughly with fork. Knead well on lightly floured surface, wrap in wax paper, and chill 30 minutes. Roll out on lightly floured surface until paper thin. Cut into 2½" circles, drop on small spoonful of desired filling (see below), and press edges firmly together with fork. Drop about 16 pierogi at a time into a 4-qt. kettle of rapidly boiling water (salted) and boil approximately 12 minutes. Drain. Serve with butter or fry in butter and onions after draining. Also delicious topped with sour cream.

Potato filling: Saute 2 small, chopped onions in 2½ tbsp. butter. Add 2 cups mashed potatoes; mix well. Salt and pepper to taste.

Sauerkraut filling: Saute 1 medium, chopped onion in 1½ tbsp. butter. Add 1¾ cups rinsed, drained, and dry sauerkraut. Cook 3 minutes. Remove from heat and add 2½ tbsp. sour cream.

Sausage filling: Combine thoroughly 10 oz. skinned and chopped Polish Kielbasa, ½ cup grated cheddar cheese, 1 egg, 4 tbsp. fine bread crumbs.

Many church groups here in New Castle get together and make pierogi to sell to raise funds for their church. Many residents look forward to filling their freezers with these home-made delicacies. Just another reason that confirms that ''New Castle is the Right Place.''

continued

New Castle became a thriving community rapidly due to its natural deposits of coal, limestone, iron ore, and clay. For further information turn to page 35.

Rouladen

Mayor Elizabeth C. Hoffman
North Tonawanda, New York

3 slices thin round steak
prepared mustard (any kind)
½ lb. bacon (cooked)
1 medium onion (chopped)
3 dill pickles (washed and chopped)
salt and pepper
1-2 tbsp. flour (optional)

3-6 servings

Cut 3 slices of round steak in half (about 3"x4"). Wash and allow to air dry. Spread mustard sparingly over steaks, salt and pepper to taste.

Drain cooked bacon and cut into small pieces. Mix the bacon, onion, and pickles together in a bowl. Spread 2 tbsp. of mixture on each of the mustard-covered round steaks. Roll and secure with toothpicks. Bake in a heavy cast iron pan with 4 tsp. of oil in a preheated 300° oven for 2 hours. Add hot water for gravy after the Rouladen is removed. If gravy is too thin, combine 1-2 tbsp. all purpose flour with an equal amount of cold water. Stir into sauce. Cook and stir until thickened and bubbly.

This is an old German dish. I am sure you will love it as much as we do.

Some of the attractions that make **North Tonawanda**, New York, a great place to live, work, and play are the 1916 Allan Herschell carousel and carousel museum and the Botanical Gardens, which gained acclaim through the Blindergarten Topiary Garden (garden for the visually impaired to touch and smell).

Sauerkraut Salad with Hot Dogs

Mayor David J. Wenzel
Scranton, Pennsylvania

1 16 oz. can sauerkraut
½ cup vegetable oil
1 large onion (chopped finely)
dash of pepper
8 hot dogs
beer

8 servings

Squeeze sauerkraut dry (homemade or canned sauerkraut may be used). Add ½ cup of vegetable oil, 1 large onion chopped finely, and good dash of black pepper. Mix.

Cook hot dogs in beer. Serve with sauerkraut salad and hard-crusted, seeded rye bread. Garnish hot dogs with Dijon mustard.

Scranton is the fifth largest city of Pennsylvania with a population of over 88,000. The "friendly city" has diversified interests, which include industry, renowned recreational facilities, and growing commercial concerns. It is also the home to Steamtown USA, the largest collection of steam-driven locomotives and memorabilia in the nation.

Shrimp a la Marion

Mayor Marion Barry, Jr.
Washington, D. C.

1 lb. fresh medium-sized shrimp
¼ lb. butter or margarine
1 cup white cooking wine
3 tbsp. all purpose flour
seasoned salt
Old Bay seafood seasoning
bay leaf

4 servings

Shell, wash, and devein shrimp. Cover shrimp with water, add a dash of Old Bay seafood seasoning, and boil for 3 minutes. Set aside.

In a frying pan, melt butter or margarine, add flour, and stir until smooth. Add cookng wine and 1½ cups of liquid from shrimp, stirring constantly. Sauce should be thick enough to coat spoon (add or decrease liquid as necessary). Season with dash of seasoned salt and bay leaf. Add boiled shrimp to mixture and simmer for 5 minutes. Serve over cooked rice.

This dish can also be prepared for large groups. I have served it at fundraising gatherings in my home several times. You will be surprised how much more "generous" the guests will be after feasting on "Shrimp a la Marion." This recipe can be used for all types of fun events—fundraising, political, and social.

Washington, D.C. is a Capital City, the center of national and international power, the seat of democracy, hometown to 630,000 residents, and a great deal more! It is a city of world-class hotels; a city of restaurants, offering over 110 ethnic cuisines; a city of theaters, bringing you a variety of outstanding Broadway shows and neighborhood repertory; a city which hosts the largest East Coast street festival, Adams-Morgan Day; and a city of sights, offering some of the nation's greatest museums and galleries. All this and more await you on your next visit to the Capital City.

Shrimp in Garlic Butter

Mayor Thomas M. Whalen, III
Albany, New York

2 cups deveined fresh jumbo shrimp
½ cup butter
1 can anchovy filets, drained on paper toweling
1 full head garlic, finely chopped

6 servings

Saute garlic in ¼ cup of the butter over low heat. Add additional butter as needed. When garlic is softened well and combined with butter, raise heat and add shrimp. Turn frequently and baste with garlic butter for 3-4 minutes or until done.

Serve over rice (cooked ahead and kept warm, about 2 cups for 6 people). Garnish with anchovies and a few sliced green olives.

As the second oldest city in the United States, **Albany** is a unique combination of architecture, neighborhoods, and people. The city is the center for education and government and a cross-roads for rail, water, and highway transportation. Given this complex mixture of people and perspectives, the Empire State's capital city is a great place to visit and an even better one to live in.

CITY TRIVIA QUESTION #10

City where Larry Bird, NBA Boston Celtic and MVP played his college basketball at Indiana State University.

Answer on page 103.

Spaghetti Al Pesto

Mayor Louis J. Tullio
Erie, Pennsylvania

1 lb. uncooked capellini #12 spaghetti (or any other type desired)

PESTO SAUCE:

2 cloves garlic

5 bunches fresh basil (well washed; about 4 cups packed)

½ cup walnuts or pignoli nuts (or mixture of both)

8 tbsp. grated parmesan cheese

8 sprigs Italian parsley

1 tsp. salt

½ tsp. pepper (or to taste)

1 cup olive oil

4 servings

Sauce: Put all ingredients, except spaghetti, into a blender—blend to obtain proper sauce consistency. Let sauce stand at room temperature until capellini is ready.

Bring 4 qts. of water to boiling—add capellini pasta, and 1 tbsp. salt; cook uncovered until pasta is tender, yet firm (al dente style)—cooking time is approximately 5 minutes. DO NOT OVERCOOK. Drain pasta immediately, transfer to serving bowl and pour pesto sauce over capellini (or other type of pasta). Mix well and serve immediately.

You don't have to be Italian to enjoy this dish—anyone who loves Italian cooking will find it delicious!

Erie, the third largest city in Pennsylvania, is situated in the northwest section of the Commonwealth on the southern shore of Lake Erie on a fine natural harbor. It provides the Commonwealth with its only lake and world port. It is a leading industrial area and business service center of northwest Pennsylvania. Shipbuilding played an important role in Erie's and our nation's history with the ships used by Commodore Oliver Perry in the War of 1812.

Foremost among Erie's amenities is Presque Isle State Park, a 7½ mile peninsula of sandy beaches and numerous swimming, boating, and picnicking facilities, visited yearly by 5 million people.

Steamed Maryland Blue Crabs

Mayor William Donald Schaefer
Baltimore, Maryland

12 large or 18 medium live Maryland blue crabs

2 cups water (or 1 bottle beer)

1 cup vinegar

½ cup Old Bay seasoning

4-8 servings

In a very large pot, place a rack which will allow the crabs to be gently steamed and kept above the liquid level. Put water and vinegar in bottom of pot. Add the live crabs a layer at a time. (Usually a layer consists of 4 crabs.) Sprinkle liberal amounts of seasoning on each layer. Place the lid on the pot and bring to a boil. Allow crabs to steam 25-30 minutes, or until crab shells turn bright red.

Remove the crabs and you are ready to begin the true Maryland experience of eating crabs. You'll need plenty of napkins and hungry participants. It is great with corn on the cob and blueberry pie—perfect for a hot summer's night feast. Enjoy!

Baltimore, the largest city in Maryland, is known worldwide for its renaissance. For many visitors, the Inner Harbor, with its modern pavilions, superb Aquarium, and other attractions stands as a shining example of the renovation and rebirth of our city. It is also the home port to the nation's oldest Navy floating ship, the *Constellation*, and was the home of Edgar Allan Poe and Babe Ruth. But if you really want to know Baltimore, you must go into our neighborhoods, where you'll find Baltimore's strength.

Stuffed Fish Filets

Mayor Dorothy Storm
Incorporated Village of Freeport, New York

6 large fish filets (sole, flounder, haddock)
2 lb. frozen spinach (chopped), or 1 bag fresh
1 10 oz. pkg. feta cheese
1/8 tsp. garlic powder
Pepper to taste
½ stick butter
1 tbsp. lemon juice

6 servings

Cook spinach enough to defrost—not to change color (allow to remain deep green). Drain and allow to cool.

In medium-size bowl crumble feta cheese with fork or fingers; add pepper and garlic powder. Add spinach to cheese and mix. Take mixture and spread about ¼" thick along filet; roll up and seal with toothpicks. Repeat procedure with all 6 filets.

Take square of foil paper, place filet in middle with square of butter on bottom, and seal ends to make boat-type shape around the filet with top open. Place another square of butter on top and sprinkle each with lemon juice (about ½ teaspoon). Place 6 filet "boats" in baking dish and place in 350⁰ oven. After about 10 minutes prick the side of boats to allow liquid to escape; then cook for about 15 minutes longer. Remove and serve immediately.

Since we are a seaside village, I submit this recipe which highlights the most popular food from our waterfront and dockside fishing boats.

Freeport, population 40,000 is known as "The Boating and Fishing Capital of the East." Only 25 miles from Manhattan, it has 8½ miles of residential and commercial waterfront and quick access to the Great South Bay of the Atlantic Ocean. It is home port to thousands of pleasure craft, commercial fishing boats, and a charter fishing fleet. The Nautical Mile, a working port with fresh fish sales, marine showrooms, boatyards, seafood restaurants, clam bars, and boutiques, is a popular metropolitan area tourist attraction.

CITY TRIVIA QUESTION #11

Garrison Keillor, author of *Lake Wobegon Days*, has established a permanent home for his tales in this Minnesota city.

Answer on page 114.

CITY TRIVIA QUIZ

Scoring System

Throughout *The Mayors Cookbook* there are 62 City Trivia questions with 130 answers. Answer each question, follow the instructions to the page with the answer, and tally your results.

Correct Answers	Level of Knowledge
0—25	Municipal Rookie
26—50	City Gazer
51—75	Metropolitan Marvel
76—100	City Slicker
101 and up	Urbanologist

Stuffed Flank Steak

Mayor Michael C. O'Laughlin
Niagara Falls, New York

1 3 lb. flank steak (butterflied)

MARINADE:

¼ cup olive oil

¼ cup soy sauce

¼ cup lemon juice

2 cloves garlic

1 tbsp. powdered rosemary

1 tsp. powdered thyme

1 tbsp. salt

2 tsp. pepper

STUFFING:

8 slices bacon, cooked and crumbled (reserve 4 tbsp. grease)

1 cup finely chopped yellow onion

¾ cup unpeeled, grated zucchini squash

¾ cup unpeeled, grated yellow squash

¼ tsp. oregano

½ cup fresh bread crumbs

2 tbsp. finely chopped fresh parsley

1 tbsp. lemon juice

1 egg, slightly beaten

¼ tsp. salt

¼ tsp. pepper

4-6 servings

Lightly pound steak with a meat tenderizer. Place steak in a large shallow roasting pan.

In a small bowl, combine all marinade ingredients, mix well, and pour over steak. Cover with foil and refrigerate 24 hours, turning several times. Remove from refrigerator at least 1 hour prior to cooking.

In a Dutch oven, heat grease; saute onion, stirring 5 minutes. Add squash and oregano; saute, stirring 5 minutes. Remove from heat and add bacon, bread crumbs, parsley, lemon juice, egg, salt, and pepper. Moisten with 3 tbsp. reserved marinade; mix well.

Preheat oven to 450°. Place steak flat and spread stuffing to within 1" of each edge. Roll, jellyroll fashion, and with thick string, tie tightly at 1"-2" intervals. Return steak to roasting pan, and baste with marinade. Roast 20 minutes for rare, 30 minutes for medium rare, or 40 minutes for medium. Every 10 minutes, turn and baste. Carve in ½" slices; arrange on a heated platter and serve.

Few people in the world have not heard of **Niagara Falls**, New York, one of the world's wonders, where God and nature provide one of the most awesome spectacles of magnificence, power, and beauty, the thunderous cascades of Niagara Falls, and where hospitality abounds. Seeing is believing and I urge you to make our city a part of your travel plans.

Veal Piccata

Mayor Alfred Del Vecchio
White Plains, New York

2 lb. veal cutlets (pounded thin)
⅔ cup flour
1 tsp. salt (may be omitted)
½ tsp. ground black pepper
⅔ stick of butter or margarine
¼ cup lemon juice
2 tsp. chopped Italian parsley
2 tbsp. chicken broth

6 servings

Dip cutlets into flour to which salt and pepper have been mixed. Melt half butter. Brown cutlets until golden, adding butter as needed. Remove to a hot platter, sprinkle with lemon juice and parsley. Pour chicken broth into pan. Scrape bottom and stir. Pour over cutlets. Serve with rice pilaf.

White Plains, settled in 1683, is located in the south central portion of West Chester County about 22 miles north of Grand Central Station in New York City.

The city is the headquarters of a number of major international corporations and is a regional retail shopping center. Its historic properties include the Purdy House, one of the headquarters of George Washington during the Revolutionary War.

ACCOMPANIMENTS

Broccoli Delight

Mayor Sharpe A. James , Jr.
Newark, New Jersey

1 10 oz. pkg. frozen broccoli (thawed and drained)
¼ cup onion, chopped
½ tsp. garlic salt
2 tbsp. butter
1 10 oz. can condensed cream of mushroom soup
1 cup (4 oz.) Swiss cheese, shredded
1 cup skim milk
8 oz. vermicelli (cooked according to directions on box)

4 servings

Cut broccoli into ½" pieces; saute in a 10" nonstick skillet with onion and garlic salt in butter or margarine until tender, but not brown. Add soup, cheese, and milk. Heat and stir until cheese melts. Lightly toss vermicelli with cheese and broccoli sauce.

This is the "Sharpe Change" for the "Athletic Mayor" who is trying to watch his weight. Only 490 calories—check it out!

Newark, the "Gateway City," is the largest city in the state of New Jersey. Revitalization and rebirth are in evidence everywhere in Newark. A city and people on the move. The home of Stephen Crane, Melba Moore, Sarah Vaughn, and many more.

49

Broccoli Salad

Mayor T. Urling Walker
Watertown, New York

1 can Eagle brand condensed milk
1/8 tsp. salt
1 egg
½ cup vinegar
3 tbsp. prepared mustard
4 cups broccoli
¼ cup raisins
¼ cup sweet onion (chopped)
4-8 slices cooked bacon (crumbled)

8 servings

Combine first 5 ingredients in blender until mixture is stiff (like mayonnaise).

Wash broccoli well. It may be used raw or steamed only long enough to bring out green color. Dry broccoli well. Mix all ingredients together just before serving.

The City of **Watertown**, with a population of approximately 29,000, is located centrally in Jefferson County, with a population of approximately 90,000. It sits in the middle of one of the largest producing milk sheds in the country. Syracuse is 65 miles south, to the west is the War of 1812 village of Sackets Harbor on the shore of Lake Ontario, to the north is Canada and the St. Lawrence River with its beautiful Thousand Islands, and to the east is the great Adirondack Park embracing probably one of the largest park areas in the world with its streams, high mountains, and bountiful flora and fauna.

German Potato Salad

Mayor Arnold Addison
State College, Pennsylvania

2 lb. potatoes	⅓ cup bacon drippings
½ tsp. salt	¼ cup cider vinegar
¼ tsp. pepper	1 tsp. instant minced onion
6 slices crisp, cooked bacon (crumbled)	

6-8 servings

Cook potatoes in boiling, salted water. Potatoes may be cooked sliced or cooked whole and sliced after cooking. Cook until tender.

While potatoes are cooking, heat bacon drippings, vinegar, onion, salt, and pepper in small saucepan.

In large bowl, combine hot potato slices, bacon, and dressing. Serve at once or at room temperature.

State College, located in the center of Pennsylvania, is the home of the Nittany Lions, of the Pennsylvania State University. In the surrounding area one finds a growing number of high tech organizations and an abundance of state and municipal park and recreational facilities.

Irish Soda Bread

Mayor James D. Griffin
Buffalo, New York

3 cups flour
3 tsp. baking powder
1 tsp. baking soda
dash of cream of tartar
3 tbsp. sugar
1 cup raisins (plumped in boiling water and drained)
½ cup butter or margarine
1 egg (lightly beaten)

1 loaf

Sift together flour, baking powder, soda, salt, and cream of tartar. Add sugar. Cut dry ingredients into butter to make crumbs. Add buttermilk and lightly beaten egg. Fold in drained raisins and knead gently to make a light dough. Place dough in a buttered loaf pan. Bake at 350⁰ for 20-30 minutes or until done.

Buffalo, located at the northern end of Lake Erie, has a strong and diverse ethnic heritage in addition to its vibrant neighborhoods. Buffalo has been the setting for a number of movies, including *The Natural* starring Robert Redford. Buffalo wings, a chicken dish, was originated at the Anchor, a local bar. The city's waterfront is used for shipping goods all over the world. Buffalo is truly "The City of Good Neighbors."

Pine Nut Casserole

Mayor Carl Eilenberg
Rome, New York

6 tbsp. margarine
⅓ cup pine nuts or slivered almonds
1 cup medium pearled barley
1 onion (chopped)
½ cup minced fresh parsley
¼ cup minced chives or green onions
¼ tsp. salt
¼ tsp. pepper
3½ cups chicken broth

6 servings

Grease a 1½ qt. casserole dish.

In deep saucepan, melt 2 tbsp. margarine. Add pine nuts and stir fry until lightly toasted. Remove nuts and set aside. Add remaining margarine and saute barley and onion, stirring constantly until tender (about 5-7 minutes). Remove pan from heat.

Stir in nuts, parsley, chives, salt and pepper. Spoon into greased casserole. Heat broth to boiling and pour over barley mixture and stir.

Bake at 375⁰ for 1 hour until barley is tender and liquid is absorbed.

Good with holiday meals. It's the nuts. Everybody will ask for this recipe.

Rome is a community of approximately 50,000, nestled in central New York State. For further information on Rome, turn to page 39.

Rice Dressing for Cornish Hens

Mayor James L. Usry
Atlantic City, New Jersey

½ cup white raisins	6 tbsp. butter
¼ cup cognac	¼ cup onions (chopped)
¼ cup green peppers (chopped)	
½ tsp. salt	
1½ cups boiled rice	1½-2 cups milk
2 cups bread crumbs	¼ tsp. nutmeg

6-8 servings

Soak raisins in cognac for 10 minutes. Drain, reserving cognac, and saute them in butter. Add onions and green peppers. Combine the above and toss lightly with salt, rice, and nutmeg. Moisten bread crumbs to this mixture with the drained cognac.

Serve with cornish hens or other poultry.

Atlantic City, New Jersey, is the number one tourist attraction in the world. Approximately 1 million people visited the resort in 1985.

It was originally conceived as a health resort, but with the coming of the Atlantic City-Philadelphia railroad, the city quickly grew and became one of the premier vacation places in the country.

In the mid 1970s, New Jersey voters approved legislation permitting casino gambling in Atlantic City. The city now boasts eleven casinos and two more are under construction.

Atlantic City is also famous for its world renown "Boardwalk" and the Miss America Pageant. The popular board game Monopoly uses the names of Atlantic City streets and former railroads, the first ferris wheel was built in Atlantic City, the word "airport" was coined in Atlantic City in reference to its flying field, and the first picture post cards were colored views of Atlantic City.

Salt Potatoes

Mayor Thomas G. Young
Syracuse, New York

1 lb. small new potatoes
¼ lb. salt (approximately)
Melted butter and salt to taste

4-5 people

Scrub but do not peel potatoes. For extra salty flavor, pierce skin with fork. Fill a large pot with enough water to cover potatoes. Add enough salt to make a potato float on the water. Bring to a boil; boil for ½ hour or until potatoes are cooked. Drain but DO NOT RINSE. Serve with lots of melted butter and, if desired, additional salt.

Recipe can be expanded easily; especially good for clam bakes and barbeques.

Syracuse is at the crossroads of New York State—in the middle of everything. The Greater Syracuse area has been a center of activity in the northeast since 1570 when the Iroquois Confederacy of Indian Nations was formed on the shores of Onondaga Lake, through the Erie Canal days in the 19th century to the present time.

A community of diverse cultures and lifestyles, Syracuse is both urban and rural, modern and historic. The city is home to a major art museum, symphony orchestra and opera theater, several theater troupes, and the New York State Fair.

Since its early days as a salt producing center, Syracuse has been known as the Salt City. Construction of the Syracuse University Carrier Dome Stadium has added the nickname "Home of the Dome."

Zucchini Pudding

Mayor Robert G. Smith
Piscataway, New Jersey

2 cups zucchini (shredded)
3 eggs (or egg substitute for low cholesterol version)
⅔ cup complete pancake mix
⅓ cup parmesan cheese (grated)
2 tsp. oil

8-10 servings

Preheat oven to 350⁰. Put the 2 tsp. oil on bottom of glass baking dish and spread evenly. Mix remaining ingredients well and pour into oiled dish. Bake 1 hour. Serve warm; delicious with meats.

Very easy to prepare. Grated zucchini may by frozen when in good supply for winter use. Time and temperature may be varied slightly for cooking with roasts.

Piscataway Township was founded in 1666, and has a long, rich colonial history, with homes still standing from that period. General George Washington rested his weary Continental troops in Piscataway after the Battle of Monmouth in 1778. Today Piscataway has working farms, alongside high-tech corporations and has won awards for the city's livability and beautification programs.

DESSERTS

Anisette Cookies

Mayor Robert W. Singer
Township of Lakewood, New Jersey

1 stick butter	2 tsp. baking powder
¾ cup sugar	1 tsp. vanilla
3 eggs	½ tsp. salt
2½ cups sifted flour	1 tsp. anisette flavoring
½ cup filberts (walnuts may be substituted)	

4-5 dozen

Cream together butter and sugar, adding eggs one at a time. Sift together flour, baking powder, and salt. Add to cream mixture along with vanilla and anisette flavoring. Add filberts (will make a soft dough). Form dough into four loaves approximately 8"x3". Brush with egg yolk. Bake at 350⁰ until light brown. Cut into slices, approximately ½" wide. Put slices cut-side down on greased cookie sheet and bake again at 300⁰ for approximately 15 minutes or until golden brown.

Lakewood is known in New Jersey as the "Garden Spot of the Garden State." It is uniquely endowed with natural beauty—in its parks, recreational areas, and lakes. It is a chosen community for retirement. No less than the prestigious publication of *U.S. News & World Report* has praised Lakewood by declaring it among the "10 Great Places to Spend Your Retirement" in the country.

Apple or Cherry Coffee Cake

Mayor Ann A. Mullen
Gloucester, New Jersey

¼ lb. butter
1 cup sugar
2 eggs
½ cup milk
1 tsp. vanilla
2 cups flour
2 tsp. baking powder
Pinch of salt
TOPPING:
⅓ cup flour
¼ cup sugar
1 tsp. cinnamon
3 tsp. butter
FILLING:
1 can or jar of either prepared apple or cherry pie mix

12 servings

Cream butter and sugar together; add eggs and vanilla. Add dry ingredients alternately with milk. Beat 1½ minutes until thick. Pour ¾ of the batter into a greased 10"x10" pan. Please note: this batter is very thick and may need to be spread with a spatula. Spread apples or cherries and top with remaining batter. Sprinkle on topping. Bake 1 hour at 350⁰.

Gloucester Township is a rapidly growing bedroom community of approximately 50,000 people. It is strategically located near several major highways. Gloucester Township boasts of one of the finest year-round recreation programs and the largest and finest elementary school district in the state.

There is always something to do in Gloucester Township, from senior citizen programs to visiting the many parks and playgrounds to unlimited social programs.

Banana Cake

Mayor Steven Van Grack
Rockville, Maryland

1½ cups sugar
1 stick margarine
2 eggs (well beaten)
2 bananas (ripe and mashed)
4 tbsp. sour cream
1 tsp. baking soda
1½ cups flour
1 tsp. vanilla

6-8 servings

Mix sugar and margarine with electric beater. Add eggs and mix. Add bananas and mix. Add sour cream, baking soda, and vanilla. Add and mix flour. Pour into greased and floured loaf pan. Bake 50 minutes to over an hour at 350°. Test center with toothpick.

Rockville is the second largest city in Maryland and county seat in Montgomery County. Located 12 miles northwest of Washington, D.C., the city is a vigorous, growing community of 45,000. Residents of Rockville enjoy a distinctive lifestyle that combines the community values and convenience of a small city with the urban cultural amenities of the nation's capital. Among the city's most interesting historic landmarks are the 1817 St. Mary's Catholic Church and the adjoining cemetery where F. Scott and Zelda Fitzgerald are buried.

CITY TRIVIA QUESTION #13

City that is the home of the Queen Mary and Howard Hughes' Spruce Goose.

Answer on page 206.

54

Chocolate Ice Box Cake

Mayor Steven B. Carlson
Jamestown, New York

2 4 oz. bars German sweet chocolate
4 eggs (separated)
2 tbsp. confectioner's sugar
½ cup chopped walnuts
½ pt. whipping cream (1 cup)
1 prepared angel food cake
½ pt. whipped cream or 9 oz. whipped topping (for frosting)

6 servings

Melt chocolate in a double boiler. Add 2 tbsp. water and blend. Remove from heat and add 4 egg yolks, one at a time. Beat until smooth. Add 2 tbsp. confectioner's sugar and nuts. Fold in 4 stiffly beaten egg whites and whipped cream very gently.

Line deep 3½ qt. serving bowl with ¼" slices of cake. Cover bowl completely. Pour in half of chocolate mixture. Place more cake slices in middle layer. Fill with remaining chocolate. Add layer of cake to completely cover across the top of the bowl. Refrigerate overnight. Turn upside down on serving plate. Frost with whipped cream or whipped topping.

Chocolate Ice Box Cake is a heavenly delight which has been served in my family at Thanksgiving and Christmas dinners since before I was born. It is a chocolate cake which tastes like ice cream and melts in your mouth.

Jamestown, New York, a community where industry and recreation meet, is located on beautiful Chautauqua Lake in southwestern New York State. The city serves as the industrial, commercial, financial, and recreational hub for a metropolitan area of 70,000 people and a market area of 175,000. Jamestown's "balanced community living" reflects the commitment of both public and private sector forces to provide the highest possible quality of life.

Chocolate Whiskey Fondue

Mayor Richard S. Caliguiri
Pittsburgh, Pennsylvania

1 cup granulated sugar
½ cup cold water
3 oz. semi-sweet chocolate
3 oz. unsweetened chocolate
¼ cup unsalted butter
2 tbsp. whipping cream
¼ cup Scotch whiskey
Strawberries

6-8 servings

Mix first 2 ingredients over medium heat for 5 minutes; cool until just warm. Cut chocolate in small pieces and then melt with butter in double boiler. Add whipping cream after chocolate and butter are completely melted. Slowly blend this with the warm sugar water. Set aside. (Mixture can be made ahead of time up to this point). Reheat mixture, slowly add scotch.

Wash strawberries; do not remove green tops. Dip only ½ the strawberry so that the chocolate, strawberry, and green top are showing.

Pittsburgh, the third largest corporate headquarters city in the nation and regarded for many years as one of the world's industrial giants, has made dramatic physical and environmental changes over the past 40 years. No longer the Smoky City, the New Pittsburgh is a community of aesthetic beauty and cultural refinement. During the past 8 years, over $3 billion has been invested in massive central city and neighborhood Renaissance II improvements. Pittsburgh's dynamic progress was recognized nationally by the Rand McNally Places Rated survey, which has designated it as America's Most Livable City.

Cool Long Branch Pie

Mayor Philip D. Huhn
Long Branch, New Jersey

1 prepared graham cracker pie crust
vanilla and chocolate ice cream (approximately 1 pt. each, softened)
bananas (sliced)
strawberries (hulled and sliced)
½ cup of pecans, walnuts, and coconut, crushed
whipped cream

6 servings

Spread a layer of softened vanilla ice cream in pie crust. Layer with sliced bananas. Spread a layer of chocolate ice cream on top of bananas. Follow with a layer of strawberries. (Depending upon depth of pie crust, you may repeat a layer of ice cream and fruit.) Freeze.

Slice and top with whipped cream and nut mixture (optional). Of course, hot chocolate topping goes well with this too!

Long Branch, centrally located on the North Jersey Coast, is often referred to as the "Presidential Resort City," as seven U.S. Presidents have enjoyed our three miles of beaches and resort and sporting atmosphere. Today, Long Branch with its ocean, beaches, salt air, boardwalk, and amusement attractions, continues to be a resort; however, the city also enjoys several retail business districts, specialty shops, and fabulous restaurants, which all create a progressive lifestyle for residents and visitors alike.

Crabb-Apple Pie

Mayor Juanita M. Crabb
Binghamton, New York

FLAKY PASTRY for 2-crust pie:	
2 cups sifted all-purpose flour	
1 tsp. salt	
⅔ cup lard	
4-5 tbsp. ice water	
FILLING:	
1½ cups sugar	1 tsp. nutmeg
2 tsp. cinnamon	1 tsp. lemon juice
4 tbsp. flour	4 tbsp. butter or margarine
dash salt	
6 cups thinly sliced, pared, tart cooking apples (2 lb.)	

Makes 1 pie

Sift flour with salt into a medium bowl. With pastry blender or 2 knives, cut in lard using a short cutting motion until mixture resembles coarse cornmeal. Quickly sprinkle with ice water, 1 tbsp. at a time, over the pastry mixture, tossing lightly with fork after each addition and pushing dampened portion to side of bowl; sprinkle only dry portion remaining. (Pastry should be just moist enough to hold together, not sticky.) Shape pastry into a ball; wrap in waxed paper, and refrigerate until ready to use. Divide in half; flatten half with palm of hand.

On lightly floured surface, roll out half of pastry into an 11" circle. Use to line 9" pie plate; crust should hang over edge of pie plate, do not trim. Refrigerate with rest of pastry until ready to use. Preheat oven to 425⁰.

In small bowl, combine sugar, cinnamon, nutmeg, flour, and salt, mixing well. Add to apples in large bowl, tossing lightly to combine. Turn into pastry-lined pie plate, mounding high in the center; dot with butter and sprinkle with lemon juice.

Roll out remaining pastry into an 11" circle. Make several slits near center for seam vents; adjust over filling; trim. Bring edge of bottom crust over top crust; press together with fingertips. Crimp edge decoratively. Bake 15 minutes at 425⁰; lower oven to 325⁰ and bake 60 minutes or until apples are tender and crust is golden brown. Cool partially on wire rack; serve warm.

Binghamton is a beautiful city nestled in the hills of New York's Southern Tier. It is a proud industrial and manufacturing city on the threshold of a renaissance. Home of IBM, its traditions were shaped by the people who forged our country's modern industrial heritage and led us into space. Binghamton is fast becoming the prototype of what a modern American city can be.

Flan

Mayor Robert Menendez
Union City, New Jersey

4 eggs	8 oz. whole milk
1 can condensed milk	3 tbsp. sugar
1 tsp. vanilla extract	

6 servings

Put sugar in saucepan and heat it to make caramel. Let cool. Take eggs, vanilla, and milk and blend for 1 minute. Pour over caramelized sugar.

Fill bottom of a double boiler with water. Cook mixture for 1 hour. Chill. To serve, flip "flan" over onto a large plate.

To serve, place on plate. Can be topped with coconut.

Union City is a densely populated city with over 60% of our residents being Cuban and Hispanic. Our main avenue, Bergenline, has many Spanish restaurants and cafeterias where "flan" is sold frequently.

Grandma's Noodle Pudding

Mayor Joan Shapiro
Newburgh, New York

1 8 oz. box medium noodles
¼ lb. melted butter (generous)
8 eggs
1 pt. cottage cheese
1 pt. sour cream
1 cup sugar
pinch salt
dash cinnamon
2 peeled and sliced apples or 1 pt. applesauce (optional)
cornflakes

8-10 servings

Cook and drain noodles. Mix all other ingredients together and add to noodles. Mixture should be loose (consistency of pudding before it sets up). If it is stiff add more eggs. Put mixture into casserole.

Crush and sprinkle 2 handfuls of cornflakes over casserole, dot with additional butter. For soft texture, bake at 350⁰ for 45 minutes; for firm texture, bake for 1 hour. To test for doneness, see if it is bubbling around the edges. Let stand for a few minutes and serve warm, or refrigerate and serve cold. Slice and serve with strawberries or raspberries, sour cream, whipped cream, or plain.

Newburgh, located in New York's scenic Hudson River Valley, is a small city with a rich history and promising future. Nearly half of the city is an Historic District, which includes Washington's headquarters at the conclusion of the Revolutionary War and a variety of 18th and 19th century residential, industrial, and commercial structures, many of which were designed by Andrew Jackson Downing. Excellent transportation links Newburgh to major Eastern markets add to its appeal as a business location.

Ice Cream Tortoni

Mayor Thomas G. Young
Syracuse, New York

⅓ cup toasted almonds (chopped)
3 tbsp. melted butter
1 cup fine vanilla wafers (crushed)
1 tsp. almond extract
3 pts. vanilla ice cream (softened)
1 12 oz. jar apricot preserves

10-12 servings

Combine almonds, butter, crumbs, and almond extract; mix well. (Set aside ¼ cup of crumb mixture for top.)

Sprinkle half of remaining crumb mixture over bottom of an 8" square pan that has been lined with aluminum foil. Spoon half th ice cream over crumb mixture; drizzle with half the preserves and sprinkle with remaining crumb mixture. Repeat to use remaining ice cream and preserves. Sprinkle reserved ¼ cup crumb mixture over top.

Store in freezer until ready to serve. Cut into squares.

Syracuse has been known as the "Home of the Dome" since construction of the Syracuse University Carrier Dome Stadium. For further information on Syracuse, turn to page 52.

CITY TRIVIA QUESTION #14

Texas city that gets its name from "The Pass," a gateway used by early Spanish explorers.

Answer on page 148.

Old World Apple Cake

Mayor Olga Boeckel
Middletown, New Jersey

FILLING:

3 lb. cooking apples (about 11)
1/3 cup sugar
1/2 cup water
2 slices lemon

PASTRY:

2 cups flour (sifted)
1 1/4 cups sugar
1 1/2 tsp. baking powder
1/2 cup butter or margarine
2 egg yolks

8 servings

Filling: Peel and slice apples. Cook with sugar, water, and lemon until tender (not mushy); drain and cool.

Pastry: Mix flour, sugar, and baking powder. Cut in butter with pastry blender until crumbly. Mix in egg yolks.

Reserve 1 1/4 cups for topping. Put remainder of mixture on bottom and sides of greased 9" springform pan. Fill with apples and sprinkle with reserved topping. Dot with two tbsp. butter, and sprinkle with 1 tbsp. sugar. Bake at 350° for 1 hour. Let cool completely before removing from pan.

Middletown Township, the largest municipality in Monmouth County, New Jersey, is more than 300 years old, having been founded on December 14, 1667. It is bounded by beautiful beaches that look across Raritan Bay to the New York City skyline and is just minutes from Sandy Hook, which is part of the Gateway National Recreation area, for swimming, boating, and fishing.

Middletown has beautiful rolling hills speckled with farmland and recreation areas, keeping it a rural suburbia. Adding to Middletown's warmth and charm are the many historic areas with quaint old homes and quiet tree-lined streets. Middletown is definitely a wonderful place to visit and an even better place to live.

Philadelphia Cream Cheese Pound Cake

Mayor W. Wilson Goode
Philadelphia, Pennsylvania

2 sticks butter
1 8 oz. pkg. cream cheese
3 cups sugar
6 eggs
3 cups sifted flour
1 tsp. vanilla extract
1 tsp. lemon extract
confectioner's sugar

1 cake

Mix together butter and cream cheese. Add sugar and blend until light and fluffy. Add eggs, one at a time, beating well after each. Add vanilla. Mix in flour, one cup at a time. Beat well. Add lemon and beat well again.

Pour mixture into well greased and floured bundt cake pan. Bake at 325° for 75 minutes. Cool in pan for 10 minutes. Dust generously with confectioner's sugar.

Philadelphia, "The City of Brotherly Love" and home of Independence Hall, is not just one of America's most historic cities...it is also a mecca for fine dining, with many world-class restaurants. From American to Continental to nouvelle cuisine, we have it all. Come to Philadelphia in 1987 when it will lead the nation and the world in a celebration of the 200th Anniversary of the U.S. Constitution. "Philadelphia: Get To Know Us."

Schaefer's Wafers

Mayor William Donald Schaefer
Baltimore, Maryland

2 egg whites (room temperature)
⅔ cup sugar
½ tsp. vanilla
6 oz. chocolate chips

Makes 50

Beat egg whites until stiff. Add ⅓ cup sugar and beat for 3 minutes. Add remaining sugar and beat another 3 minutes. Add vanilla and fold in the chocolate chips. Drop by teaspoonfuls onto a cookie sheet. Preheat oven to 375^0. Place sheet in oven, count to 10, then turn off the oven. Leave cookies in the oven overnight.

These terrific cookies began on the campaign trail. Three young supporters of Mayor William Donald Schaefer sold them on the street corner in one of Baltimore's neighborhoods. They called them "Schaefer's Wafers," and in this way announced who their favorite candidate was.

Baltimore, the largest city in Maryland, is the home town of Babe Ruth and Edgar Allan Poe. For further information on Baltimore, turn to page 46.

CITY TRIVIA QUESTION #15

Match these California cities with
their known food product:

____Oxnard	A. Grapes
____Fresno	B. Strawberries
____Riverside	C. Raisins
____Modesto	D. Asparagus
____San Leandro	E. Garlic
____Stockton	F. Naval Oranges
____West Hollywood	G. Cherries

Answers on pages 187, 184, 185, 214, 212, 183, 192.

Whiskey Cake

Mayor Stephen R. Reed
Harrisburg, Pennsylvania

1 cup walnuts (finely chopped or ground)
1 box white cake mix
1 box vanilla instant pudding
¼ cup whiskey
¾ cup milk
4 eggs (slightly beaten)
½ cup oil
TOPPING:
¼ cup butter
¾ cup sugar
¼ cup whiskey

12 servings

Mix all ingredients, just until thoroughly blended, and pour into a greased and floured tube or bundt pan. Bake at 350^0 for 1 hour or until top springs back when touched.

Topping: Mix topping ingredients and bring to a boil. Boil for 5 minutes. Pour hot topping directly over warm cake and let stand for 30 minutes to allow the flavor to soak in.

Harrisburg, the capital of Pennsylvania, is nestled at the base of the Appalachian Mountains, on the banks of the serene Susquehanna River. For further information on Harrisburg, turn to page 40.

SOUTHEAST

"First you start with this much"
Mayor John Rousakis
Savannah, GA

"Oh shucks!"
Mayor Pat Screen
Baton Rouge, LA

*"Hey good lookin',
what you got cookin'?"*
Mayor Sidney Barthelemy
New Orleans, LA

"Come and get it"
Mayor James W. Holley III
Portsmouth, VA

STARTERS

Hugging the shores of Sarasota Bay, **Sarasota** is home to an assortment of cultural activities all year long, including the Ringling Museums, the Van Wezel Performing Arts Hall (built in the shape of a *purple* shell), Arts and Crafts Festivals, a Medieval Fair, opera, dance, theaters, water sports galore, dog racing, major league baseball, etc. World travelers have likened Sarasota to the French Riviera and our white sandy beaches have been voted among the top six in the world! "Circus City" is a beautiful place to visit and even better to be able to live here!

Ark Soup

Mayor Kerry Groom Kirschner
Sarasota, Florida

2 tbsp. butter
2 onions (peeled and chopped)
2 leeks (sliced)
2 medium turnips (cubed)
2 peeled potatoes (cubed)
2 shallots (chopped)
2 stalks celery (sliced)
2 carrots (sliced)
2 cloves garlic (halved)
2 sprigs parsley
2 cans chicken broth
2 cups half-and-half
salt and pepper to taste
dill weed to taste (optional)

6-8 servings

Saute all the vegetables in a large soup pot with the 2 tablespoons butter until vegetables are limp. Add chicken broth and simmer until turnips are tender. Cool slightly, then process a little at a time through a blender. Return soup to the pot and add the half-and-half. Reheat gently and serve hot, garnished with a sprig of fresh dill.

Easy and delicious on a cold, winter night—yes, we do have a couple of them each year!!!

Black Bean Soup

Mayor Xavier L. Suarez
Miami, Florida

1 lb. black beans
10 cups water
⅔ cup olive oil
1 large onion (chopped)
4 cloves garlic (chopped)
1 bell pepper (chopped)
4 tsp. salt
2 tsp. oregano
⅓ cup vinegar

8 servings

Wash beans and soak in water with pepper. When beans are swollen boil until soft (approximately 45 minutes).

In a pan heat oil and saute onion, garlic, and pepper. Put approximately 1 cup of beans in the pan and smash them. Pour mixture into boiling pot; add salt and oregano. Let boil approximately 1 hour, then add vinegar. Simmer for 1 more hour or so until it thickens.

This soup is best served over white rice.

Miami is a city with a unique blend of natural beauty and multiethnic diversity. In the public schools in Greater Miami, there are 114 nationalities represented. This multicultural, multilingual spice adds to the vibrance of a young, energetic and exciting community, all mixed together, topped off with a tropical breeze to get "Miami Nice," "Come See It Like A Native."

Chili Dip

Mayor Bill Vines
Fort Smith, Arkansas

2 lb. ground beef
1 cup chopped onions
1 cup ketchup
5 tsp. chili powder
2 tsp. salt
2 16 oz. cans refried beans
1 tsp. comino seed
2 cups cheddar cheese (grated)
½ cup onion (chopped)

6-8 servings

Brown meat and 1 cup onions. Stir in ketchup, chili powder, salt, and comino seed. Add beans and mix well and heat thoroughly. (Can be frozen at this point.)

When ready to serve, put in chafing dish and garnish top with cheese and ½ cup onions. Use tostados or corn chips to dip.

Great to serve while watching football games.

Fort Smith is the industrial capital of Arkansas with over 200 industries supporting the economy. It continues to be the center of one of the most rapidly growing economically developed areas in the nation, boasting retail sales in excess of $1.5 billion per year. It has one of the lowest crime rates to be found anywhere in the country and with its climate and being surrounded by the Ouachita, Boston, and Ozark mountains, we have the greatest area livability to be found anywhere in the nation.

Cocktail Loaf

Mayor Mara Giulianti
Hollywood, Florida

1 loaf French bread (crisped, cut in half, and ends cut off and scooped out leaving the crisp crust)
1 cup baked ham (diced)
1 cup turkey breast (diced
1 cup pepperoni (diced)
1 cup Swiss cheese (diced)
1 cup mild cheddar cheese (diced)
½ cup pistachio nuts (chopped)
2 tsp. capers
3 anchovy fillets (mashed)
2 tbsp. Dijon mustard
salt and pepper to taste
¾ lb. butter (creamed)
3 egg yolks (hard-cooked and mashed)

6-8 servings

Into the creamed butter mix the egg yolks and mustard. Then add all the rest of the ingredients and mix well. Pack mixture into the bread crusts tightly. Refrigerate for 4 hours until firm.

To serve, slice loaf in ¼" slices.

I serve this at political cocktail parties—fundraisers—in fact, we served this for our congressman and county commissioner's fundraiser!

Aptly called the "Diamond of the Gold Coast," **Hollywood** is a vibrant coastal community strategically located midway between Miami Beach and Fort Lauderdale in Broward County, Florida. Its assets include: six miles of glistening public beach with the famous "Boardwalk," enjoyed by walkers, joggers, and bicyclists...Florida's largest indoor arena...greyhound racing...Seminole Indian Village...beautiful state and county parks. Hollywood's mild, subtropical climate lures visitors as a vacation city or permanent residence.

Conch Chowder

Mayor Tom Sawyer
Key West, Florida

18 conchs
lime juice
5 potatoes
1 oz. olive oil
½ lb. bacon (diced)
1 large can tomato sauce
3 onions (chopped)
1 small sweet pepper (chopped)
3-4 cloves garlic
2 bay leaves
pinch oregano
flour or instant potatoes

6-8 servings

Scald conch meat with water and lime juice to cut slime; drain and grind up conch coarsely. Return to pot in 4 quarts water; while cooking fry spices and bacon until soft, not brown. Pour off excess grease; add olive oil and tomato sauce and simmer. Add diced potatoes and mix all with conch meat in soup pot. Cook 1 hour. Thicken before serving using flour or instant potatoes.

Situated at the farthest tip of the Florida Keys is **Key West**, continental America's southernmost city. The ambiance of this two by four mile subtropical island—closer to Havana, Cuba, that to Miami—is embodied in its quaint, palm-studded streets and historic gingerbread mansions built a century ago. Key West's main street is said to be the "longest in the world" since it reaches from the Atlantic Ocean on one side of the island to the Gulf of Mexico on the other. Many Key West natives, who call themselves "Conchs," claim Bahamian ancestry. Add Yankee and Southern transplants and visitors from all over the world and Key West features a unique and delightful mix of cultures and customs.

Conch Fritters

Mayor Tom Sawyer
Key West, Florida

1 lb. conch (ground)
1 tbsp. garlic salt
1 cup self-rising flour
1 green pepper
1 onion
¼ tsp. black pepper
1 tbsp. tabasco sauce

6-8 servings

Chop onion and green pepper. Combine all ingredients with self-rising flour. Mix until thick batter is formed, adding water a little at a time until batter has consistency of dough. Over a medium to high flame, fry in deep fat in deep pot, spooning out batter by the tablespoon into hot fat. The conch fritters will rise to the top of the hot fat. Turn fritters until browned evenly. Serve hot with a tabasco sauce, if desired.

Key West, is America's southernmost city. See above for additional information on the city.

Crabmeat Dip

Mayor James L. Eason
Hampton, Virginia

16 oz. cream cheese
2 tbsp. milk
1 tbsp. Worcestershire sauce
1 lb. backfin crabmeat
4 tbsp. green onions (chopped)

Makes about 3 cups

In a double boiler, heat cream cheese, milk, and Worcestershire sauce. Add crabmeat and onions. Serve in chafing dish with crackers or small patty shells.

This is quick and very good.

Hampton, Virginia, is a 375-year-old city. Hampton was America's first continuous English settlement, as well as America's first site of free education, America's first training ground for the astronauts, and many other national firsts.

Hot Crab Dip

Mayor G. D. Williamson
Hattiesburg, Mississippi

1 lb. white crab meat
1 stick margarine
2 tbsp. flour
½ cup green onions (chopped)
1 pt. half-and-half
½ lb. Gouled Swiss cheese (Swiss cheese only)
½ cup cooking sherry

Makes 1½ quarts

Melt margarine; saute onions and flour. Add half-and-half and cheese; simmer about 5 minutes. Then add crab and sherry and heat through. If mixture is thicker than desired, add enough whole milk to obtain desired thickness. Serve hot, keep warm while serving.

Hattiesburg, which began as a lumber town, is called the Hub City because of its central location between the gulf coast and the state's capital. Many of the outstanding homes within the city have been designated as historical sites by the National Trust for Historic Preservation. Hattiesburg is the home of Southern Mississippi University and William Carey College.

Marinated Flank Steak

Mayor T. Patton Adams IV
Columbia, South Carolina

2 flank steaks, 1½-2 lb. each
⅔ cup vegetable oil
⅓ cup soy sauce
garlic salt to taste
1 tbsp. Worcestershire sauce (approximately)
⅓ cup tarragon vinegar

15-20 servings

Pierce flank steaks with fork. Sprinkle liberally with garlic salt. Mix remaining ingredients and pour over steaks. Marinate for 6 hours or overnight.

Broil or grill 6 minutes on each side. Slice thin diagonally across the grain of the meat. Serve hot or cold with toothpicks.

Wonderful served hot or cold as an hors d'oeuvre or picnic food.

The "recipe" for **Columbia** dates back to 1786, when the city was founded as the capitol of South Carolina. All the ingredients of this city have been blended to produce a repast sure to please any visitor. Let your eyes feast on the beauty of a sunrise on the historic Columbia Canal or a sunset on Lake Murray. The daytime menu offers a hearty mix of business, government, education, culture, and industry. For appetizers, you'll enjoy a veritable cornucopia of exciting events and interesting sites, from historic homes and nature preserves to a five star zoo and a wide range of cultural and recreational happenings. For dessert, there's golf, tennis, boating, and athletic events at the University of South Carolina. For an evening buffet, you can choose from a wide variety of international cuisine topped off with Columbia's colorful nightlife!

Oyster and Bacon Roll-Ups

Mayor Robert Jones
Virginia Beach, Virginia

1½ dozen fresh Lynnhaven oysters (shucked)

bacon

6 servings

Cut strips of bacon in half crosswise. Wrap each half around oyster. Secure with a toothpick. Broil about 5 minutes, turning once. Serve hot.

These delicious morsels are also known as ''angels on horseback.''

Virginia Beach has something for everyone. Our beaches and boardwalk provide leisure in the sun, our historical sites date back to 1607 with the First Landing of the Jamestown expedition, and our new Virginia Marine Science Museum offers unique family entertainment and has experienced record attendance. Virginia Beach truly has something for everyone and is a great place to vacation and live.

Party Ham Biscuits

Mayor Harry A. Connor
Gastonia, North Carolina

¼ lb. butter (room temperature)

2 tbsp. poppy seeds

2 tbsp. prepared hot mustard

2 tsp. Worcestershire sauce

1 small onion (grated)

1 pkg. (20) Pepperidge Farm party rolls

4 oz. cooked ham (sliced)

1 4 oz. pkg. sliced Swiss cheese

20 servings

Mix first 5 ingredients, split rolls and spread with mixture (on both sides), top each half with ham, then one half with small slice of cheese. Close halves. Heat in 350⁰ oven only until cheese melts. (May be frozen before heating.)

This recipe is a big hit with the men.

Gastonia is a city of 53,000 located in the heart of the Piedmont Crescent of the two Carolinas. Because of Gastonia's leadership role in commerce and industry, we have been known as the "Pacemaker of the Piedmont." Gastonia is strategically located between the coast, the mountains, and the major markets of the Southeast. The slogan for the city is "A Commitment to Excellence."

CITY TRIVIA QUESTION #16
Home of the United States Coast Guard Academy.
Answer on page 26.

Piedmont Cheese Soup

Mayor Carlton B. "Buddy" Holt
Albemarle, North Carolina

3 strips bacon
2 tbsp. onion (chopped)
1 cup celery (chopped)
1 cup carrots (chopped)
2 cups potatoes (cut up)
2 cups broccoli (cut up into flowerets)
2-3 cups milk
¼ lb. Velveeta

6-8 servings

Cook bacon; reserve. Saute onion until clear; add celery and carrots and 2 cups of water. Cook about 15 minutes, add potatoes, cook another 15 minutes. Add broccoli, cook until done and water is gone. Add milk (do not boil); just before serving add cheese and allow to melt. Crumble bacon on top.

Albemarle—a most beautiful place—located centrally in Piedmont North Carolina—just a few hours away from the mountains and the beaches.

CITY TRIVIA QUESTION #17

California city that serves as the "Western White House" when President Reagan vacations at his ranch.

Answer on page 203.

MAIN DISHES

Bayou Seafood Casserole

Mayor Pat Screen
Baton Rouge, Louisiana

1 8 oz. pkg. cream cheese
1 stick margarine or butter
1 lb. shrimp (peeled)
1 large onion (chopped)
1 bell pepper (chopped)
2 ribs celery (chopped)
2 tbsp. butter
1 can mushroom soup
1 can mushrooms (drained)
1 tbsp. garlic salt
1 tsp. tabasco
½ tsp. red pepper
1 pt. crabmeat
¾ cup cooked rice
sharp cheese (grated)
cracker crumbs

8 servings

Melt cream cheese and butter using a double boiler. Saute shrimp, onion, pepper, and celery in 2 tablespoons butter; add to the first mixture. Add soup, mushrooms, seasonings, crabmeat, and rice. Mix well, place in a 2 quart casserole, and top with cheese and cracker crumbs. Bake at 350° 20-30 minutes until bubbly. Freezes well.

The Mississippi River gently flows through **Baton Rouge** serenading the richness of life here—from the savory Cajun cooking, the arts and festivals, the moss-draped oaks, and friendliness of the people, to the excitement of LSU and Southern football, Catfish Town Marketplace, and the State Capitol. Baton Rouge successfully combines a vibrant metropolitan center with the graceful surroundings of our rich Southern heritage, making "Red Stick" a great place to live.

Beef Stroganoff

Mayor James C. Wallace
Chapel Hill, North Carolina

2 lb. tender beef
salt and pepper to taste
5 tbsp. butter
1 tbsp. flour
2 cups beef stock
2 tsp. prepared mustard
2 tbsp. ketchup
4 tbsp. sour cream
3 cups mushrooms (thinly sliced)
1 onion (thinly sliced)

4-6 servings

Cut beef into narrow strips ½" thick and 2" long. Season with salt and pepper, and let meat stand for 2 hours in refrigerator.

Blend 2 tablespoons butter with 1 tablespoon flour over low heat until mixture bubbles and is smooth. Stir in 2 cups beef stock and simmer until mixture begins to thicken. Boil for 2 minutes and stir in 2 teaspoons prepared mustard, 2 tablespoons ketchup, and 4 tablespoons sour cream. Simmer gently, without boiling.

Brown the pieces of meat in 3 tablespoons butter. In separate pan, saute lightly mushrooms and onion in butter. Add meat, mushrooms, and onion

to the sour cream sauce. Cover the saucepan and put it over hot water for 20 minutes. Serve hot.

Chapel Hill is a charming and unique community, an oasis surrounded by the beauty of an expanding greenway, different in each of the four distinct seasons: the dogwood of spring (redbud and wisteria, too); the pleasant temperatures of summer; the radiant colors of fall; and the occasional snowfall ushering in the moderate cold of winter. The winding streets, rock walls, and subtle village atmosphere give us a sense of privacy while having people from around the world residing in every neighborhood. Ours are a cosmopolitan people, many affiliated with the Greater University of North Carolina, and internationally known seat of higher learning. Chapel Hill is the home of the Tar Heels of North Carolina, who are also internationally known for their athletic prowess.

Biloxi Boiled Shrimp

Mayor Gerald Blessey
Biloxi, Mississippi

6 qts. water
5 lb. shrimp
1 tsp. liquid Crab Boil seasoning
1 tbsp. salt
3-4 celery leaves
orange peel from half an orange
1 bay leaf

4 servings

Bring to boil all ingredients; add shrimp. When water comes back to boiling point, cover pot and simmer for 12 minutes. Pour off water at once. Serve hot or cold. Peel as you eat.

On the first weekend in June each year, Biloxians celebrate the Blessing of the Shrimp Fleet and the Shrimp

Festival. On Saturday, ten thousand tourists and residents gather to crown the Shrimp King and Queen and to eat Biloxi boiled shrimp. On Sunday, the Bishop of Biloxi blesses the fleet in Biloxi harbor with thousands of family and friends on board approximately 500 vessels.

Biloxi is the shrimp capital of the world. Founded in 1699 by French colonists, Biloxi is a melting pot of fishermen and seafood workers of European, Asian, and African descent. In the heart of America's Riviera, Biloxi is host to hundreds of conventions and thousands of tourists who visit its twelve miles of beach annually.

Home of Keesler Air Force Base, the Air Force's electronics training center, Biloxi is proud of its role in America's defense.

Cajun Pork Tenderloin

Mayor William D. Workman, III
Greenville, South Carolina

3-4 lb. boneless pork tenderloin
¾ cup celery (chopped)
¾ cup onion (chopped)
½ cup green bell pepper (chopped)
4 tbsp. margarine
1 tsp. black pepper
1 tsp. red pepper
1 tsp. white pepper
½ tbsp. salt

6 servings

Saute chopped celery, onion, and green pepper in margarine over medium heat for 10 minutes. Remove from heat and add ground peppers and salt. Deeply score the tenderloin every 2" and stuff with the sauteed mixture. Bake at 325⁰ for 1½-2½ hours, depending on size of roast.

Greenville is a down home, comfortable, vigorous city of 60,000 located in the northwest corner of South Carolina. Once known as the textile center of the world, Greenville now boasts a variety of businesses and industries. One of our most popular community events is Fall for Greenville—a downtown food and entertainment festival that draws over 50,000 people to downtown Greenville on a Sunday afternoon in October.

Charleston Shrimp Pilau

Mayor Joseph P. Riley, Jr.
Charleston, South Carolina

4 slices bacon
1 cup rice (uncooked)
3 tbsp. butter
½ cup celery (finely diced)
¼ cup green pepper (chopped)
1 lb. shrimp (shelled and deveined)
salt and pepper to taste
1 tsp. Worcestershire sauce
1 tbsp. flour

6 servings

Fry bacon until crisp; set aside. Add bacon drippings to water in which you cook rice and cook according to directions.

In another pot, melt butter; add celery and green pepper and cook for a few minutes. Add shrimp, which have been previously sprinkled with Worcestershire sauce and dredged in flour. Stir and simmer until flour is cooked. Season to taste with salt and pepper. Add cooked rice and mix until well blended; stir in the crumbled bacon. Serve hot.

Charleston, South Carolina, the historic colonial city on the Atlantic Coast, caters to the craving of the palate for fine seafood. Charleston's many historic sites of interest include Fort Sumter where the Civil War began in 1861, and perhaps the best-preserved collection of 18-19th century buildings in this country. Charleston is the American home of the Spoleto Festival.

Chicken with Dumplings

Mayor Alex Daoud
Miami Beach, Florida

CHICKEN:
1 4½-5 lb. stewing chicken (cut up)
1 medium onion studded with 3 whole cloves
3 celery tops
1 carrot (sliced)
2 bay leaves
1 tbsp. salt
3 cups hot water
DUMPLINGS:
1⅓ cups all purpose flour
2 tsp. double-acting baking powder
1 tsp. chopped parsley
1½ tsp. salt
⅔ cup milk
2 tbsp. salad oil

4 servings

Chicken: In 8 quart saucepot over high heat, heat chicken, neck, giblets, and remaining ingredients to boiling. Reduce heat. Cover; simmer for 2-2½ hours. Discard onion, celery, and bay leaves.

Dumplings: In a large bowl, stir dry ingredients with fork until mixed. In a cup, combine milk and oil. Slowly stir into flour until soft dough forms. Drop by heaping tablespoon onto chicken and broth. Cook uncovered for 10 minutes. Cover and cook for 10 more minutes. With slotted spoon, remove dumplings. Spoon chicken into serving dish and top with dumplings.

The City of **Miami Beach** has some of the most beautiful beaches in the world, covering a three mile stretch of sand and sun, available for visitors and residents year-round. In the southern portion of the island and facing the Atlantic Ocean is the Art Deco District, recently placed in the National Register of Historic Places and one of the most outstanding displays of period architecture to be found in the United States.

The sunny climate and balmy breezes found in Miami Beach make the city a perfect vacation spot during any season, and you can always find exciting events going on in our parks and beaches, as well as four star hotels and restaurants to please even the most extravagant traveler.

Chicken with Rice

Mayor Raul L. Martinez
Hialeah, Florida

2 whole chickens (2 lb. each)
1 tbsp. margarine
½ cup onions (chopped)
½ lb. ground ham
1 cup tomato sauce
4 cups chicken broth
1 lb. rice (preferably Valencia)
½ tsp. salt
¼ tsp. pepper
⅓ cup Parmesan cheese (grated)
1 cup canned petit pois (small peas)
½ cup sliced pimientos

6 servings

Debone chicken; cut into large pieces. Saute onions in butter. Cook chicken, ham, tomato sauce, and onions over low heat for 5 minutes, stirring frequently. Add the rest of the ingredients with the exception of the cheese, peas, and pimientos. Bring ingredients to a boil. Cover and simmer for 30 minutes or until chicken and rice are cooked. Garnish with cheese, peas and pimientos. Serve with fried plantains.

With 160,000 residents, **Hialeah** is the fifth largest city in Florida. The city is rich in ethnic diversity. About 85 percent of the residents are Hispanic, about 14 percent white, and about 1 percent black. We have a large manufacturing sector. Centrally located and easily accessible, Hialeah is located about 10 minutes from Miami International Airport. In addition to many parks and recreation centers, Hialeah is home to world-famous Hialeah Park, a race course that also is an Audubon bird sanctuary with a large band of flamingos.

Crab Norfolk Casserole

Mayor Joseph A. Leafe
Norfolk, Virginia

1 lb. crabmeat
½ cup sherry
3 slices soft white bread
½ cup mayonnaise
½ cup light cream (half-and-half is fine)
½ stick butter (melted)
juice of ½ lemon
1 tsp. Worcestershire sauce

4 servings

Marinate crabmeat in sherry (may add more to moisten thoroughly) for several hours. Break bread into small pieces and add to crabmeat with mayonnaise, melted butter, light cream, lemon juice, and Worcestershire sauce. Bake at 350⁰ for 20 minutes.

May be served in shells as entree or in chafing dish with crackers as a hot hors d'oeuvre.

Norfolk is the cultural, economic, and business hub of the Greater Hampton Roads area. Tall ships and character vessels from all over the world visit the city's newly revitalized downtown waterfront, a place where people can enjoy the sights and sounds of one of the world's busiest harbors. The Chrysler Museum at Norfolk houses one of the south's finest art collections and one of the finest collections of glass in the world. Other popular visitor attractions include the General Douglas MacArthur Memorial, the Virginia Zoological Park, and The Waterside festival marketplace.

Crawfish Elegante

Mayor Pat Screen
Baton Rouge, Louisiana

1 lb. crawfish tails
1½ sticks butter or margarine
1 small bunch green onions
½ cup parsley (chopped)
1 pt. half-and-half
3 tbsp. sherry
salt and red pepper to taste
3 level tbsp. flour

4 servings

In skillet saute crawfish tails in ½ stick butter or margarine for 10 minutes. In another skillet saute green onions and parsley in 1 stick of butter or margarine. Blend in flour gradually; add half-and-half, stirring constantly, to make a thick sauce. Add sherry, then crawfish tails, being careful not to include fat in bottom of skillet. Season with salt and red pepper to taste. Serve in pattie shells or over rice. Will freeze well.

NOTE: Before cooking crawfish tails, lay on paper towels and wipe gently to remove some of the fat.

Baton Rouge, the state capital of Louisiana, is located on the Mississippi River. For further information on Baton Rouge, turn to page 66-67.

Enchiladas

Mayor Richard H. Fulton
Nashville, Tennessee

1 recipe taco meat (see below)
1 can green chilies (chopped)
2 tbsp. parsley (chopped)
8 oz. Monterey Jack cheese (grated)
12 tortillas
1 pt. sour cream
1 jalapeno pepper (seeded)
1 tsp. salt
TACO MEAT:
1 lb. ground beef
1 medium onion (chopped)
½ tsp. ground cumin
1 tbsp. chili powder
1 tsp. salt
¼ tsp. pepper
2 cloves garlic (minced)
1 can Ro-Tel brand tomatoes and green chilies

6 servings

Enchiladas: Dip each tortilla into hot oil in skillet for 2-4 seconds to soften. Place 2 tablespoons taco meat on each tortilla and roll. Place close together in ungreased baking dish. Combine chilies, parsley, pepper, sour cream, and salt in blender and mix well. Spread over enchiladas and top with cheese. Bake 15-20 minutes at 350° or until cheese is melted and bubbly.

Taco Meat: Cook beef and onion in skillet about 5 minutes. Add remaining ingredients and stir over medium heat, mashing tomatoes and mixing well. Reduce heat, cover, and simmer about 30 minutes, stirring occasionally.

Nashville, Tennessee's capital city, settled on the banks of the Cumberland River in 1779, is home to 475,000, 14 colleges and universities, the world renown Grand Ole Opry, the historical Hermitage landmark honoring President Andrew Jackson and is known as the "Athens of the South." Downtown revitalization, along with diversified industry throughout the area, is pushing the city forward as a "Boom Town" in the '80s.

Flanagin Soup

Mayor Ted Crozier
Clarksville, Tennessee

2 lb. lean ground beef
1 small head cabbage (chopped)
1 large onion (chopped)
3-4 carrots (sliced)
6 cups water
1 bay leaf
pinch of thyme
dash of oregano
salt and pepper to taste
4 beef bouillon cubes
¼ cup barley
2 stalks celery (sliced)
1 2 lb. can tomatoes (sliced)
3-4 medium potatoes (cubed)
½ cup macaroni

Makes 6 quarts

Brown beef and drain off excess fat. Add next 12 ingredients; cook for 1 hour. Add potatoes, macaroni, and enough water to make 6 quarts of soup; cook an additional 30 minutes.

This is my favorite soup; it is really hearty—sticks to the ribs!

continued

Clarksville, the Queen City of the Cumberland River, brings a rich history to a rapidly growing metropolitan area. From its early history as the hub of the tobacco industry in the southeast, Clarksville has evolved into a multifaceted city. Clarksville is home to the 101st Airborne Division, "Screaming Eagles" stationed at the Fort Campbell Military Reservation. Although the city is looking to a future of continued growth and expansion, it has not forgotten its past. The city has paid particular attention to the preservation of the many historic buildings in its central business district while expanding its role as a river city that provides a good location to live, work, and play.

Jambalaya

Mayor Sidney Barthelemy
New Orleans, Louisiana

1½ lb. Andouille (hot sausage)
1½ lb. smoked sausage
2 onions (chopped finely)
1 bell pepper (chopped finely)
1 stalk celery (chopped finely)
4 cloves garlic (chopped finely)
10 oz. can tomato sauce
10 oz. can whole tomatoes
6 cups rice (cooked)
salt to taste
1 tbsp. cayenne pepper
½ tsp. basil
½ tsp. thyme

6 servings

Steam rice separately. Saute first six ingredients in small amount of oil for about 6 minutes. Add tomato sauce and whole tomatoes; simmer 10 minutes. While sauce is simmering, add the cayenne pepper, basil, and thyme to cooked rice. Serve in oblong baking dish over rice.

This Jambalaya is one of the best around!

New Orleans is a city of skyscrapers, a thriving, busy, urban place. It is a city of quiet, stately houses in the Garden District, and the noise and bustle of Bourbon Street. New Orleans is the Mississippi River, the stern-wheelers and the sidewheelers and steamboat lore, and it is the big, sprawling international port, second largest in the U.S. It is the Superdome, the Superbowl, the French Quarter, streetcars, jazz, and the finest food in the world. It was also the site for the 1985 World's Fair with its theme of water.

Lasagna

Mayor Joe Viterisi
Paducah, Kentucky

1 lb. ground beef
1 onion (chopped)
2 tsp. garlic (chopped)
1 15 oz. can tomato sauce
1 6 oz. can tomato paste
salt and pepper to taste
1½ tsp. oregano
½ 16 oz. box lasagna noodles
1 egg (beaten)
1 tsp. salt
1½ cup large curd cottage cheese
1 lb. mozzarella cheese (grated)
⅓ cup Parmesan cheese (grated)

6 servings

Brown beef, onion, and garlic. Drain fat and add tomato sauce, tomato paste, oregano, salt and pepper to taste. Simmer 1 hour. Cook noodles in boiling, salted water until tender; drain. Combine egg, cottage cheese, and 1 teaspoom salt, mix well. In greased 3 quart baking dish arrange alternate layers of half the noodles, half the meat sauce, half the cottage cheese, half the mozzarella, and half the Parmesan cheese. Repeat layers. Bake at 375⁰ for 30 minutes. Let stand 15 minutes before serving.

Paducah, Kentucky, is a community rich in heritage, dynamic in spirit, and generously endowed with warm southern hospitality. Founded on the site of a Chickasaw Indian village, Paducah was named after the tribe's colorful Chief Paduke. The city rests in the middle of Kentucky's western waterland paradise. Being surrounded by rivers—the Ohio, the Tennessee, the Cumberland—and by the largest man-made lakes in the world, Lake Barkley and Kentucky Lake, works a special magic on natives and visitors alike. Thousands visit Paducah annually, home of former U.S. Vice President Alben "The Veep" Barkley and humorist Irvin S. Cobb, to tour the historic district, sample the famous southern cuisine, visit the many tourist attractions, and to enjoy the beautiful scenery. "Paducah, easy to get to and hard to leave."

Mother's Dirty Rice

Mayor Aaron F. Broussard
Kenner, Louisiana

| 1 lb. country sausage |
| 1 lb. ground chuck |
| 1 extra large can mushrooms (stems and pieces) |
| 3 onions (chopped) |
| 1 small bunch green onions (chopped) |
| 1 green pepper (chopped) |
| 2 cans mushroom gravy |
| 2 cups uncooked rice |

10 servings

Cook rice and set aside. Cook sausage, drain grease, and set aside. Cook ground chuck and set aside. Saute onions and pepper until glossy.

Mix all ingredients and place in covered pan; cook at 375⁰ for 20-30 minutes.

The City of **Kenner** is located ten miles west of New Orleans. It is embraced by the grandeur of the Mississippi River on the south and the greatness of Lake Pontchartrain on the north and in the corridor of these bodies of water, Kenner possesses the glory of alluvial soil and is the nation's leading producer of okra.

Paella Valenciana

Mayor Sandra Freedman
Tampa, Florida

| ½ lb. pork (cut in chunks) |
| ½ lb. fryer chicken (cut into pieces) |
| 1 lb. lobster (cut in chunks) |
| ½ lb. shrimp (peeled) |
| 8 oysters (shucked) |
| 8 scallops |
| 8 muscles |
| 4 clams in shells |
| 4 stone crab claws |
| 1 lb. red snapper (cut in chunks) |
| 6 cups chicken stock or bottled clam juice |
| 1 onion (chopped) |
| 1 green pepper (chopped) |
| 3 garlic cloves (chopped) |
| 1 bay leaf |
| ½ cup whole tomatoes |
| ½ cup olive oil |
| 1½ cups rice |
| 1 tsp. salt |
| 1 pinch saffron |
| ¼ cup white wine |

4 servings

Pour oil in heavy casserole; add onion and pepper and fry until limp but not brown. Add garlic, bay leaf, pork and chicken and saute until tender, stirring to prevent sticking or burning. Chop tomatoes in blender and add to mixture; simmer for 5 minutes.

Add seafood, stock, rice, and saffron and stir. Allow to come to boil; cover and bake at 350⁰ for 20 minutes.

When ready to serve sprinkle with white wine. Garnish with fresh vegetables such as small green peas, asparagus, or sliced pimientos.

This extremely versatile dish allows you to use any native seafood in lieu of stated ingredients. This is the National Dish of Spain!

Tampa and the surrounding Bay area located along Florida's central west coast, represents one of the fastest growing metropolitan areas in the nation. While tourism remains an important part of the local economy, the establishment of new high technology and service industry operations in the area have provided the city with a new growth-oriented image. Primary attractions include the warm climate, proximity to the beaches of the Gulf of Mexico, a busy harbor and seaport, and two major universities. In addition, the cost of living and tax burden of the area are relatively low.

Although the Sun Belt boom-town image dominates Tampa's character, the city has retained significant elements of its past. Ybor City—the Latin Quarter—was a center for major trade with Latin America and home of a once-thriving cigar manufacturing industry. The elegant Henry B. Plant Hotel—now the University of Tampa campus—is the most visible reminder of the influence of early-Florida land speculation as well as the important role of tourism. The city served as the headquarters for Teddy Roosevelt and his Roughriders before the Spanish-American War.

Palmetto Chicken
Mayor Elizabeth D. Rhea
Rock Hill, South Carolina

6 boned chicken breasts
3 cans mushroom soup
2 pkgs. dried beef
bacon

8 servings

Cut chicken breasts in half; wrap with bacon. Line casserole dish with dried beef. Place wrapped chicken breasts on dried beef. Pour mushroom soup over chicken. Bake uncovered for 1½ hours at 350⁰. Serve with wild rice.

From our beautiful Glencairn Garden, inspiration for our annual 10-day Come See Me Festival, to our innovative Cherry Park, a 68-acre leisure facility, **Rock Hill** has a lot to offer everyone! As the "gateway to South Carolina," Rock Hill is ready to welcome you on your way to Myrtle Beach, Charleston, and points south.

Patitas de Cerdo
Mayor Angel Leon-Martinez
Juana Diaz, Puerto Rico

3 lb. salted pork feet
4 medium sized potatoes
1 large onion (chopped)
1 green pepper (chopped)
6 cloves garlic
1 can chick peas
1 4 oz. can tomato sauce
½ lb. hot Spanish sausage
¼ tsp. ground oregano

1 tbsp. salt

½ tsp. black pepper

6 servings

The night before serving, wash pork thoroughly and place it in a large saucepan filled with hot water.

The next day change the hot water; pork is ready when it is desalted. Cook under pressure in 3 quarts of water for 20 minutes, or until soft. Remove from pressure cooker and put into 5-quart saucepan, and add potatoes, onion, green pepper, and sausage. Grind garlic with salt, pepper, and oregano; add to pan and cook over medium high heat for about 20 minutes. Add tomato sauce and chick peas and cook about 10 more minutes. Serve over rice.

Best when served with Puerto Rican style white, short or medium grain rice. A tomato and lettuce salad is welcome.

Juana Diaz is a friendly and pleasant city located on the southern coast of Puerto Rico. It houses over 50,000 within its valley and surrounding mountains. During its 184 years, Juana Diaz has been characterized by a high sense of traditionalism. There are four major celebrations throughout the year, all of which reflect our cultural heritage. Juana Diaz has a sculpture of the Three Kings in the Public Square, representing our three races of origin—colonization by the whites, slavery by the blacks, and our native Indian Taino. The purest white marble in America is found in the Juana Diaz mountains.

CITY TRIVIA QUESTION #18

The oldest city under the American flag in the western hemisphere.

Answer on page 77.

Pernil Asado (Roast Pork)

Mayor Victor M. Soto Santiago
Toa Baja, Puerto Rico

10 lb. roasting pork (hind quarters)	
10 garlic cloves (crushed)	
2 tbsp. black pepper	
4 tbsp. salt	
3 tbsp. oregano	
3 tbsp. vinegar	
¼ cup olive oil	

8 servings

Thoroughly wash pork. With a sharp knife pierce the meat, making ¼" incisions all around the roast. Place in a deep baking dish and set aside. Prepare marinade; stir together the garlic, black pepper, salt, oregano, vinegar, and oil. Pour over the roast being sure to cover all incisions.

Place in refrigerator overnight or for a minimum of 4 hours. Remove from refrigerator, cover with aluminum foil and place in preheated oven at 350⁰. Roast 4 hours or until meat thermometer reads 185⁰. (Serve with Arroz con Gandules.)

Although not exclusively reserved for Christmas Season, this dish is a typical food served throughout the island during the holidays. (This recipe can be increased or decreased according to the number of people being served.)

This 241-year-old city, ninth largest on the island, yet only 24 square miles in size, grew up in back of a church due to a change in the coarse of Rio La Plata. Thus, **Toa Baja** holds the distinction of being the only town so situated in all of Puerto Rico. Home of historic sites, diverse modern industries, beautiful beaches, and the fresh fish center of the North Coast, Toa Baja proudly boasts of being truly "The City as Friendly as a Small Town."

Picadillo

Mayor Xavier L. Suarez
Miami, Florida

¼ cup olive oil
1 onion (chopped)
1 bell pepper (chopped)
1 clove garlic (chopped)
½ lb. ground beef
½ lb. ground pork
½ lb. ground ham
¼ cup capers
1 tsp. salt
1/8 tsp. pepper
½ cup tomato sauce
¼ cup dry wine

6 servings

Heat oil and saute onion, garlic, and pepper. Add meats and cook for a few minutes, constantly stirring so it does not stick. Add other ingredients and cook for 20 minutes over medium heat until cooked through. Serve with rice on the side.

Miami is a city with a nice blend of natural beauty and multiethnic diversity. For further information on Miami, turn to page 61-62.

Pigeon Marinade (Squab)

Mayor Benjamin Cole
Mayaguez, Puerto Rico

4 pigeons (1 lb. each)
2 spoonfuls salt
½ tsp. black pepper
2 bay leaves
½ lb. onion (grated)
¼ cup vinegar

1 cup oil
2 bell peppers
4 spoonfuls butter

4 servings

Season pigeons with salt and pepper. Brown in oil and top with onion, butter, bay leaves, and vinegar. Cover pan and cook at low heat until tender. Add the bell peppers and cook uncovered for 5 minutes. Serve with white rice.

Mayaguez is located on the western coast of Puerto Rico on the Caribbean. According to historians the city was founded in 1760. Mayaguez is also the birthplace of the Puerto Ricans national anthem, "La Borinquena." For years, Mayaguez has been an important center of industrial activity, and has perhaps the largest needlework industry in the world. Also, the sugar mills are an important source of economic activity for the area's residents. Because of its location, Mayaguez is a recreational and tourist attraction.

Pinon (Stuffed Ripe Plantains)

Mayor Baltasar Corrada-del Rio
San Juan, Puerto Rico

1 cup tomato sauce
1 onion (chopped)
2 garlic cloves (chopped)
¼ cup oil
1 green pepper (chopped)
1½ lb. lean ground meat
3 ripe plantains
½ cup vegetable oil
1 can French cut green beans
6 eggs
½ cup milk

salt and pepper to taste

parmesan cheese (optional)

6 servings

Place the first five ingredients in heavy pan and cook for a few minutes until tender. Add ground meat and cook until brown, then cover and simmer for 10 minutes. Add strained can of green beans and salt and pepper. Peel the ripe plantains and cut thin slices lengthwise. Fry in hot oil. Beat eggs and add ½ cup milk. In buttered baking dish add ¼ part of the beaten egg mixture, then cover with plantains. Add meat mixture and pour ¼ part of the eggs. Sprinkle with parmesan cheese if desired and then cover with the rest of the plantains and eggs.

Place in 350⁰ oven for 30 minutes and serve hot.

San Juan, the capital city of Puerto Rico, is the oldest city under the American flag in the Western Hemisphere. Founded in 1540, San Juan is a thriving center of culture, commerce, and tourism. The city has a pleasant blend of old Spanish architecture, modern office buildings, and oceanfront hotels. Today San Juan Proper includes the zones of Santurce, Hato Rey and Rio Piedras, and the entire metropolitan area encompasses some 300 square miles and a third of the island's three million residents.

Seafood from the Bayou
Mayor Andrew Young
Atlanta, Georgia

1 lb. fresh shrimp (peeled and deveined)
1 lb. fresh crayfish (peeled and deveined)
1 lb. crabmeat
1 pt. oysters with liquid
1 large bunch scallions
1 stick butter

½ cup celery (minced)
½ pt. cream
½ cup flour
1 tsp. creole seafood seasoning
1 tsp. Worcestershire sauce

6 servings

Remove shells from oysters. Trim and chop scallions; melt butter in large pot with scallions and celery. Saute until wilted but not browned. Add shrimp and crayfish tails and cook for 5 minutes. Add crabmeat, oysters, and oyster liquid. Cook for 10 minutes longer. Mix cream with flour and stir into seafood mixture. Cook and stir on low heat until thickened. Stir in seasoning. Serve over freshly cooked pasta.

Atlanta is a universally recognized city of international prominence characterized by an even blend of modern economic vitality, social progress, and cultural diversity. With the establishment of Hartsfield International Airport, the largest and busiest air terminal in the world, Atlanta has been able to develop a strong business community that transcends national limits. Approaching its 150th birthday, Atlanta, once known as Terminus because of its railroad heritage, is a big city with a small town air and a population proud of its long-established reputation for southern hospitality.

Seafood Pie
Mayor Robert A. Dressler
Fort Lauderdale, Florida

9″ pie shell (unbaked)
¼ cup onions (diced small)
¼ cup green peppers (diced small)
¼ cup butter
1 clove garlic (minced)

continued

1 tomato (seeded and chopped)

6 oz. Jarlsburg cheese (grated large)

1 egg yolk

2 oz. crabmeat (diced small)

9 oz. cooked shrimp (diced small)

2 oz. cooked lobster (diced small)

1½ tbsp. mayonnaise

1 tbsp. chopped parsley

1 tsp. oregano

1 tsp. basil

1 tsp. salt

½ tsp. black pepper

2 tbsp. bread crumbs

1 tsp. paprika

8 servings

Saute the onions and green peppers in butter; when the vegetables are almost tender, add the garlic and finish cooking; allow vegetables to cool. Combine vegetables, tomato, cheese, egg yolk, seafood, mayonnaise, parsley and seasonings; mix together gently. Cover and place mixture in refrigerator for 1 hour. Fill pie shell with the mixture; sprinkle with bread crumbs and paprika. Bake at 425⁰ for approximately 25 minutes. Do not overbake. Cut seafood pie into 8 equal portions and serve.

Fort Lauderdale, "The Venice of America," truly serves as the yachting capital of the world with abundant waterway dining, night life, business and residential areas. The picturesque New River winds its way through the city serving as an historical link between a revitalized downtown and the beach area. A Winterfest Boat Parade, New River Street Dance, Seafood Festival, and River Raft Race are but a few of the water-oriented annual events that residents and visitors enjoy in Fort Lauderdale.

Seafood Stew

Mayor James W. Holley, III
Portsmouth, Virginia

¼ cup salt pork (diced)

1 large onion (coarsely chopped)

3 stalks celery (coarsely chopped)

½ medium green pepper (coarsely chopped)

1 lb. can tomatoes (coarsely chopped)

1 qt. fish stock

½ cup white wine

½ pt. oysters with juice

1 tsp. salt

½ tsp. lemon pepper

½ tsp. thyme

1 can potato soup

1½ lb. fish (boiled, drained, and flaked)

6-8 mussels (in shells)

6-8 clams (in shells)

6 servings

Saute salt pork in medium-sized pot for 10 minutes or until golden. Add chopped onion, celery, and green pepper and continue cooking on medium heat until clear. Add tomatoes, stock, wine, and seasonings. Continue cooking over slightly lowered heat for 10-15 minutes. Add potato soup, fish, mussels, clams, and oysters with juice. Cover and continue cooking until mussels and clams open. (Can use scallops, crabmeat, shrimp.)

Located in the heart of Hampton Roads, **Portsmouth**, Virginia, is indeed one of the finest cities in America. This historical maritime community offers a wealth of activities and attractions to its citizens and visitors alike. The Portsmouth Museums, which include the Lightship, the Naval Shipyard, and a "hands on" Children's Museum, preserve the diverse history and culture of the city. Moreover, the downtown waterfront has been transformed into a festive marketplace with an array of shops, dining areas, and entertainment activities. Adjacent to this beautiful area lies Olde Towne, site of one of the largest collections of antique houses in the country. There is something for everyone to see and do in Portsmouth.

Seranata Multicolor

Mayor Juan M. Higgins Santana
Humacao, Puerto Rico

2 lb. salted cod fish
2 lb. onions (sliced)
2 lb. tomatoes (sliced)
4 hard-cooked eggs (sliced)
2 avocados (sliced)
stuffed green olives (as desired)
SAUCE:
1 cup olive oil
½ cup vinegar
½ tsp. salt
¼ tsp. pepper

6-8 servings

Soak cod fish in water for 4 hours. Drain and add 2 liters of fresh water. Boil fish for 15 minutes; rinse and remove skin and bones. Tear fish into small pieces. Mix in bowl with onions, tomatoes, eggs, avocados, and olives. Add sauce and stir to mix. Serve cold. This dish is often accompanied with plantains, patatas (very small white potatoes), or yautias (yucca root).

Make sure fish is free of bones. Great for a luncheon.

Established in 1793, **Humacao** was named after the Indian Chief Jumacao. The town also is known as the Gray City. If you're ever in Puerto Rico come down to Humacao and visit our beautiful city.

Shrimp and Oyster Pilaf

Mayor John P. Rousakis
Savannah, Georgia

2 cups onion (chopped)
2 sticks butter
1 15 oz. can tomato sauce
1 15 oz. can whole tomatoes
3 cups chicken broth
2 cups Uncle Ben's Converted brand rice
1½ lb. shrimp (peeled and deveined, if large, cut in bite size pieces)
1 qt. oysters (drained)
salt and pepper

6-10 servings

Place onion in a 4 quart size pot, brown slightly with 1 stick butter. Add tomato sauce and whole tomatoes, mashed thoroughly. Let simmer for about 15 minutes. Add chicken broth, salt and pepper to taste, and let simmer for an additional 30 minutes. Bring to a boil and add rice, shrimp, and oysters. Stir well. Reduce heat *immediately* to very low, cover pot, and cook without removing top for 20 minutes.

While this is cooking, place 1 stick butter in a skillet and burn until black. Take pot off fire, remove top, and stir well. Then pour hot, burnt butter into pot, stir again, and serve.

Each year, I auction two dinners for 16 people for the Annual Savannah Symphony Auction. This dish, which combines some local seafood with a Greek flair, is one of the most popular selections. I will prepare this along with five other courses in the home of the winning group.

Savannah was the only Southern city saved on General Sherman's march to the sea. For further information on Savannah, turn to page 84.

Shrimp and Rice Casserole

Mayor Vicki Chastain
Marietta, Georgia

2½ lb. fresh shrimp
1 tbsp. lemon juice
·3 tbsp. vegetable oil
1 cup raw rice
2 tbsp. butter
¼ cup green pepper (chopped)
¼ cup onion (chopped)
1 tsp. salt
1/8 tsp. pepper
1/8 tsp. red pepper
1 can tomato soup
1 cup half-and-half
½ cup sherry
¾ cup almonds (toasted and sliced)

6 servings

Boil and peel shrimp. Cook rice. Cook onion and green pepper in butter until soft. Combine remaining ingredients with the above mixture. Bake uncovered at 350⁰ for 45 minutes.

Marietta, Georgia, located just north of Atlanta, is a city rich in history. Founded in 1834 and carved from Cherokee Indian territory, Marietta has evolved into a growing, thriving city with over 40,000 residents. Today, stately, antebellum homes and a beautifully restored historic district and city park provide the perfect contrast to the sleek new shopping and business centers and exciting amusement parks. Skillfully blending the old with the new, Marietta offers the best of both worlds.

Smoked Turkey

Mayor J. W. ''Bill'' Feighner
Columbus, Georgia

1 15-17 lb. turkey
1 large onion
4-5 cloves garlic
½ lb. melted margarine or butter
2 oz. Worcestershire sauce
2 oz. Liquid Smoke
3 tsp. salt
1 tsp. black or white pepper
1 tsp. tabasco
1 glass cooking wine
2 oz. vinegar

8 servings

Blend onion and garlic in blender until as mushy as possible; add all the rest of the ingredients and blend thoroughly. Place turkey over slow fire or grill, using a revolving spit if available. DO NOT prick with fork to turn, use pot holders if you don't have a spit. Baste with sauce often during cooking time. Cooking time is 4-4½ hours, but well worth it. You will never want another oven baked turkey.

Excellent dish with rice casserole, hot biscuits and fruit salad with poppy seed dressing.

Columbus, Georgia, is the second largest city in the state of Georgia and was Georgia's first consolidated government formed in 1971. Columbus is part of a tri-city area with the Ft. Benning reservation and Phenix City, Alabama, across the river. Columbus has a number of Civil War era buildings, including a naval museum containing Confederate Civil War artifacts.

Snappy Salmon

Mayor Richard Arrington, Jr.
Birmingham, Alabama

1 15 oz. can red salmon
1 cup onion (coarsely chopped) not scallions
½ cup margarine
½ cup sour cream
2 tbsp. lemon juice
1 tsp. garlic salt
¼ tsp. dill weed
¼ tsp. white pepper
4 large sprigs parsley
2 envelopes unflavored gelatin
½ cup water

5-6 servings

Drain salmon; remove and discard skin and bones. Place salmon and all other ingredients (except gelatin and water) in container of blender or food processor (with metal blade). Run on low speed until smooth and well blended.

Sprinkle gelatin over cold water in small saucepan to soften. Place over low heat and stir constantly until gelatin is dissolved. Cool and add to blended mixture. Pour into lightly oiled 5 cup fish mold. Chill until firm; unmold and garnish as desired. (Mold will set very quickly if set in freezer for the first 20 minutes.)

Richard's Snappy Salmon is Mayor Arrington's favorite, original recipe. This dish has been one of the staples in his cuisine for over 30 years. Richard's Snappy Salmon won Mayor Arrington the Gourmet Gala, a benefit for the March of Dimes, in 1984.

Birmingham's history is unique in the South because it was established after the Civil War as part of the industrialization of the southeastern United States. It was dubbed the "Magic City" due to the rapid population growth after the realization that iron could be produced easily in Birmingham where iron ore, limestone, and coal—the major resources necessary for the production of iron—were in abundance. The city's economic base has diversified through the years with the health care industry employing the largest number of people today.

Vulcan, the god of fire and forge, is the city's symbol and keeps watch from atop Red Mountain in a city park. The second largest statue in the United States, Vulcan was Birmingham's entry in the World's Fair in St. Louis where it was awarded first prize.

Tennessee Country Ham and Gravy

Mayor Kyle C. Testerman
Knoxville, Tennessee

3 slices country ham (center cut)
2 cups black coffee

6 servings

Trim most of the fat from slices of country ham. Cut in serving pieces. Place ham in baking dish and pour the two cups of black coffee over this. Cover. Bake at 350⁰ for 1 hour. Serve hot.

This method of preparation is easy and the ham is very tender.

Knoxville, Tennessee is truly a "sense-sational" city to call "home" and visit! You can *see* the awesome beauty of the Smoky Mountains contrasted with the peaceful reflections of surrounding lakes. You can *hear* the harmony of bluegrass and symphony. You can *smell* the honeysuckle competing with fresh mown hay. You can *taste* the country ham and the sweet golden honey. You can *feel* the warmth and hospitality of its people. A visit to Knoxville can be a "sense-sational" experience.

Tried and True Meat Loaf

Mayor John Starr
Hot Springs, Arkansas

1½ lb. ground chuck or round beef

1 onion (chopped)

1 bell pepper (chopped)

crackers (preferably chicken seasoned)

3 eggs

salt, pepper, garlic powder to taste

1 can Hunt's tomato sauce special

ketchup

8-10 servings

Mix together beef, onion, pepper, crackers, eggs, and seasoning. Add ½ to ⅔ can tomato sauce special. Form into 2 loaf pans and pour remaining sauce on top. Bake for 30 minutes at 375⁰. Pour ketchup on top and bake another 30 minutes.

Hot Springs is an historic resort nestled in the Ouachita Mountains in Central Arkansas. It is virtually surrounded by lakes and is famous for its natural thermal waters.

Hot Springs hosts more than 500 conventions annually, and is the home of Oaklawn Park, one of the leading thoroughbred tracks in the nation and home of the world-renowned Arkansas Derby.

ACCOMPANIMENTS

Arroz con Gandules (Rice with Pidgeon Peas)

Mayor Victor M. Soto Santiago
Toa Baja, Puerto Rico

½ cup corn oil

1 lb. cooking ham (chopped)

2 large green peppers (chopped)

2 large onions (chopped)

1 small can of tomato paste

5 garlic cloves (crushed)

¼ tsp. oregano

¼ tsp. black pepper

4 cups white rice

2 16 oz. cans pidgeon peas

3½ cups water

salt to taste

8 servings

In a 4 quart casserole, heat oil on high and stir in ham; cook until lightly browned. Add green peppers, onions, garlic, oregano, black pepper, salt, and tomato paste. Stir until it begins to boil, then add rice, pidgeon peas, and water; continue to stir until completely mixed. Cover and cook over medium high heat, until all water is absorbed (approximately 15 minutes). Stir occasionally, then reduce heat to low and cook 20 minutes. Serve hot with roast pork (Pernil Asado).

continued

Toa Baja grew up behind a church when there was a change in the direction of the La Plata River. For further information on Toa Baja, see page 75.

Barriguitas De Vieja (Old Lady's Tummy)

Mayor Angel Leon Martinez
Juana Diaz, Puerto Rico

3 lb. fresh pumpkin (cut in pieces)
2 eggs
¼ tsp. ground cinnamon
2 drops vanilla extract
½ cup sugar
1 cup all purpose flour
oil for deep frying

6 servings

Boil pumpkin in lightly salted water for 15 minutes or until tender. Mash pumpkin. Slowly add ingredients in the order above, mixing while adding. Preheat oil for frying at high temperature. Use 1 tablespoon of mixture to form patty. Fry your first patty to test consistency; if it breaks up, add one more ounce of flour. (NOTE: A patty may break up if oil is extremely hot.) Form additional patties. Fry at medium-high temperature for 2 minutes on each side, or until brown. Drain excess oil and serve.

Juana Diaz is a friendly and pleasant city located on the Southern coast of Puerto Rico. For further information on Juana Diaz turn to page 75.

Curried Fruit

Mayor Kyle C. Testerman
Knoxville, Tennessee

1 29 oz. can sliced peaches (drained)
1 17 oz. can apricot halves (drained)
1 16 oz. can pear halves (drained)
1 15 oz. can pineapple chunks (drained)
1 jar maraschino cherries (drained)
½ cup slivered almonds (toasted)
⅓ cup margarine or butter (melted)
1 cup firmly packed brown sugar
1 tbsp. curry powder

8-10 servings

Place drained fruit in 13″x9″x2″ baking dish. Sprinkle almonds over fruit. Combine butter, brown sugar and curry powder.

Place mixture on top of fruit. Bake 1 hour at 325⁰. Serve warm.

This recipe is good to serve for a brunch or breakfast.

Knoxville is a potpourri of activity during the many festivals held each year. For further information on Knoxville, please turn to page 81.

CITY TRIVIA QUESTION #19

This North Carolina city was one of the first places where gold was discovered in the United States and became the gold mining capital of the United States. (Hint: It's named after the wife of George III of England.)

Answer on page 87.

83

Grape Nuts Bread

Mayor James P. Moran, Jr.
Alexandria, Virginia

½ cup Grape Nuts cereal (soaked 20 minutes in 1 cup sour milk)*

1 egg

1 cup brown sugar (scant)

1½ cups flour

1 tsp. baking soda

1 tsp. baking powder

8-10 servings

Mix the cereal, egg, and brown sugar. Add flour, baking soda, and baking powder. Bake in greased loaf pan at 350⁰ for 30-35 minutes.

*Sour milk can be made by adding 1 tablespoon of vinegar to one cup of milk.

Alexandria has a small town atmosphere in a large, sophisticated, urban metropolitan area. Winner of the 1984 All America City Award for the efforts of its citizens and their contributions, Alexandria was home to George Washington and Robert E. Lee. Today it is home to congressmen and senators, as well as a diverse ethnic, economic, and social population.

CITY TRIVIA QUESTION #20

Texas city where oil was first struck in 1901 touching off the oil boom in Texas.

Answer on page 158.

Greek Collards and Ham Hocks

Mayor John P. Rousakis
Savannah, Georgia

---

2 bunches collards

1½ lb. ham hocks (cut up)

2 medium size onions (minced)

1 can whole tomatoes

1 tbsp. vinegar

1 tbsp. sugar

½ stick butter

salt and pepper

---

6 servings

In 5 quart kettle braise ham hocks in butter and minced onion until slightly browned.

Pick collards from stem and add to kettle on top of onion and ham hocks. Cook on very low heat (about 200⁰) for 2 hours. Add tomatoes, vinegar, sugar, salt, and pepper. Turn well, mixing ham hocks with collards. Continue cooking for another 2 hours or until collards are tender. Turn frequently while cooking.

Savannah, a city with both a Revolutionary and Civil War legacy, combines old Southern charm with modern-age convenience. Savannah is known for its cobblestone streets, hanging moss and azalea-filled town squares, and its restored Victorian-style homes. The city was the only Southern city saved on General Sherman's march to the sea and was given by Sherman as a Christmas present to President Lincoln. Savannah has the largest historic district of any city in the country. Its riverfront cotton warehouses have now been converted into shops and restaurants.

Green Chili Rice

Mayor Robert E. Powell
Monroe, Louisiana

3 cups sour cream
½ cup chopped sweet green chilies (or more to taste)
½ cup chopped hot green chilies (or more to taste)
salt and pepper to taste
3 cups cooked rice
¾ lb. Monterey Jack cheese (cut into strips)
½ cup cheddar cheese (grated)

6-8 servings

Mix sour cream, chilies, salt, and pepper. Add cooked rice. Butter a 2 quart casserole. Place half of the rice mixture in the bottom of the dish, top with half of Monterey Jack cheese. Repeat. Sprinkle grated cheddar cheese on top. Bake at 350⁰ for about 25 minutes, or until cheese is melted and bubbly.

A good make-ahead dish, and can be frozen.

Monroe, located on America's second most scenic river, the Ouachita, is an historic old city dating back to the French and Spanish settlements in 1783. In the heart of the rich agricultural Delta, surrounded by mossy bayous and lakes, Monroe is the cultural, recreational, and urban trade center for our neighboring 14-parish Northeast Louisiana.

CITY TRIVIA QUESTION #21
What Ohio city did Johnny Appleseed call home?
Answer on page 137.

Linguine Aglio e Olio (Spaghetti with Garlic and Olive Oil)

Mayor Frank R. Branca
Miramar, Florida

¾ cup olive oil
8 large cloves garlic (minced)
1 cup fresh parsley (chopped)
1 cup black olives (pitted and sliced thin)
salt and pepper to taste
1 lb. linguine spaghetti
Parmesan cheese (optional)

4 servings

Put olive oil and minced garlic in saucepan over very low heat; cook for a few minutes, but do not brown garlic. Meanwhile, cook spaghetti according to directions on package. Toss together oil mixture, spaghetti, olives and parsley, salt and pepper to taste. Serve hot. Sprinkle with Parmesan cheese if desired.

Quick and easy to prepare. Very tasty—if you like garlic.

Miramar, located in Broward County, Florida, got its name from the Spanish word meaning "Garden View of the Ocean." The city is located five miles from the ocean and is becoming known in Florida as the "City of Trees." Today, thousands of trees bloom where none did 31 years ago. The city received national recognition in 1985 for leadership in sponsoring community awareness and involvement in wearing safety belts.

Onions au Gratin

Mayor Richard C. Hackett
Memphis, Tennessee

2 large sweet onions (sliced)
¾ cup beef broth
salt, pepper, and thyme
2 tbsp. butter (melted)
½ cup fresh bread crumbs
½ cup cheddar cheese (grated)

4-6 servings

Place onion slices, overlapping, in baking dish; sprinkle with salt, pepper, and thyme. Bake covered for 20 minutes at 350⁰. Then mix together melted butter, bread crumbs, and beef broth. Sprinkle over onions. Top with grated cheese and bake for 10 more minutes, uncovered.

Memphis, the home of southern hospitality, lies on the banks of the mighty Mississippi River. The city's emergence as a distribution hub has given rise to new recognition as "America's Distribution Center." A city rich in musical heritage, Memphis is known throughout the world as the home of the blues and the birthplace of rock and roll. Hundreds of thousands of visitors annually visit Elvis' home, Graceland, and Beale Street, where W.C. Handy wrote and played the blues. Memphis' history, closely linked to the Mississippi River, is explored at the unique riverfront Mud Island Park. An historical museum and scale replica of the father of rivers highlight this truly unusual experience of life on the Mississippi.

CITY TRIVIA QUESTION #22

Only non-Sunbelt city in the United States to host a Super Bowl game.

Answer on page 134.

Ozark Dinner Rolls

Mayor Terry Hartwick
North Little Rock, Arkansas

2 pkgs. dry yeast
1½ cups water
½ cup sugar
1 tsp. salt
6 cups all purpose flour
⅓ cup vegetable oil
1 egg

Makes 24

Mix yeast, salt, and water until dissolved. Add 2 cups flour and mix well. Add vegetable oil and egg and beat well. Add 4 cups flour to make the dough stiff. Place in warm area until it doubles in size.

Knead the dough on a floured surface. Roll it out with a rolling pin and cut it to fit size of roll pans. Let it rise again until it doubles in size.

Bake at 400⁰ until brown.

Originally called "Silver City" and then "Argenta," the Latin word for silver, **North Little Rock** was founded in 1901 near the site of a small silver vein in central Arkansas. It is a city which wrestled its freedom from its overpowering giant neighbor, Little Rock, first by breaking the chains of oppression, and then for years continuing its fight to protect its independence.

This city is known for its fine city parks and recreation facilities—some of the finest in the south—featuring an unusual lighted golf course for those who prefer a late night tee off time, a water theme park, and fantastic hotels. The people of North Little Rock are proud of its heritage and are excited about its future.

Pretzel and Strawberry Salad

Mayor Edward L. Cole, Jr. M.D.
St. Petersburg, Florida

2 small pkgs. or 1 large pkg. strawberry jello
2 cups pretzels (crushed)
8 oz. cream cheese
1 pkg. dream whip or 8 oz. whipped topping
2 cups pineapple juice
1 cup sugar
1½ sticks margarine
2 pkgs. frozen strawberries

12 servings

Crush pretzels with rolling pin. Mix with 1½ sticks melted margarine and 1 tablespoon sugar. Spread mixture in a 9"x13" pan and bake for ten minutes at 375°. Cool.

Blend cream cheese with sugar; fold in whipped topping and spread over cooled pretzels.

Dissolve jello with 2 cups boiling pineapple juice. Add strawberries. Pour over mixture; chill until firm.

St. Petersburg is a major city of nearly a quarter of a million people, the fourth largest city in Florida by population. It is located 25 miles west of Tampa on the tip of Pinellas County's peninsula on Florida's west coast. With an average of 361 days of sunshine a year, the city is affectionately known as the "Sunshine City."

Set in a clean, relaxed atmosphere, the 58-square-mile city contains 2,400 acres of preserved parkland in 102 parks, including seven miles of downtown waterfront parkland, which has been described by *Time* magazine as the "nation's loveliest urban waterfront."

Pull-Apart Bread

Mayor Harvey B. Gantt
Charlotte, North Carolina

2 sticks butter
1 cup milk
1 pkg. yeast
¼ cup warm water
2 eggs
½ cup sugar
½ tsp. salt
3 cups flour

8-10 servings

In saucepan melt 1 stick butter in milk. Dissolve yeast in warm water. Beat eggs, sugar, and salt together in mixer. Add butter and milk mixture. Add 1½ cups flour. Beat well. Add yeast. Let rise 30 minutes. Add 1½ cups flour. Blend. Cover with cloth in refrigerator for 6 hours or overnight.

Butter bundt pan well. Pull off dough in small pieces (should have enough pieces for 2 layers) and dip in melted butter. Pour any remaining butter over top. Cover with cloth and let rise 40-60 minutes. Bake at 375° for 20-30 minutes.

Charlotte is located at the "foot of the mountains" in the Piedmont section of North Carolina. Named for Queen Charlotte, wife of George III of England, Charlotte played a key role in the Revolutionary War. When gold was discovered in 1799, Charlotte became the gold mining capital of the United States and since that time has been the financial center for much of the Southeast. Charlotte offers its citizens a rich heritage, cultural amenities, excellent climate, cleanliness, and a progressive environment in which to conduct business.

Red Molded Salad

Mayor Leslie H. Garner
Greenville, North Carolina

8 oz. cream cheese (softened)
¾ cup celery (finely chopped)
½ cup mayonnaise
¾ cup nuts (chopped)
6 oz. pkg. cherry gelatin
2 cups hot water
1 can applesauce
dash of cinnamon

10-12 servings

Dissolve gelatin in water. Add applesauce and cinnamon. Put half of mixture in 9"x13" baking dish. Place in refrigerator and let set. Save remaining mixture at room temperature.

Let cream cheese soften. Add celery, mayonnaise, and nuts. When gelatin layer is set, spread cream cheese mixture over it. Then top with remaining gelatin and let set. Cut in squares and serve on lettuce.

Greenville, known as the "Hub of Eastern Carolina," is home to East Carolina University and the world's largest tobacco warehouse. It serves as the center for the region in business, agriculture, education, and medicine. "Greenville, North Carolina, Has It All."

CITY TRIVIA QUESTION #23

This North Carolina city is in the heart of tobacco country and has the largest tobacco warehouse in the world.

Answer on page 88.

Squash Casserole

Mayor Bill Frederick
Orlando, Florida

2 lb. yellow squash (cut up)
2 cups extra sharp cheddar cheese (grated)
1 egg
½ cup saltines (crushed)
½ cup evaporated milk
¼ cup water
salt and pepper to taste

6 servings

Boil squash in salted water until tender. Drain well. In the same pan add cheese and cover until the cheese is melted. With a fork, mix and mash squash. Add remaining ingredients, (except saltines), mix well, and pour into buttered casserole dish. Dot with butter and sprinkle with cracker crumbs and paprika. Bake at 350⁰ for 30 minutes.

Freezes well.

Orlando, home to Sea World and Walt Disney's Magic Kingdom and EPCOT Center, is America's number one tourist destination. The city's economy, based solidly in tourism and citrus production, is rapidly diversifying. Spurred by high tech industries developing in the shadow of the neighboring Kennedy Space Center, Orlando is expected to lead the nation in the growth rate of new jobs through the end of this century. Lush in subtropical foliage and dotted with 74 lakes and more than 600 acres of public parks and recreation areas, Orlando has rightfully claimed its title as "Florida's City Beautiful."

Southern Cheese Grits

Mayor Wib Gulley
Durham, North Carolina

1 cup grits
1 stick butter
1 roll Kraft jalapeno pepper cheese
1 roll Kraft garlic cheese
3 eggs (well beaten)
2/3 cup milk
1 cup sharp cheddar cheese (grated)

6 servings (Southerners);
8-10 servings (non-Southerners)

Cook grits as directed on package; remove from heat and stir in butter, jalapeno cheese, and garlic cheese. Let mixture cool for a few minutes, then add milk and beaten eggs.

Pour into a greased 2 or 3 quart casserole dish and cover. Top generously with grated cheese. Bake in 350⁰ oven for about 45 minutes or until set. Let stand for 5-10 minutes before serving.

This dish tastes wonderful, better than a non-Southerner would ever expect.

Durham, once a sleepy southern town known primarily for the production of tobacco products and textiles, is now one of the major urban centers of the Southeast. Durham's attractions include being a center for high technology, research, health care, education, and the arts, which allow for a diverse community. Durham's location adds to its attractiveness as a place to live. It is bounded on the west by mountains and on the east by the coast, either of which can be reached in three hours. The temperate climate and lush countryside add to the beauty of the City of Durham.

Sweet Potato Supreme

Mayor Neil Stallings
Jonesboro, Arkansas

2 large cans sweet potatoes (heated, drained, and beaten with mixer)
2 cups marshmallows
3/4 stick butter or margarine
1 cup sugar
1 cup whipped cream or whipped topping
2 eggs
TOPPING:
1 stick melted butter or margarine
1 cup brown sugar
1 1/4 cups crushed corn flakes
1/2 cup chopped pecans

12 servings

Beat sweet potatoes with mixer. Mix butter and marshmallows; add to sweet potatoes. Add sugar, eggs, and cream. Pour into large Pyrex dish.

Topping: Melt margarine in saucepan. Add brown sugar, stirring constantly for 1-2 minutes. Add pecans and crushed corn flakes to sweet potatoes. Pour sauce over all

Bake at 400⁰ for 20 minutes.

Jonesboro is a truly great place to live! Located in the northeastern corner of the beautiful state of Arkansas, this city is the home of Arkansas State University. While the university makes it an educational center, its two fine hospitals have made Jonesboro the medical hub of the surrounding area as well. The friendliness of its residents and the underlying wholesome respect that they hold for one another has helped to foster Jonesboro's reputation as an exceptional city.

Incidently, Olympic bronze medal winner and one-time world record pole vaulter, Earl Bell, hails from Jonesboro.

Taco Salad

Mayor William P. A. Nicely
Parkersburg, West Virginia

1 head lettuce
2 tomatoes (diced)
1 green pepper (chopped)
1 onion (chopped)
1 lb. ground beef (fried and drained)
1 can red kidney beans (drained)
1 cup mild cheddar cheese (shredded)
1 pkg. Original Recipe tortilla chips (crumbled)
California Onion or Toasted Onion Dressing

15-20 servings

Mix all ingredients together in a large bowl. Add tortilla chips just before serving. Dressing may be added to entire dish before serving or diners may add their own.

Parkersburg, located on the majestic Ohio River in west central West Virginia, is truly a city of diversity. While it boasts a growing tourism industry with such attractions as Fenton Art Glass and Blennerhassett Island Historical Park, Parkersburg also enjoys an active manufacturing and industrial economy. Twenty-three of the nation's Fortune 500 companies have facilities in the area. Parkersburg is also the "Savings Bond Capital of the World" with the Treasury Department's Bureau of Public Debt processing every bond sold and redeemed in the United States through its Parkersburg facility. All this, combined with outstanding educational, recreational, and transportation systems, places Parkersburg on the threshold of "the century of progress and prosperity" as the city celebrates its bicentennial during 1985-86 and looks forward to the future.

Top o' the Mornin' Irish Soda Bread

Mayor Kathy Kelly
Clearwater, Florida

3 cups flour
⅔ cup sugar
1 tbsp. baking powder
1 tsp. baking soda
1 tsp. salt
1½ cups raisins
2 beaten eggs
1¾ cups buttermilk
2 tbsp. melted butter

12 servings

Sift flour, sugar, baking powder, baking soda, and salt 3 times. Stir in raisins. Combine eggs, milk, and butter in a separate bowl. Add liquid to dry ingredients. Mix until flour is moist.

Grease a loaf pan. Pour in mixture. Bake at 350⁰ for 90 minutes. Remove and allow to cool.

"The top o' the mornin' t'you!"

Clearwater's sparkling beaches and beautiful Gulf waters make it a great place for the city's annual Fun 'N Sun Festival...and you're sure to find plenty of both here! A thriving city of tourism and industry, Clearwater is proud of the efforts made to manage its tremendous growth while maintaining the high quality of life our residents enjoy. With all this to offer, it's no wonder so many of our visitors keep coming back year after year!

DESSERTS

Almond Puff

Mayor David Kaminsky
Lauderhill, Florida

1 cup butter (softened)
2 cups flour
1 cup plus 2 tbsp. water
1 tsp. almond extract
3 eggs
¾ cup walnuts (chopped)
GLAZE:
1½ cups confectioner's sugar
2 tbsp. butter (softened)
1½ tsp. almond extract
1-2 tbsp. warm water

10-12 servings

Heat oven to 350º. Cut ½ cup butter into 1 cup flour. Sprinkle 2 tablespoons water over mixture and mix with fork. Shape into ball and divide in half. Form each half into a 12"-13" strip and place the strips about 3" apart on an ungreased baking sheet.

In medium saucepan, heat ½ cup butter and 1 cup water to rolling boil. Remove from heat and quickly stir in almond extract and 1 cup flour. Stir vigorously over low heat until mixture forms a ball, about 1 minute. Remove from heat and beat in eggs until smooth. Divide in half and spread over strips evenly, covering completely. Bake 60 minutes or until topping is crisp and golden. Cool, frost with glaze, and sprinkle with chopped nuts. When dry cut into strips.

Glaze: combine all ingredients until smooth.

The City of **Lauderhill** is located in the western section of Broward County and is composed of fine single-, and multi-family dwellings, flourishing businesses, and concerned, active citizens and government. It has a population of over 42,000 enjoying social, recreational, and entertainment abundance. It is the home of the beautiful Inverrary Golf Course. Lauderhill has a strong government and is sensitive to the community's needs. New parks have been and are in the process of being developed.

Banana Nut Ice Cream

Mayor Jimmy Kemp
Meridian, Mississippi

6 eggs
1½ cups sugar
2 tsp. vanilla
4 bananas
1 pt. whipping cream
1 can condensed milk
2 qt. (or less) milk
2 cups nuts (preferably pecans)

8 servings

Beat eggs until creamy; add sugar and vanilla. Beat thoroughly. Add whipping cream and condensed milk; mix and then add milk, beaten bananas, and nuts. Freeze as usual in ice cream freezer.

Meridian, nestled in the foothills of the Appalachians, is a city of gently rolling hills, historic architecture, and unrivaled beauty when the azaleas bloom in spring. Meridian is also a modern, thriving trade center serving the retail, medical, and educational needs of a large trade area encompassing East Central Mississippi and West Central Alabama.

Bien me Sabe (Coconut Delight)

Mayor Baltasar Corrada del Rio
San Juan, Puerto Rico

| 1 15 oz. can cream of coconut |
| 1½ cups sugar |
| 2 cups water |
| 6 egg yolks |
| 1 sponge cake (sliced) or lady fingers |

10 servings

Mix water and sugar. Bring to a boil, stirring until syrup is formed. Let stand for a few minutes.

In a saucepan mix the cream of coconut and egg yolks. Add syrup gradually, while beating at medium heat until the sauce thickens. Let stand for a few minutes until cool. Pour in bottle and refrigerate until ready to use.

Pour sauce over sponge cake slices or lady fingers.

San Juan, the capital of Puerto Rico, is the oldest city under the American flag in the Western Hemisphere. For further information on San Juan, turn to page 77.

Bourbon Pie

Mayor Leroy Urie
Gulfport, Mississippi

| 1 box confectioner's sugar |
| 1½ sticks margarine |
| 6 tbsp. bourbon |
| 1 box vanilla wafers (crush for 2 pie crusts) |
| 2 eggs |
| 1 pt. whipped cream |
| 1 can crushed pineapple (drained) |
| ¼ cup pecans |

Makes 2 pies

Cream confectioner's sugar and margarine. Add bourbon, then eggs one at a time. Spread on vanilla wafers crust for two pies. Mix whipped cream and spread over above. Spread pineapple and sprinkle pecans on top with a few crumbs of crushed vanilla wafers. Chill pies 10 hours before serving.

Gulfport, located halfway between New Orleans and Mobile, is the center of the longest man-made beach in the world—26 miles. Being located in the geographic center of the Mississippi Gulf Coast, its port is one of the largest banana and fruit terminals in the world. Gulfport hosts the world's largest fishing rodeo each July. In Gulfport, we take our fun seriously!

CITY TRIVIA QUESTION #24
City where a famous Tea Party was held.
Answer on page 19.

Chocolate-Pecan Kentucky Pie

Mayor Jerry Abramson
Louisville, Kentucky

1 cup chocolate chips
½ cup flour
1 stick butter (melted)
1 cup pecans (chopped)
1 cup sugar
2 eggs (beaten)
1 tsp. vanilla
1 unbaked 9″ pie shell

6 servings

Mix flour and sugar; add all other ingredients and pour into unbaked pie shell. Bake at 350° for 30 minutes. Serve warm with whipped cream or vanilla ice cream.

Louisville, Kentucky has the unique distinction of being the home of the Kentucky Derby. We are a centrally located city that has effectively combined the old and the new and maintains the excitement of the Kentucky Derby year-round.

Florida Fresh Coconut Cake

Mayor Jake M. Godbold
Jacksonville, Florida

¼ cup fresh coconut (grated)
1 cup coconut milk (see below)
3 eggs (separated)
1½ cups sugar
¾ cup shortening
½ tsp. vanilla
2¼ cups pastry flour
2¼ tsp. baking powder
½ tsp. salt
FROSTING:
¾ cup sugar
2 tbsp. water
1/8 tsp. cream of tartar (or 1 tsp. light corn syrup)
few grains salt
1 egg white
½ tsp. vanilla
¾ cup fresh coconut (grated)

8-10 servings

For fresh coconut and coconut milk: Pierce eyes of fresh coconut and let milk drain into a bowl. Set coconut in a 400° oven for 20 minutes. Tap with hammer to loosen shell. Split with a heavy knife; pry out the white meat with a sharp knife. Pare off dark skin and grate white meat. A medium-sized coconut yields 3-4 cups grated coconut.

Preheat oven to 375°. Lightly grease two 9″ cake pans. Prepare fresh coconut as above, grate 1 cup, and reserve coconut milk. Separate three eggs and beat whites until they form soft peaks. Gradually add ½ cup sugar; set aside. Beat egg yolks until thick; set aside.

Sift together pastry flour, baking powder, and salt; set aside. Cream together shortening, vanilla, and gradually add 1 cup sugar. Stir in egg yolks and ¼ cup fresh coconut. Beat well; alternately add flour mixture and 1 cup coconut milk. Fold in egg whites. Pour into prepared cake pans and bake for 25 minutes.

Frosting: In the top of a double boiler, mix ¾ cup sugar, water, cream of tartar (or 1 teaspoon light corn syrup), salt, and 1 egg white. Beat 1 minute. Set over boiling water and beat until stiff enough to form stiff peaks, approximately 4 minutes. Remove from heat and continue to beat until thick enough to spread. Add vanilla and ¼ cup grated coconut. Frost the cake and sprinkle remaining fresh coconut on the top and sides.

Jacksonville, Florida...the largest city in the continental United States in land area with 840 square miles. It is bordered to the east by the Atlantic Ocean while the heart of the city sits on the beautiful St. Johns River. It is experiencing tremendous economic growth especially in downtown redevelopment. One of the newest attractions to enhance the downtown area is the Southbank Riverwalk, a 1.1 mile boardwalk located along the St. Johns River. Jacksonville is, by far, a magnificent city on "Florida's First Coast."

Florida Pound Cake

Mayor Mary Bonner
Dunedin, Florida

1 cup butter
2 cups sugar
2 cups all purpose flour
5 eggs
1 tbsp. vanilla extract

10-12 servings

Cream butter and sugar; add eggs, one at a time, beating well after each addition. Add flour and vanilla extract. Pour batter into greased and floured 10" bundt or tube pan. Bake at 325⁰ for about 1 hour or until done.

Variation: 1 tablespoon lemon extract or almond extract may be substituted for vanilla extract.

Dunedin, a quiet village-like city situated midway down the west coast of Florida, was founded in 1870 and named after Edinburgh, Scotland. Proud of its Scottish heritage, Dunedin hosts a Highland Games and Festival every March. From its cultural atmosphere, tree-lined brick streets, historic buildings, and scenic waterfront vistas, this city offers unique appeal to visitors and residents alike.

Fudge Cakes

Mayor John B. Hussey
Shreveport, Louisiana

4 eggs
½ lb. butter
2 cups sugar
1 cup flour
3 squares bitter chocolate (melted)
1 tsp. vanilla
1 cup chopped pecans
ICING:
1 lb. confectioner's sugar
3 tbsp. bitter chocolate (melted)
1 tsp. vanilla
enough cream or milk to make icing spreadable

12 servings

Cream butter and sugar. Beat eggs together and add to butter and sugar, mixing well. Mix in flour, melted bitter chocolate, and vanilla; continue beating until well mixed. Fold in pecans.

Bake in greased pan (approximately 11½"x17"x2½") at 350⁰; DO NOT OVERCOOK. Test with toothpick after 15-20 minutes; done when batter cakes on toothpick.

Icing: Mix all ingredients well and ice while cake is hot. Cover pan and allow to cool overnight before cutting. If desired, put pecan halves on each square.

Tucked quietly into the Northwest corner of Louisiana, **Shreveport** comes alive with attractions, festivals, and great food. The city combines the cultures of the United States and France with the flavor of Texas, the beauty of Arkansas, and the jazz of Louisiana. Shreveport is the home of the American Rose Center, America's largest rose garden; the Shreveport Captains, the state's only professional baseball team; the River Rose Paddlewheeler, beautiful parks, and museums; and some of the world's finest restaurants. But for visitors, the most attractive thing about Shreveport is friendly people rolling out the red carpet treatment and good ole' Southern hospitality.

miles, and has a population of 45,000. A unique blend of diverse industries including thoroughbred horses, manufacturing, tourism, and agriculture along with the area's abundant natural resources for recreational activities provides a superb quality of life for Ocala's citizens.

Golden Apricot Squares

Mayor Wayne L. Rubinas
Ocala, Florida

1 stick butter (softened)
1 cup sugar
1 egg
1 tsp. vanilla
2 cups plus 1 tbsp. flour
¼ tsp. salt
1⅓ cups flaked coconut
½ cup walnuts (or pecans)
1 12 oz. jar apricot preserves (for a less rich dessert use 9 oz.)

20 servings

Beat softened butter and sugar until fluffy. Beat in egg and vanilla. Sift together flour and salt and beat into butter mixture. Use wooden spoon to add coconut and nuts. (May use hands—dough crumbles like pie crust but is still sticky).

Grease 8" or 9" square cake pan. Add ½ the dough; press flat with spoon; spread sparingly as you need enough to cover the top well. Then spread the apricot preserves over this layer. Top with remaining dough mixture. Pat lightly with wooden spoon. Bake in oven at 350° for 35 minutes. Cool on rack. When cool cut into squares.

Ocala, named after the Indian Providence of Ocali, is located in Central Florida, covers 30 square

Hootenany Cake

Mayor Everett B. Reeves
Ashland, Kentucky

1 box yellow cake mix
1 box instant toasted coconut pudding
1 cup water
4 eggs
½ cup oil
1 tsp. vanilla
½ tsp. baking powder
NUT MIXTURE:
1 cup chopped nuts
4 tsp. sugar
2 tsp. cinnamon
GLAZE:
½ stick margarine
½ tsp. vanilla
½ cup light brown sugar
2 tbsp. milk

8-10 servings

Grease bottom of tube pan. In large bowl mix first 7 ingredients and beat for 5 minutes.

Mix nuts, sugar, and cinnamon together. Put ⅓ nut mixture into bottom of tube pan, then add ½ the cake batter. Add another ⅓ of the nut mixture and the remaining cake batter, finishing off top with the remainder of the nut mixture. Bake at 350° for 50-60 minutes.

Combine glaze ingredients and cook for 1 minute. Pour over cake.

Ashland, named after famous statesman Henry Clay's home, lies in the northeastern part of the state of Kentucky. Ashland is home to large corporations, such as Ashland Oil and Armco Steel, but still provides the beautiful surroundings for a happy family life.

Hot Milk Coconut Cake

Mayor Wayne A. Corpening
Winston-Salem, North Carolina

| 1 box pudding cake mix |
| 2 cups milk (hot) |
| ¾ cup confectioner's sugar |
| 2 tsp. vanilla |
| 14 oz. coconut |
| 1 cup heavy cream |

8-10 servings

Mix pudding cake mix according to instructions on box, adding 6 ounces coconut to batter. Bake in 8"x12" pan according to directions. Take from the oven and pour a mixture of the milk and 1 teaspoon vanilla over the hot cake. Let cool.

Beat heavy cream with confectioner's sugar and 1 teaspoon vanilla. Spread over cake and sprinkle remaining cocount.

Winston-Salem, in the foothills of North Carolina, is a city of two centuries, the 18th century Moravians who settled the congregational town of Salem and the 20th century corporate giants who make the city a financial and commercial center.

The restored village of Old Salem welcomes visitors year-round in a colonial restoration with the oldest continuing college for women in the country. Not far away stands the headquarters of a number of major corporations including RJR/Nabisco and Piedmont Airlines. The city has four outstanding colleges—Wake Forest University, Salem College, Winston-Salem State U., and N.C. School of the Arts, the only one of its kind in the nation.

Winston-Salem is a cultural center, an educational center, an historical-experience, and a world business leader.

Japanese Fruit Pie

Mayor Charles Hardcastle
Bowling Green, Kentucky

| 3 eggs (slightly beaten) |
| 1½ cups sugar |
| ½ cup butter (melted) |
| ½ cup coconut (shredded) |
| ½ cup light raisins |
| ½ cup almonds (chopped) |
| 1 tsp. vanilla |
| 1 deep-dish 9" pie shell |

6 servings

In bowl, combine all ingredients. Pour mixture into pie shell. Bake in a preheated 400⁰ oven for

---

CITY TRIVIA QUESTION #25

Match event/place with the right city:

____Miss America Pageant	A.	San Antonio, TX
____Graceland	B.	Springfield, MA
____Alamo	C.	Nashville, TN
____Grand Ole Opry	D.	Atlantic City, NJ
____Independence Hall	E.	Memphis, TN
____One of the Wonders of the World	F.	Canton, OH
____Rock-n-Roll Museum	G.	Independence, MO
____Football Hall of Fame	H.	Philadelphia, PA
____Basketball Hall of Fame	I.	Beverly Hills, CA
____Home of Harry Truman	J.	Cleveland, OH
____Rodeo Drive	K.	Niagara Falls, NY

Answers on pages 52, 86, 163, 71, 58, 48, 118, 113, 19, 133, 219.

---

15 minutes; reduce oven temperature to 350⁰ and continue baking 20-25 minutes longer. Cool.

Bowling Green, the home of Duncan Hines, has much for you to see and enjoy: historic sites, cultural events, recreational opportunities, and shopping centers. Our city is known for "Southern Hospitality" and its progressive nature. Western Kentucky University, the Home of the Hilltoppers, is located in Bowling Green.

Key Lime Pie

Mayor Tom Sawyer
Key West, Florida

partially baked pie shell
6 eggs (separated; save whites for meringue)
1 can sweetened condensed milk
½ cup key lime juice
4 tbsp. sugar
1 tsp. vanilla
½ tsp. cream of tartar

6-8 servings

Blend slowly egg yolks and sweetened condensed milk; add key lime juice slowly to taste. Pour into partially baked pie shell.

Meringue: Beat egg whites until stiff adding sugar slowly until peaks form; add vanilla and cream of tartar. Spread over pie mixture and bake at 350⁰ until golden brown. Refrigerate until thoroughly chilled.

Key West, situated at the farthest tip of the Florida Keys, is continental America's southernmost city. For further information on Key West, turn to page 63.

Million Dollar Pie

Mayor Noel C. Taylor
Roanoke, Virginia

2 graham cracker pie shells
1 large container of non-dairy whipped topping
2 tsps. lemon juice
2 16 oz. cans sliced peaches (drained)
2 small cans crushed pineapple (drained)
1 small can shredded coconut
1 can condensed milk
2 small cans mandarin oranges (drained)
1 large jar maraschino cherries

Makes 2 pies

Combine non-dairy whipped topping, lemon juice, peaches (cut in small pieces), crushed pineapple, maraschino cherries (sliced in half), mandarin oranges (cut in half), coconut and condensed milk. Stir well, spoon one-half mixture in pie shells, garnish top with maraschino cherries.

For best results, refrigerate 2 hours before serving.

The City of **Roanoke** is known as the "Star City of the South." Our stardom comes from not only the huge electric star on Mill Mountain, but from the fact that we believe people are the stars in Roanoke. In 1982, Roanoke celebrated its 100th anniversary and our progress in the areas of rehabilitation, restoration, and preservation surpass any efforts experienced in the past to make Roanoke a better place in which to live and work.

Molasses Cookies

Mayor Paul Noland
Fayetteville, Arkansas

3½ cups all purpose flour

1 cup shortening

1 cup brown sugar

1 cup dark molasses

1 tsp. cinnamon

1 tsp. ginger (optional)

2 tsp. soda dissolved in 2 tsp. of vinegar

Makes approximately 48

Combine all ingredients and chill. Roll out the dough, cut into rounds, and bake at 325⁰.

Fayetteville, Arkansas, is surrounded by the natural beauty of the Ozarks. The trees, hills, lakes, and streams enhance the lifestyle of our congenial residence. Our community has a desirable balance of retirees, University of Arkansas employees, industrial workers, professionals, and those engaged in agricultural industries.

Peanut Butter Pie

Mayor Bill J. Dukes
Decatur, Alabama

1 baked 9″ pastry shell

¾ cup confectioner's sugar

⅓ cup peanut butter

⅓ cups all purpose flour

3 egg yolks (slightly beaten)

½ cup sugar

1/8 tsp. salt

2 tbsp. butter or margarine

1 tsp. vanilla

2 cups milk (scalded)

MERINGUE:

3 egg whites

½ cup sugar

¼ tsp. cream of tartar

1 tsp. cornstarch

6-8 servings

Blend peanut butter with confectioner's sugar until mealy. Sprinkle mixture over baked pie shell. Combine flour, ½ cup sugar, and salt in the top of a double boiler. Stir in scalded milk. Cook over boiling water, stirring constantly, until thickened. Stir a small amount of cooked filling into egg yolks. Combine with remaining hot mixture and cook several minutes longer. Add butter or margarine, and vanilla. Pour into pie shell. Top with meringue.

Meringue: Beat egg whites until stiff, add cream of tartar. Gradually add sugar mixed with cornstarch. beat until stiff and shiny. Pile on pie and bake. Cool pie before serving.

Decatur, a city of approximately 45,000 people, is set along the banks of the Tennessee River, which sets the stage for recreation, relaxation, and year-round enjoyment. Decatur offers a variety of interesting places for families to visit and fun ways to spend a weekend. Only in Decatur can you enjoy ocean waves, hot air balloons, and outdoor ice skating.

Pecan Pie

Mayor Dale Danks, Jr.
Jackson, Mississippi

CRUST:
1 cup flour
½ tsp. salt
⅓ cup shortening
water
FILLING:
⅓ cup Crisco
½ cup sugar
½ cup milk
3 eggs
½ tsp. salt
1 cup corn syrup
1 cup pecans (chopped)
½ tsp. vanilla

8 servings

Line pie pan with crust and set aside.

Cream Crisco and sugar. Add other ingredients and blend. Pour into prepared pie crust. Bake in oven at 425⁰ for 10 minutes. Turn oven down to 350⁰ and bake for 25 more minutes.

Jackson is a major Sunbelt urban center constantly planning for a greater future. As a dynamic distribution center and the seat of state, local, and federal government, Jackson is a vibrant city of change superimposed upon a gracious and congenial neighborhood lifestyle.

Plum Cake

Mayor Cecil W. Bradbury
Pinellas Park, Florida

2 cups self rising flour
2 cups sugar
3 eggs
1 cup salad oil
1 jar junior size baby food: plums with tapioca
1 tsp. each of cinnamon, nutmeg, cloves, ginger
1 cup chopped nuts or raisins (optional)

24 servings

Blend all ingredients in large bowl. Do not overbeat. Turn into a lightly greased and floured 10" tube pan. Bake at 350⁰ for 45-60 minutes.

May be served with whipped cream, powdered sugar, or ice cream. Store leftovers covered; they will stay moist for days.

This cake is easy to carry to meetings to be shared, or for surprise birthdays.

The active, growing city of **Pinellas Park**, in the heart of Pinellas County, comprises approximately 43,000 citizens, living in an area of 13.5 square miles—people who care, and actively participate in the continued betterment of their community. Pinellas Park will hold its centennial celebration in 1990, and has grown from a Pennsylvania-settled farm community to a municipality of fine residents and constant commercial, manufacturing and residential growth.

CITY TRIVIA QUESTION #26

This city is the home of the 1985 world baseball champions. (Hint: It also has more fountains than any other American city and ranks third in the world behind Rome and Mexico City.)

Answer on page 123.

Quick Blueberry Cobbler

Mayor J. Larry Durrence
Lakeland, Florida

| 2 cups blueberries (fresh or frozen) |
| 1 pkg. yellow cake mix (8 oz.) |
| 3½ tbsp. butter or margarine |

4-6 servings

Grease loaf pan with margarine or butter. Put in two cups of blueberries; then pour the dry cake mix from the carton over blueberries and pat lightly with fork until level. Cut butter or margarine into 8 pats and arrange evenly on top of the cake mix. Place in preheated oven at 325° for 25 minutes or until golden brown.

Allow to cool for 30 minutes before serving, with or without vanilla ice cream.

It is possible to substitute 2 cups of fresh peaches for the blueberries, sprinkling 1 teaspoon of sugar over the peaches before adding cake mix.

Lakeland, a lovely city containing 21 lakes, is located in central Florida. While it is called "the World's Citrus Center," this dynamic community of 63,700 has become a major medical center in Florida as well as a manufacturing/distribution center with more than 200 industries. It also has three institutions of higher education, including Florida Southern College, whose campus was designed by Frank Lloyd Wright.

Suffolk Peanut Pie

Mayor Johnnie Mizelle
Suffolk, Virginia

| 3 eggs |
| ½ cup sugar |
| 1½ cups dark corn syrup |
| ¼ cup butter (melted) |
| ¼ tsp. salt |
| ½ tsp. vanilla |
| 1½ cups roasted peanuts (chopped) |
| unbaked pie shell |

6 servings

Beat eggs until foamy. Add sugar, syrup, butter, salt, and vanilla; continue to beat until thoroughly blended. Stir in peanuts. Pour into unbaked pie shell. Bake in preheated 375° oven for 45 minutes. Delicious served warm or cold. May be garnished with whipped cream or ice cream.

Suffolk, Virginia's largest city in area (430 square miles), is internationally known as the peanut capital of the world. Planters Peanuts was founded here by Amedeo Obici. "Surprising Suffolk" is the marketing slogan currently being used by the city.

Tomato Soup Cake

Mayor Dorothy Thomson
Coral Gables, Florida

| ¾ cup margarine |
| 1½ cups sugar |
| 1 cup canned tomato soup |
| ¾ cup water |
| 1 tsp. baking soda |
| 3 cups flour |
| ¾ tsp. salt |
| 3 tsp. baking powder |
| 1½ tsp. cinnamon |
| 1 tsp. cloves |
| 1½ tsp. nutmeg |
| ¾ cup walnuts (chopped) |
| FROSTING: |
| 1 small pkg. cream cheese |
| 1 egg yolk |

1½ cups powdered sugar

½ tsp. vanilla

8-10 servings

Blend margarine and sugar in bowl. Combine tomato soup with water and baking soda in a separate bowl, and add to first mixture, alternating with dry ingredients, which have been sifted. Stir in nuts. Pour mixture into a well-greased bundt pan and bake at 375⁰ for 30 minutes, or until done.

Frosting: To 1 small package of cream cheese, slowly add 1 egg yolk and 1½ cups powdered sugar. Add ½ tsp. vanilla. Spread on cooled cake.

This is an old family recipe which my grandmother handed down to my mother from Peekskill, NY, and one which my children have grown up with and adopted as a family favorite for get-togethers.

Coral Gables is unique. In 1986 it has achieved much that its founder, George Merrick, conceived in the early twenties; there are broad, sunny boulevards, residences great and small in the Mediterranean style he fostered. The University of Miami in Coral Gables, where over 30,000 students are enrolled, thrives on the land he donated. Fifteen minutes from the central business district of the city is the largest tropical garden in the continental United States, Fairchild Tropical Garden, 83 acres of exotic trees, rare plants, vines, and flowers.

Velvety Chocolate Cake

Mayor Roy A. West
Richmond, Virginia

| ½ cup buttermilk |
| 1 tsp. baking soda |
| 2 cups all purpose flour |
| 2 cups sugar |
| ¼ tsp. salt |

| ½ cup butter |
| 1 cup water |
| 4 tbsp. cocoa |
| 2 eggs (beaten) |
| FROSTING: |
| ½ cup butter |
| ¼ cup plus 2 tbsp. milk |
| 4 tbsp. cocoa |
| 1 16 oz. pkg. confectioner's sugar |

8-10 servings

Cake: Combine buttermilk and soda; set aside. Combine flour, sugar, and salt in mixing bowl. Combine butter, water, and cocoa in a saucepan, bring to boil. Pour over flour mixture. Mix well; cool. Add eggs and buttermilk mixture, stirring well. Pour into 2 greased and floured 8" pans. Bake at 350⁰ for 25-30 minutes. Cool on wire racks and frost with velvety chocolate frosting.

Frosting: Combine butter, milk, and cocoa in a saucepan, bring to boil. Remove from heat; add confectioner's sugar, stirring well. Spread warm frosting on sides and top of cake.

Richmond, the capital of the Commonwealth of Virginia, lies along the banks of the James River, where at the fall line, Christopher Newport planted a cross nearly 380 years ago to mark the first journey up river from Jamestown. Richmond's Renaissance, a remarkable rebirth, has spurred renewed economic growth and expanded cultural offerings and a host of revitalization projects that enhance Richmond's stature as a booming corporate, cultural, and historic southeastern urban center.

CITY TRIVIA QUESTION #27

City that is govened by the Dean of American Mayors—26 years in office.

Answer on page 115.

MIDWEST

"Hudnut helps hack huge
Hoosier hoagie"
Mayor William Hudnut
Indianapolis, IN

"Say cheese"
Mayor Harold Washington
Chicago, IL

"Udderly delightful"
Mayor Stephen Daily
Kokomo, IN

"Ein Prosit!"
Mayor Henry Maier
Milwaukee, WI

STARTERS

Artichoke Spread

Mayor Betty Gloyd
Village of Hoffman Estates, Illinois

1 cup mayonnaise	
1½ cups mozzarella cheese	
1 cup parmesan cheese	
2 cans artichoke hearts (chopped and drained)	
2 tsp. garlic powder or salt	

Makes 2½ cups

Mix together and bake at 350⁰ for 25 minutes; sprinkle with paprika and serve with crackers.

A growing community of 41,000 people, the Village of **Hoffman Estates** is nestled amidst 4,000 acres of forest preserves and boasts a well-balanced economy. This thriving community includes an extensive variety of housing, manufacturing, office and research complexes, making it an ideal place to live.

Bayia

Mayor P. Pete Chalos
Terre Haute, Indiana

4 average potatoes (peeled and diced)	
1 cup celery (chopped)	
1 cup carrots (chopped)	

½ lb. Codfish or Orange Roughy (sliced into 1" cubes)

parsley to taste

salt and pepper to taste

5 servings

Boil potatoes until half-cooked; add celery and carrots. Bring to boil for 15 minutes. Add fish and parsley; cook on slow heat until finished. Add salt and pepper as desired.

Terre Haute's name is derived from the French meaning "High Ground." Terre Haute was the home of Eugene V. Debs, a major figure in the history of labor unions who was a perennial candidate for the presidency on the Socialist ticket. It was also the home of Paul Dresser, composer of many numbers, among them "On the Banks of the Wabash," and "My Gal Sal." NBA MVP Larry Bird played his college years at Terre Haute's Indiana State University.

Cheese Soup

Mayor Gary K. Anderson
Decatur, Illinois

1 cup celery (diced)	
1 cup onion (chopped)	
2 chicken bouillon cubes	
1 qt. water	
1 cup carrots (diced)	
2½ cups red potatoes (diced)	
1 8 oz. pkg. frozen vegetables (mixed)	
2 cups cream of chicken soup	
1 lb. Velveeta	

6-8 servings

Simmer celery, onion, bouillon, and water in large pot for 20 minutes. Add remaining vegetables and simmer for an additional 40 minutes. Add soup and cubed cheese. Heat through until cheese is melted and soup hot. Stir often.

This is the recipe from a local restaurant famous for its cheese soup.

Decatur, Illinois, with a population of 94,000, is the largest of 13 cities and towns named after U.S. Naval hero Commodore Stephen Decatur. The Lincoln log cabin courthouse and Governor Richard Oglesby mansion are a few of the historic sites around our city. Decatur is an industrial and processing center for corn and soybeans from our rich prairie surroundings. We're proudly designated as Decatur...Pride of the Prairie.

Cocktail Wieners

Mayor Richard J. Schneider
Sheboygan, Wisconsin

2 1 lb. pkgs. bite-size smoky links	
1 cup brown sugar	
1 medium onion (thinly sliced)	
1 medium apple (diced)	
2 tbsp. water	

12-15 servings

Place brown sugar in a crockpot with onions and apple. Add 2 tablespoons water and stir until blended. Add smoky links and simmer all day.

Excellent for large parties, barbeques, very little work.

Sheboygan, located on the shores of Lake Michigan, has a population of 50,000, excellent schools and parks, and great sportfishing. We are known for our homemade bratwurst.

Cream Cheese Soup

Mayor Clyde F. Johnson
Clinton, Iowa

1 cup potatoes (diced)	2 cups milk
1 cup carrots (diced)	3 cups chicken broth
1 cup celery (diced)	½ tsp. pepper
1 cup onion (diced)	12 oz. American cheese
4 tbsp. butter	1 tbsp. parsley
½ cup flour	
2 cubes or 1 tsp. chicken bouillon	

8 servings

Cook or microwave vegetables. Mix butter, flour, and milk as for a white sauce. Add chicken broth, bouillon, pepper, cheese, and parsley. Heat slowly together with vegetables.

All your friends will want this recipe. My brother served this in his restaurant years ago.

Clinton, Iowa, named after De Witt Clinton, former governor of New York, at one time had more millionaires per capita than any city in the United States. The city's major festival is "Riverboat Days," drawing thousands of visitors each year to the city's Mississippi River banks and to the showboat "Rhododendron."

Grilled Shrimp Wrapped in Bacon

Mayor J. Michael Houston
Springfield, Illinois

½ cup olive oil	
2 tbsp. champagne vinegar or good white vinegar	
3 tbsp. fresh dill (chopped)	
2 garlic cloves (minced)	

1 lb. large shrimp (13-15 per lb.; peeled and deveined, with tails intact)

5 slices very lean bacon (sliced very thin)

13-15 pieces

Combine oil, vinegar, dill, and garlic in a bowl. Add shrimp and marinate overnight.

Cut each slice of bacon into thirds and wrap a piece around each drained shrimp, securing well with a toothpick. Grill over hot coals until the bacon is crisp and shrimp is cooked through, 7 to 8 minutes. You can also grill them under a hot broiler, 4 minutes on each side, being careful not to burn the bacon or overcook the shrimp.

Springfield, Illinois, the state's capital city, is "Mr. Lincoln's Hometown." In keeping with that historical distinction, the city still offers its visitors the same hospitality experienced in that bygone era when Mr. and Mrs. Lincoln entertained here. This recipe will give you the opportunity to do the same in true midwestern style.

Hummos

Mayor Joe Alkateeb
Farmington Hills, Michigan

1 can chick peas

⅓ cup tahineh (sesame seed paste)

juice of 1 or 2 lemons

1 clove garlic (minced)

salt to taste

3 tbsp. olive oil

10 servings

Boil chick peas in juice for 5 minutes on medium heat; drain, reserving liquid. Place drained chick peas in food processor with enough liquid to form smooth paste (begin with 2 tablespoons and add more if needed). Add minc-

ed garlic and process 3-4 seconds. Add tahineh and process 3 more seconds; then add lemon and salt. Process to make an almost smooth thick paste.

Spread on a platter or place in wide bowl. Drizzle olive oil over dip. Serve with pita bread or crudites.

Very popular Middle Eastern appetizer. Can be served with pita bread and/or vegetables to dip.

Farmington Hills, located northwest of Detroit, was incorporated in 1973 and was the fastest growing community in Michigan in 1985. The city was the site of an underground railroad station during the Civil War. Today the community is largely residential and service industry-oriented.

Mama's Gefilte Fish

Mayor Charlotte M. Rothstein
Oak Park, Michigan

2 lb. pickerel or trout

3 lb. whitefish (skinned and boned; save skins and heads)

2 hard-cooked eggs

6 large onions

4 whole eggs

3 carrots (sliced)

white pepper, salt, and sugar to taste

Makes 6 patties or 20 balls

Grind eggs in grinder 2 times. Grind 3 onions with hard-cooked eggs 2 times and set aside. Grind fish 2 times. Combine ground eggs, onions, and fish in wooden chopping bowl and chop by hand with ½ cup water. Sprinkle with pepper and ½ teaspoon salt; add 1 tablespoon sugar. Put 4 whole eggs in blender and beat until light. Add eggs to fish mixture and continue hand chopping until mixture is smooth and pulls clean from the chopper.

continued

Prepare heavy, deep cooking pot with ½ cup water. Place fish heads and skin on bottom; add 3 diced onions and 3 sliced carrots. Set aside 1 small bowl of cold water and dip your hands in it. With a large spoon, dip into fish mixture and form pattie. Smooth this pattie with moist hands so it is sealed and place in the pot. Continue until the rows of fish are below the water line (add water slowly to do this). If you are making small fish balls, cooking time will be cut in half.

Cover pot, bring to boil, then cook on medium for 2 hours. Take pot off stove when done and carefully place patties or balls in wide-mouthed canning jars. Pour fish juice over fish and seal. Cool and serve or refrigerate up to two weeks.

May be served with horseradish.

Makes a delicious entree or delightful hors d'oeurve.

Oak Park, Michigan, has a population of 31,500 and covers 5.5 square miles. A "family city" with a multitude of ethnic diversities, Oak Park was one of the first planned communities and is located adjacent to Detroit. It features good schools and a variety of ethnic festivals.

CITY TRIVIA QUIZ

Scoring System

Throughout *The Mayors Cookbook* there are 62 City Trivia questions with 130 answers. Answer each question, follow the instructions to the page with the answer, and tally your results.

Correct Answers	Level of Knowledge
0—25	Municipal Rookie
26—50	City Gazer
51—75	Metropolitan Marvel
76—100	City Slicker
101 and up	Urbanologist

Mock Turtle Soup

Mayor Paul R. Leonard
Dayton, Ohio

3 large onions
1 12 oz. can tomatoes
6 hard-cooked eggs
2 large potatoes
1 green pepper
1 lb. green beans (preferably fresh)
4 stalks celery
3 carrots
2 lb. veal
salt and pepper to taste
1 box pickling spice (small box if various sizes are available)
1 lemon (for juice only)
2 lemons
1 cup flour

6-8 servings

Cook veal until it is done in 2 quarts water (boil for approximately 3 hours). Grind following in food processor: onions, tomatoes, eggs, pepper, green beans, celery, carrots, and two lemons. Cube potatoes. Remove veal from broth; grind veal and reserve broth. Add ground veal and vegetables, cubed potatoes, and juice from 1 lemon to reserved broth. (You will probably need to add more water to broth.) Add pickling spice by placing in cheesecloth and tying shut.

Brown 1 cup of flour in a pie tin about 20 minutes at 350⁰ (until it reaches a pretty brown), and then make a paste out of flour by adding a small amount of water. Add paste to veal and vegetable mixture. (NOTE: Be sure to remove the bag containing pickling spice prior to serving soup.)

It is recommended that this recipe be prepared in the morning so that it can simmer the balance of the day, until your evening meal.

Dayton, Ohio, the birthplace of aviation, situated at the crossroads of America, is a highly cosmopolitan center just 90 minutes from most North American cities. Its highly traveled citizens have developed sophisticated and discerning tastes. We extend our best wishes for Bon Appetit.

Peppy Pecans

Mayor James T. Ryan
Arlington Heights, Illinois

½ lb. pecan halves
2 tbsp. butter (melted)
½ tsp. salt
1½ tbsp. Worcestershire sauce
1/8 tsp. tabasco sauce

1½ cups pecans

Mix pecans, butter, and salt in shallow baking pan. Bake at 325⁰ for 10 minutes. Add Worcestershire and tabasco sauces, mixing well. Bake 15-20 minutes longer, stirring twice. Cool before serving.

Arlington Heights, "The City of Good Neighbors," will be celebrating 150 years as a community. Our convenient location and excellent highway system give citizens easy access to neighboring states. The village's outstanding school system sends three-quarters of its graduates on to colleges and universities. There's a lot to be proud of when you say you are a resident of Arlington Heights, and as our village sticker proclaims, we're still "Reaching for New Heights."

Sweet and Sour Meatballs

Mayor James P. Perron
Elkhart, Indiana

1 lb. hamburger
½ cup dry bread crumbs
¼ cup milk
2 tbsp. onion (finely chopped)
1 tsp. salt
½ tsp. Worcestershire sauce
1 egg
SWEET AND SOUR INGREDIENTS:
½ cup brown sugar
1 tbsp. cornstarch
1 13¼ oz. can pineapple chunks
⅓ cup vinegar
1 tbsp. soy sauce
1 small green pepper (coarsely chopped)

25-30 meatballs

Mix ingredients for meatballs, shape into 1½" balls, and brown over medium heat for about 20 minutes. Remove from pan and drain fat.

Mix brown sugar and cornstarch in skillet, stir in pineapple (with syrup), vinegar, and soy sauce. Heat to boiling. Reduce heat and add meatballs. Cover; simmer, stirring occasionally, 10 minutes. Stir in green peppers; cover and simmer until tender, approximately 5 minutes.

Can be used as a main dish served with rice. Can be used as hors d'oeurves when served with other small dishes.

Elkhart, is a bustling community with an overwhelming spirit of entrepreneurship that has helped to make our city one of the most progressive in the state. While we are known as the capital of the mobile home and recreational vehicle industries, band instruments, and phar-

continued

maceuticals, we believe you will find that we are also the home of warmth and friendliness that emanates from our community's residents who are ready with a helping hand to welcome visitors to the "City with a Heart."

MAIN DISHES

Asparagus Pie

Mayor George S. Freeman
Grosse Pointe Woods, Michigan

1 baked pie shell	2 cups ham (diced)
3 tbsp. butter	1 lb. hot cooked asparagus
1 tbsp. cornstarch	1 tsp. lemon juice
1 cup milk	¼ cup Parmesan cheese
½ cup mayonnaise	

6-8 servings

Make cream sauce out of butter, cornstarch, milk, and mayonnaise. Add ham and beat 5 minutes. Arrange half of hot asparagus in pastry shell. Add half of the ham mixture. Add remaining asparagus, then remaining ham. Top with cheese. Broil 3" from heat until brown. Serve immediately.

Grosse Pointe Woods is a family-oriented community known for its proximity to a beautiful lakeshore with magnificent trees. It is located on 3.2 square miles with a population of 18,880. The city provides recreational facilities with four parks,

one of which is a 55-acre facility, including one of the largest pools in the county. Our city is becoming known as a "sharing and caring" community.

Bar-B-Q Ribs

Mayor James A. Sharp, Jr.
Flint, Michigan

6-10 lb. ribs
MARINATING SAUCE:
2 cups soy sauce
1 cup water
½ cup brown sugar
1 tbsp. dark molasses
1 tsp. salt
RED SAUCE:
⅓ cup water
1 14 oz. bottle ketchup
1 12 oz. jar chili sauce
½ cup brown sugar
1 tbsp. dry mustard
2 tsp. rum flavoring

6-10 lbs. ribs

Combine all ingredients for marinating sauce and bring to boil. Let cool. Put ribs in baking pan; cover with sauce and let stand, refrigerated, overnight. When ready to cook, pour off sauce (can be reused); place ribs in baking pan and cover tightly with foil and bake at 325⁰ until tender, about 2 hours.

After ribs are cooked, dip in red sauce. Place finished ribs on charcoal pit or grill for 7-10 minutes.

Both sauces can be reused if brought to a boil and stored in containers in the freezer.

Flint, "Our new spark will surprise you" is certainly true today. This city in southeastern Michigan boasts a new $21 million festival marketplace that houses boutiques, specialty shops, and restaurants. The University of Michigan has a new downtown Flint campus. Award winning Riverbank Park is the scene of summer concerts and close by is a cultural center housing a planetarium and historical automobile museum.

Boiled Kielbasa and Kraut

Mayor Coleman A. Young
Detroit, Michigan

3 lbs. Kielbasa	4-5 medium whole potatoes
1½ lbs. fresh kraut	4-5 cloves garlic (peeled)
1 tsp. oregano	1 tsp. crushed red pepper
3-4 whole onions	2 tsp. black pepper

4-5 servings

Put potatoes, onions, and garlic in 2 quarts water; boil for 20 minutes. Add kraut, Kielbasa, and seasoning; boil over low flame for additional 30 minutes.

"The Kielbasa and Kraut is a favorite of mine because it's a complete meal and can be stored and reheated indefinitely. Best served with cornbread and buttermilk."

One thing that makes **Detroit** a special place to live is its cultural and ethnic diversity. Scores of ethnic groups continue to display their traditions proudly, giving rise to such communities as Greektown and Mexicantown and serving as the basis for our summer-long scenes of ethnic festivals, which run from early May to late September. Detroit is also on a roll with dramatic changes on our riverfront and neighborhoods. General Motors has its headquarters here and recently opened a brand new assembly facility, the most modern in the world, in the heart of the city. This is a very exciting time to be living in Detroit or to visit us.

Chicken Broccoli Casserole

Mayor William H. Hudnut III
Indianapolis, Indiana

5 chicken breasts or 2 whole chickens
3 10½ oz. cans cream of chicken soup (undiluted)
1 cup mayonnaise
½ tsp. curry powder
1 tsp. lemon juice
3 pkgs. frozen broccoli or 2 lbs. fresh
½ cup sharp cheese (grated)
1 pkg. crumbly bread dressing
¼ cup butter (melted)

6-8 servings

Cook chicken until tender; debone. Cook broccoli. Mix soup, mayonnaise, curry powder and lemon juice. Spread broccoli on bottom of well greased 13"x9" casserole. Cut up chicken and spread over broccoli. Pour soup mixture over chicken and mix slightly. Cover with cheese. Then sprinkle on dressing, which has been lightly tossed with melted butter.

Bake just before serving at 350° for 45 minutes. May be made in advance and refrigerated or frozen. (May be cut in half or third.)

Indianapolis is one of the most exciting, dynamic cities in America today. We are known as the "Crossroads of America" because more interstate highways intersect here than in any other city in the U.S. and because we are less than one day's drive from half of the American population. Our vibrant, rejuvenated downtown has earned us the titles "Cinderella City" of the Midwest again this year in *Newsweek*, and "Star of the Snowbelt" in the *Wall Street Journal*. The Indianapolis 500 motor car race is held every Memorial Day weekend and is the largest attended sporting event in the world.

Chicken Saute Sec

Mayor Robert Anstine
Macomb, Illinois

meaty parts of 2 medium frying chickens
4 cloves garlic
1 pt. fresh or canned mushrooms (thinly sliced)
6 tbsp. olive oil
¾ cup dry white wine
salt and pepper

8 servings

Heat olive oil, browning garlic as it heats. Remove browned garlic and discard. Quickly brown seasoned (salt and pepper to taste) chicken in oil, removing pieces if necessary to get all pieces browned quickly. When all chicken is browned, pour off excess oil. Return chicken to skillet. Reduce heat; add mushrooms. Add wine, cover with tightly fitting lid and cook 20 minutes or until all wine is cooked away and chicken is done.

Macomb was founded in the 1830s, during a land boom in western Illinois. It was incorporated as a village in 1841 and as a city in 1856. Agriculture is a very important part of the community as Macomb is surrounded by rich prairie soil. In 1899, Macomb was selected as the site for Western Illinois State Normal School, now Western Illinois University with a student enrollment of approximately 10,000. Abraham Lincoln was a guest in Macomb on two different occasions in 1858.

Chicken Supreme

Mayor Harold Washington
Chicago, Illinois

4 chicken breasts (boned)
1 pkg. frozen peas
1 egg (beaten)
1 can cream of mushroom soup
salt, pepper, and paprika
1 garlic clove (minced)
bread crumbs
1 cup sour cream

4 servings

Remove chicken skin; halve breasts; sprinkle with salt, pepper, and paprika. Dip in beaten egg, then bread crumbs; brown on each side in oil. Drain on paper; arrange in baking dish and sprinkle peas over chicken. Mix soup and minced garlic and spread on top of peas. Bake for 1 hour at 350⁰.

Chicago is at the crossroads of the nation and is the home of the 1986 Superbowl Champion Chicago Bears. From its diverse ethnic neighborhoods to its spectacular lakefront, the city offers a rich mix. Chicago is the home of modern architecture and great restaurants, a leader of culture, a center for jazz and blues music, and the commodities center of the nation—to name just a few of the things that make Chicago great!

Chitterlings

Mayor Robert B. Blackwell
Highland Park, Michigan

10 lb. clean frozen chitterlings	½ tsp. salt
1 whole white potato	1/8 tsp. pepper
1¼ cups vinegar (optional)	1 whole onion
1 clove garlic	1 tsp. parsley
1 medium size crushed red pepper	

20 servings

Cook chitterlings in heavy pot, season with salt, pepper, whole onion, and whole white potato.

Add vinegar to pot. Cook until tender. Cut up chitterlings in bite-size pieces and serve with coleslaw, hot sauce, and hot cornbread.

A real Southern soul gourmet.

Highland Park is home to Chrysler Corporation's world headquarters and was the site of the original Ford plant. It is the first urban city in the country to combine its police and fire departments into one public safety department. Its theme is "My Town, Highland Park."

Crescent Chicken Squares

Mayor Donna Owens
Toledo, Ohio

1 3 oz. pkg. cream cheese (softened)
3 tbsp. margarine (melted)
2 cups chicken (cooked, cubed) or 2 5 oz. cans boned chicken
¼ tsp. salt
1/8 tsp. pepper
2 tbsp. chopped pimiento (if desired)
1 8 oz. can plain or Italian crescent rolls
¾ cup seasoned croutons (crushed)

4 servings

Blend cream cheese and 2 tablespoons margarine. Add all other ingredients except crescents and croutons. Mix well. Separate crescent dough into 4 rectangles. Seal perforations. Place ½ cup chicken mixture in center of each. Pull up corners; twist on top and seal sides. Brush with remaining tablespoon margarine; sprinkle with crushed croutons. Bake on greased cookie sheet 25-30 minutes at 350⁰.

Toledo, the Glass Capital of the World, is nestled on the banks of the Maumee River and is home of the world famous Jeep, the Toledo Mud Hens, Tony Packo's, Jamie Farr, Danny Thomas, Teresa Brewer, and host city of the 1986 PGA Tournament. Toledo is Ohio's newest city with more new construction and revitalization than any other Ohio city and with the busy world accessible port on Lake Erie, which serves as a model for riverfront development throughout the nation.

God's Country Special

Mayor Albert J. Smith
Skokie, Illinois

2 cups cold water
1 can cream of chicken soup (or cream of mushroom soup)
1 box long grain and wild rice mixture
1 packet onion soup mix
10-15 pieces chicken

4-5 servings

Thoroughly mix cold water with can of cream of chicken soup (or cream of mushroom if you prefer). Set aside.

Over bottom of 12"x8" ungreased pan, spread one cup of the rice mixture (seasoning will be enclosed in the box of rice), spreading it evenly with fork or fingers. Sprinkle one packet of onion soup mix over rice mixture. Add pieces of chicken over the mixture, using as many pieces as will cover the pan. Slowly pour the soup mixture over all.

Bake in 350⁰ oven for 1 hour and 45 minutes. Serve hot from the casserole.

Skokie, has a strong ethnic and religious heritage. Located outside Chicago, the city recently opened the Holocaust Museum to accompany its Memorial to the Holocaust victims. A "Village of Vision," Skokie offers a wide diversity of commercial, cultural, and recreational opportunities.

Hamburger Pie

Mayor Verne Hagstrom
Quincy, Illinois

9" pie crust (if you desire, 1 tsp. onion powder may be added)

¼ cup ketchup

2 tsp. onion (minced)

1 tsp. salt

½ tsp. sweet basil

¼ tsp. pepper

1 lb. ground beef

1 egg (beaten)

6 tomato slices

6 wedges sliced cheese

1 cup cheddar cheese (shredded)

½ cup bread crumbs

6 servings

Cook ground beef until it loses its color. Combine ketchup, onions, salt, and herbs, and stir into beef. Add shredded cheese, egg, and bread crumbs. Turn into pastry-lined pie plate. Top with tomato slices. Bake in 400⁰ oven for 20-25 minutes. Remove from oven. Top with cheese wedges and bake for 1 minute longer until cheese melts.

There is definitely an art to good cooking, and when it comes to the arts, **Quincy** sizzles more than the juiciest steak on a barbeque grill! We love to brag that our Quincy Society of Fine Arts, established in 1947, was the first community arts organization founded in the United States. And in 1986 it became one of the best in Illinois. Twice selected as an "All-America City," Quincy is made up of people who have a strong sense of their roots, which links them with their history. At the same time, people in Quincy work extra hard to ensure that our children will inherit a healthy future.

Hawaiian Hekka

Mayor Chuck Hazama
Rochester, Minnesota

2 tbsp. salad oil

½ cup sugar

1 1/8 cup soy sauce

1 bunch green onions (cut in 1½" lengths with tops)

2 medium sized onions (sliced thin)

1 10½ oz. can bamboo shoots (sliced thin)

1½ lb. chicken, steak, or pork (cut in small slices)

1 cup water

½ lb. watercress or spinach (cut in 2" lengths)

1 10½ oz. can mushrooms (sliced thin)

1 cup celery (sliced diagonally in 1½" pieces)

1 block tofu (cut in 1" cubes)

1 bundle long rice (bean thread, soak in water until soft and cut into 1½" lengths)

6 servings

Heat oil in a heavy iron or aluminum frying pan. Fry ⅓ of the meat (pork, chicken, or steak) slightly; then add 2 tablespoons sugar. Three minutes later add ½ cup soy sauce; cook 3 minutes, then add ⅓ of the sliced onions. When onion is soft add ⅓ of the celery, mushrooms, and bamboo shoots, and ½ cup water; cook 3 minutes. Add ⅓ cup more of soy sauce and more sugar and water. Add the balance of the ingredients, vegetables, and long rice; when they are about done add the tofu and serve with hot cooked white rice on the side.

Rochester, Minnesota, is the friendliest city east of the Hawaiian Islands! The Mayo Clinic and a major IBM facility have contributed to creating an atmosphere of progress in the field of technology and service to mankind in science and medicine. With over 80 different cultures integrated in our community, the citizens of Rochester know how to express warmth and hospitality in any language!

Iowa Beef Stroganoff

Mayor Thomas W. Hart
Davenport, Iowa

1 lb. Iowa beef sirloin steak
3 tbsp. butter
3 tbsp. ketchup
1 lb. mushrooms (washed, cut in half)
1 large onion (diced)
2 cloves garlic (minced)
2 bouillon cubes
2 cups water
2 tbsp. flour
1½ cups sour cream
1 8 oz. pkg. noodles

4 servings

Cut sirloin steak into strips about 1"-1½" long. Melt butter in a large skillet, then add mushrooms and onions. Cook and stir until they are tender; remove from skillet into separate saucepan. Cook sirloin in skillet until brown; add 1 cup water and bouillon cubes to meat. Stir in ketchup and garlic; simmer on stove for 20 minutes.

Add flour to the remaining cup of water and stir into meat mixture. Add mushrooms and onions to meat mixture. Simmer for an additional 10 minutes, then heat to boiling. Reduce heat and stir in sour cream; stir for 2 minutes. Serve over boiled noodles.

I am sure that you will find this recipe a delight to cook and eat. Its main ingredients, of course, are quality Iowa beef, Iowa grown mushrooms, flavorful Iowa onions, and rich Iowa sour cream.

Davenport, Iowa, a city of 100,000, is located on the banks of the Mississippi River. 1986 marks the 150th birthday of Davenport and Sesquicentennial festivities are going on all year to celebrate. The theme, "Come Look Us Over," is an invitation to each reader of this cookbook to come and join in our year-long celebration.

Italian Spaghetti Sauce

Mayor Sam Purses   *Canton, Ohio*

½ bushel tomatoes	¼ cup salt
2 cloves garlic	8 small cans tomato paste
3 large onions	2 tbsp. oregano
3 green peppers	2 tbsp. sweet basil
3 hot peppers	4 bay leaves
2 cups oil	2 tbsp. parsley
¾ cup sugar	

Makes 8 quarts

Wash and cut up tomatoes. Heat tomatoes for 5 minutes. Strain (strain skin and tomatoes until left with just juice). Boil 2 cloves garlic, 3 large onions, 3 green peppers, and 3 hot peppers in the juice for 1 hour. Remove vegetables (optional). Add remaining ingredients and simmer 1 hour. Can or freeze.

This recipe has been used to feed thousands at the Mayor's special events for the community. The recipe can be tailored for smaller servings.

Canton is probably best known as the home of the Pro Football Hall of Fame. What is less well-known, but is something of which we are equally proud, is the strong, positive spirit of our citizens. Their "Can-Do" attitude has seen Canton through the recent devastating effects of the steel industry's employment problems—to a spectacular new downtown revitalization. We are truly feeling CANTON PROUD!

Lake Erie Perch Packets

Mayor Martha Flippen
Sandusky, Ohio

4 fresh perch fillets
1 cup broccoli flowerettes
1 cup cauliflower pieces
1 red pepper (cut in strips)
1 medium onion (sliced thin)
½ cup Hidden Valley Herb dressing

4 servings

Cut 4 12" foil squares and place a fillet and equal amounts of vegetables in each. Add 2 tbsp. dressing; fold and seal tightly. Place on cookie sheet and bake at 450° for 25 minutes or until vegetables are tender.

Lake Erie is famous for it's Perch and Sandusky for cooking it.

Sandusky, Ohio, is the largest city in Erie County. This community of 31,000 is nestled on the shores of Sandusky Bay on Lake Erie. Sandusky was settled in 1818 by German and Italian immigrants. Sandusky is highly respected in the wine industry; our Ohio weather and the lake create the perfect climate for growing grapes, with our local wines being distributed worldwide. Lake Erie is a fisherman's paradise with some of the best fishing on the Great Lakes. Sandusky is the home of one of the largest amusement parks, Cedar Point, which attracts 5 million people each year. We are a friendly, charming community and we invite everyone to visit Sandusky, Ohio.

CITY TRIVIA QUESTION #28

What city is home to Frontier Days, the world's largest outdoor rodeo?

Answer on page 172.

Lamb and Eggplant Casserole

Mayor George Latimer
Saint Paul, Minnesota

1 eggplant
3 medium onions
1 clove garlic
2 cups lamb (cut into ½" pieces)
3 large tomatoes (chopped)
salt and pepper to taste

4 servings

Chop eggplant into small cubes and saute in frying pan. Remove from pan and place in casserole. Saute onions and garlic, add to casserole.

Cook lamb until lightly browned; add chopped tomatoes to this and cook until soft. Combine remaining ingredients and pour into casserole. Cover and cook in 350° oven for 1½-2 hours.

A Lebanese favorite

For the second year in a row, **Saint Paul** has been recognized nationally for its livability. The city now boasts the new Ordway Music Theatre, home to the St. Paul Chamber Orchestra, and is considered to be one of the finest concert halls in the world. Garrison Keillor, first St. Paul's and now the nation's favorite humorist, has established a permanent home for his tales of Lake Wobegon in the restored World Theatre.

St. Paul recently won site designation for the first inland world trade center to serve the international trade capital of the Midwest. The energy and enthusiasm that St. Paul's residents put into their work and play can be shown best by the recent construction of a 15-story ice palace for the city's Winter Carnival.

Marinated Fried Fish

Mayor Henry W. Maier
Milwaukee, Wisconsin

filets of fresh fish
½ cup vinegar
1 qt. water
salt, pepper, onion salt to taste
flour
cracker crumbs or cornmeal

number of servings depends on fish used

Marinate fish overnight in vinegar and water. Drain; sprinkle with salt, pepper, and onion salt to taste. Shake in bag containing flour and cracker crumbs or cornmeal. Fry in hot corn oil.

May also be used for frog legs, pheasant, and rabbit. If doing so, add some thyme to the flour mixture.

If your spouse also fishes (as does mine), make sure he or she uses this recipe and more importantly, knows how to properly clean and filet fish!

Though traditionally known as "Beer Town USA" and "The Machine Shop of the World," **Milwaukee** is much more. This midwestern metropolis on the shores of Lake Michigan is clean, well-run, industrious, friendly, and fun-loving. Its summer panorama of ethnic festivals, parades, and Summerfest have earned it a new label—"The City of Festivals." Henry W. Maier, the dean of American mayors, has served as Milwaukee's mayor since 1960. One of Milwaukee's traditions is the Friday night fish fry, where Milwaukee's brand of Gemutlicheit abounds.

Old Ben Souffle

Mayor Stephen J. Daily
Kokomo, Indiana

2 cans green chiles (drained)
1 lb. Monterey Jack cheese (coarsely grated)
1 lb. cheddar cheese (coarsely grated)
4 eggs (separated)
⅔ cup canned evaporated milk
1 tbsp. flour
½ tsp. salt
1/8 tsp. pepper

6-8 servings

Preheat oven to 375°. Remove chile seeds and dice. In large bowl combine cheeses and chiles. Turn into a well-buttered, shallow 2 quart casserole. Beat egg whites until stiff peaks form. In small bowl combine salt, pepper, egg yolks, milk, and flour. Gently fold egg whites into egg yolk mixture. Pour egg mixture over cheese mixture; using a fork, "ooze" it through the cheese. Bake 30 minutes or until knife comes out clean. Garnish with more chiles and sliced tomatoes. Excellent served with a tomato hot sauce.

This recipe is in honor of Old Ben, the largest steer to ever live in America. You will notice this recipe includes no beef!

Kokomo is a city of 50,000 in Central Indiana with a unique blend of urban and rural lifestyles. Kokomo is widely known as "the City of Firsts" because of a long list of significant inventions including the first commercially built automobile, built by Elwood Haynes in 1894. Kokomo offers a blend of natural resources, and cultural and leisure activities, creating a pleasant environment for families and singles alike.

Oriental Pork

Mayor Robert C. Stefaniak
Calumet City, Illinois

2 whole pork tenderloins (about 12 oz. each)	
¼ cup soy sauce	
2 tbsp. dry red wine	½ tsp. ground ginger
1 tbsp. brown sugar	1 clove garlic (crushed)
1 green onion (cut in half)	
1 tbsp. honey	
½ tsp. ground cinnamon	
GINGER SAUCE:	
1 small onion	
½ cup soy sauce	
¼ cup vinegar	
1 small piece ginger root (or 1/8 tsp. ground ginger)	

6 servings

Remove and discard fat from meat. Combine soy sauce, wine, sugar, honey, cinnamon, garlic, and onion in large bowl. Add pork, turning to coat completely. Cover and let stand at room temperature for 1 hour or refrigerate overnight, turning occasionally.

Drain pork, reserving marinade. Place pork on a wire rack in baking dish. Bake in preheated 350⁰ oven about 45 minutes. Turn and baste frequently with marinade during baking. Remove pork from oven, cut into diagonal slices, and serve with ginger sauce.

Ginger Sauce: Place ingredients in blender on high for 2 minutes. Serve sauce separately.

Great, served with green salad and rice dish.

Calumet City, Illinois, a city of homes and flourishing businesses, is located 25 miles outside the teeming metropolis of Chicago, and takes pride in the River Oaks Center, one of the largest shopping plazas in the southern suburbs.

Pepper Steak

Mayor Robert Pastrick
East Chicago, Indiana

2 lb. sirloin
½ cup margarine
¼ tsp. garlic powder
½ cup onions (chopped)
2 green peppers (thinly sliced)
1 lb. mushrooms (thinly sliced)
1 can tomatoes
1 beef bouillon cube
1 tbsp. cornstarch
1 tbsp. soy sauce
1 tsp. sugar
1 tsp. salt
½ cup cooking sherry

8 servings

Slice sirloin in thin strips. Saute the meat in margarine with garlic powder. Remove meat and place in large pan; reserve drippings. Saute onions, peppers, and mushrooms, in drippings 5 minutes. Add to meat.

Blend soy sauce, sugar, salt, water, cornstarch and add to meat. Simmer over low heat 40 minutes. Add sherry before removing from heat.

Serve over cooked rice.

When people think of **East Chicago**, they may think of the city's industrial heritage, but this city is more than an excellent business community...it's also a great place to live. More than anything else, East Chicago is a city with a varied and rich cultural soul that is undeniably unique. East Chicago is also a community that really knows how to unwind. The sparkling sands of the Indiana Dunes National Lakeshore and Lake Michigan are only minutes away.

Polish Golumki (Cabbage Rolls)

Mayor Alex M. Olejko
Lorain, Ohio

3 lb. ground chuck	
½ lb. ground pork	
¾ cup rice	
1 packet dry onion soup mix	
½ tsp. season salt	
1 large onion (chopped)	
2 medium heads cabbage (cored)	
1 32 oz. can sauerkraut	
1 32 oz. can tomato juice	
5 strips bacon (chopped)	
1 tbsp. parsley flakes	

6 servings

Parboil cabbage in water to which ½ teaspoon oil has been added. Drain and separate into leaves. Bring 2 quarts water to boil, put in rice, and let stand 5 minutes. Saute onions with chopped bacon. Mix meat, rice, onion, bacon, and spices.

Put portion of meat mixture in each cabbage leaf; roll up each leaf securely. Drain and rinse sauerkraut. Put in bottom of roaster; layer cabbage rolls on top, adding sauerkraut on top of each layer of cabbage rolls except the last one. Pour tomato juice over last layer of cabbage rolls; cover with pan lid. Bake at 375⁰ for 1 hour. Lower to 325⁰ and cook for an additional 3 hours. Add additional juice or water if needed.

Lorain is known for being the "International City"—55 nationalities joining together for a community of pride and friendship. The City of Lorain is located in Northern Ohio, on the shores of Lake Erie, where our summer activities consist of fishing, swimming, sailing, and sunset fiestas with music and ethnic foods.

Polish Hunter's Stew

Mayor John B. Czarnecki
East Lansing, Michigan

1 lb. Kielbasa	
1½ lb. boneless beef chuck	
1½ lb. lean pork	2 tsp. salt
3 tbsp. vegetable oil	1 tsp. caraway seeds
2½ cups onion (sliced)	1 tsp. pepper
12 oz. mushrooms (cut in half)	
1 lb. sauerkraut (rinsed and drained)	
1 cup dry red wine (burgundy)	
8 oz. tomato sauce	

6 servings

Three hours or day before serving: Slice sausage ½" thick. Brown ⅓ at a time in heavy skillet over high heat. As they are done, transfer to a 4-5 quart casserole (not aluminum). When all the sausage is browned, add the oil to skillet. Brown the beef and pork in several batches in the hot oil; when each batch is done add to the casserole. When all the meat is browned, add onions to skillet and cook 3-5 minutes, stirring, until soft. Add to the casserole along with mushrooms, sauerkraut, wine, tomato sauce, salt, caraway seeds, and pepper.

Cover and bake 2-2½ hours at 375⁰ stirring every 30-40 minutes until meat is very tender.

A strong full-bodied red wine is a good accompaniment.

East Lansing, Michigan, is home of Michigan State University. The city's motto is "Promise, Fulfillment, Privilege and Responsibility." The older tree-lined neighborhoods make it an attractive residential community.

Pork Chops with Apples

Mayor George V. Voinovich
Cleveland, Ohio

8 loin pork chops

salt and pepper

½ cup apple juice

½ cup soy sauce

½ cup brown sugar, packed

2 tbsp. cornstarch

½ tsp. ginger

3 tbsp. ketchup

2 Golden Delicious Apples (cored and cut into 4 rings)

6-8 servings

Sprinkle chops with salt and pepper and layer in shallow pan. Bake chops at 350⁰ for 1 hour, turning after 30 minutes.

Cook next 6 ingredients over medium heat, stirring occasionally, until thickened.

After placing apple ring on each chop, pour sauce over and bake 30 minutes until chops are tender, basting with sauce from pan.

Good with fluffy white rice and fresh broccoli. A favorite in the Voinovich household for many years.

Cleveland, on Ohio's north coast, has undergone a major resurgence. It has three times been acclaimed an "All-America City" by the National Municipal League, and just recently was chosen over several other major cities as the site for the Rock-N-Roll Hall of Fame and Museum. Work begins this year on a 7.4-acre harbor development project along the Lake Erie shoreline, and plans continue for a new domed stadium downtown, which is witnessing a $1 billion building boom.

Salmon Souffle Supreme

Mayor Charlotte M. Rothstein
Oak Park, Michigan

¼ cup butter

2 cups milk

1 lb. can pink or red Sockeye salmon

⅓ cup flour

4 eggs (separated, extra large)

1½ tsp. salt

6-8 Servings

Melt butter in saucepan. Blend in flour, salt, and milk and cook, stirring constantly, until sauce boils and thickens. (This should be the consistency of a medium white sauce.)

Beat egg yolks until light. Stir in a little of the hot sauce mixture. Pour egg mixture into the saucepan. Cook 2 minutes, stirring constantly, then remove from heat.

Flake fish, mixing skin, bones, and juice together. Mix fish with sauce until well blended. Beat egg whites with pinch of salt until stiff. Fold into fish and sauce mixture. Pour into buttered 6-quart casserole and bake at 325⁰ for one hour. Serve immediately.

Oak Park was one of the first planned communities in the nation. For further information on Oak Park turn to pages 105 and 106.

Oak Park was one of the first planned communities in the nation. For further information on Oak Park turn to pages 105 and 106.

CITY TRIVIA QUESTION #29

This Boston suburb has a popular cookie named after it.

Answer on page 28.

Saumon en Papillote (Salmon Baked in Foil Packages)

Mayor Robert B. Blackwell
Highland Park, Michigan

1½ lb. skinless, boneless fillets of salmon, preferably the tail end (cut into 4 pieces of equal size)
¾ lb. carrots
½ lb. fresh mushrooms
2 tbsp. butter
juice of ½ lemon
½ cup scallions (trimmed and cut into 2″ lengths)
salt to taste (optional)
1 tbsp. tarragon (finely chopped)
6 tbsp. melted butter or oil for greasing paper or foil rounds
8 tsp. shallots (finely chopped)
4 tsp. dry white wine
freshly ground pepper to taste

4 servings

Preheat oven to 525°, or the hottest temperature possible. Place a baking sheet in the oven and let heat at least 5 minutes. Holding knife at an angle, cut the salmon into very thin slices as if you were slicing smoked salmon. Lay out a length of heavy-duty aluminum foil or non-stick kitchen parchment on a flat surface. Invert a 12″ round baking dish, such as a cake pan, on the aluminum foil and trace around the pan with a sharp knife to cut away one round. Cut 4 foil rounds.

Scrape and trim carrots and cut them crosswise into 1″ lengths. Cut each length into thin slices. Stack the slices and cut them into very thin matchstick-like strips. There should be about 3 cups. Cut off and discard the bottom of each mushroom. Cut the caps crosswise into thin slices. There should be about 2 cups.

Heat 2 tablespoons butter in a saucepan and add mushrooms. Sprinkle with lemon juice. Cook, shaking the skillet and stirring, about 1 minute. Add the carrots, scallions, and salt; cover. Cook 7-8 minutes; add the tarragon and stir. Cover and set aside.

Place each round of paper or foil on a flat surface and brush all over with butter. Spoon an equal portion of the carrot mixture slightly off center on each round, leaving an ample margin for folding over. Cover the vegetable mixture with slices of raw salmon, leaving them slightly overlapping but making a compact row that just covers the vegetables. Sprinkle each serving with 2 teaspoons of finely chopped shallots and 1 teaspoon of wine. Sprinkle with salt and pepper. Fold over each round of foil or paper to enclose the filling completely. Fold and pleat the margins of each round over and over to seal the filling as tightly as possible.

Arrange the packages neatly in 1 layer in the oven and bake 7 minutes.

Highland Park is home to the Chrysler Corporation headquarters and was the site of the original Ford plant. For further information on Highland Park, turn to page 111.

Sausage and Mushroom Quiche

Mayor James W. ''Choppy'' Saunders
Middletown, Ohio

1 lb. sausage	4 large eggs
1 lb. fresh mushrooms (sliced)	
1 large can evaporated milk	
¼ cup parsley (chopped)	
½ cup Parmesan cheese (grated)	
1 9″ pie crust (deep dish)	

6-8 servings

continued

Brown sausage, adding mushrooms halfway through browning process. Drain. Add parsley. Mix eggs, evaporated milk, and Parmesan cheese together. Combine both mixtures and pour into pie crust. Bake at 350⁰ for 25 minutes (or until filling is set).

This recipe is great for mayor's luncheons with a tossed salad, rolls and dessert. It can also be served as an hors d'oeuvre, snack, or finger food if cut into smaller portions.

Along the banks of the Miami River, midway between Dayton and Cincinnati, lies **Middletown, Ohio**. A city of friendly folks welcomes visitors, who readily feel at home. This blue-ribbon city boasts excellent schools, government, business, industry, arts and culture. A close-knit community, it extends its hands internationally through business and industry and each October hosts Middfest—An International Festival.

Seafood Sauce in Casserole

Mayor Thomas C. Sawyer
Akron, Ohio

2 7-oz. cans crabmeat or lobster or 1 lb. cooked shrimp	
SAUCE:	
½ tsp. Escoffier Diable Sauce	1 cup mayonnaise
1 tsp. Worcestershire sauce	½ cup chili sauce
few grains cayenne pepper	½ tsp. chutney
Parmesan cheese (grated)	½ tsp. paprika
3 tbsp. butter (melted)	

4-6 servings

Put two 7-ounce cans prepared crabmeat or lobster or 1 pound cooked shrimp in a quart casserole. Cover with sauce. Sprinkle with a little Parmesan cheese and the melted butter. Bake in 350⁰ oven 10-20 minutes or until nicely browned. Serve on or with buttered toast.

In preparing the sauce—taste—more seasoning can be added if you desire.

Akron is a new city built on the foundations of a historic past—a first class hotel and retail complex cut out of an old Quaker Oats mill and grain silo, a hi-tech research center built within a 70-year old tire factory, a contemporary housing development constructed around a 19th century canal.

Preserving the traditions of high quality livability, which feature the finest in educational institutions and cultural and recreational amenities, the Akron of tomorrow has emerged as a clean, safe city with record levels of employment and an affordable, affluent style of living. The city still maintains its ties to its historic past with the annual Soap Box Derby held here each spring.

As John Nesbitt, author of the best-seller *Megatrends*, recently put it, Akron is a city "moving gracefully into the future."

Sloppy Joes

Mayor J. Michael Peck   *Dolton, Illinois*

2 lbs. ground beef	salt to taste
6 oz. chili sauce	parsley flakes to taste
1 can tomato soup	
½ chopped onion or onion flakes to taste	

4 servings

Brown meat in saucepan, drain off fat. Add soup and ½ cup water, chili sauce, salt, and other seasonings. Cook on slow fire for 45 minutes.

Dolton was incorporated as a city in 1892, as a result of the Chicago World's Fair. It was a railroad town and has now become a truck garden center for Chicago. It was the first community in Illinois to install concrete sidewalks, in 1913. We are a proud community.

Special Chili

Mayor Bob Bailey
Bolingbrook, Illinois

2 lbs. ground beef	
1 medium onion	
1 16-oz. can sliced tomatoes	
1 6-oz. can tomato paste	
3 8-oz. cans tomato sauce	
1½ cups water	
2 large cans kidney beans	
1 packet chili seasoning	

6 servings

Brown ground beef in saucepan; drain off fat. Combine all other ingredients in large pot; add beef. Bring to low boil, cover pot, and simmer at least 2 hours.

Allow chili to "rest" for a few hours. Heat and serve with shredded cheese and crackers.

Chili can be spiced up with chili seasoning, but taste before adding any spices.

The Village of **Bolingbrook** was incorporated in 1965, and has evolved as one of the fastest growing communities in the Chicago area. Modern housing developments border farmland in this young community. A satisfying family life can be established in Bolingbrook centered around the excellent school system, outstanding park district facilities, and a spirit of volunteerism that exists in the community.

CITY TRIVIA QUESTION #30

This Minnesota city is the home
of the internationally famous Mayo Clinic.

Answer on page 112.

Tenderloin Stuffed with Ham

Mayor John D. Bilotti
Kenosha, Wisconsin

3 large onions (thinly sliced)	
6 tbsp. olive oil	
4 tbsp. butter	
2 cloves garlic (minced)	
1 4 oz. can chopped ripe olives	
½ cup cooked country ham (chopped)	
1 tsp. freshly ground black pepper	
1 tsp. thyme	
salt to taste	
2 egg yolks (beaten)	
2 tbsp. chopped parsley	
1 whole filet tenderloin of beef	
watercress (garnish)	

8 servings

Saute onions in olive oil and butter until limp. Add garlic, olives, ham, pepper, thyme, and salt (if necessary). Cook until mixture is well blended; stir in egg yolks and parsley. Cook a few minutes until blended.

Cut tenderloin into 8-10 thick slices—not quite through to the bottom—and spoon stuffing between the slices. At the thin tail end, fold tail over on some stuffing. Skewer tenderloin from one end to the other; freeze or refrigerate.

When ready to serve, bring to room temperature and roast on a rack at 300⁰ for 50 minutes. Brush once with oil. Let rest for 10 minutes, salt lightly, and slice through. Serve on platter garnished with watercress.

NOTE: Fifty minutes is for rare; cook to your own taste. For medium, cook 1-1½ hours, checking every 15 minutes after the first 50 minutes.

Kenosha, known as the "Gateway to Wisconsin" is a clean and attractive community with miles

continued

of recreational parkland along the beautiful Lake Michigan shore. This magnificent lake offers the pleasures of boating, fishing, swimming, and more. With four scenic seasons, Kenosha provides many opportunities for year-round activities. Our inland lakes are also recreational and scenic and that's why thousands visit our area every year.

Three Cheese Pizza

Mayor Michael A. Guido
Dearborn, Michigan

6 cups flour
1 tbsp. salt
1 egg (beaten)
2⅓-2⅔ cups water
2 pkgs. dry yeast (diluted in 3 tbsp. warm water)
vegetable oil (on hand)
2 cans Contadina pizza sauce
salt and pepper to taste
1½ lb. mozzarella cheese (grated)
4 oz. Swiss cheese (grated)
½ lb. brick cheese (grated)
2 tbsp. parsley
1 tbsp. oregano
Optional: pepperoni, green pepper, onions, mushrooms, ham, etc. (sliced thinly)

Makes 2 large pizzas

Mix flour and salt together; add egg. Add diluted yeast and water slowly to flour mixture. Knead together until mixture becomes sticky and has a dough consistency. Rub hands in oil and mold dough into a smooth ball. Place dough in a deep bowl, cover with a towel, and leave in a warm place to rise. Punch dough down after 1 hour and let rise a second time (approximately 45 minutes). Divide dough in half and spread on pizza pans with oiled finger tips. Carefully spread pizza dough to cover edge of pan.

Generously spread pizza sauce over dough, except for ½" edge around the perimeter. Sprinkle salt and pepper to taste. Add mozzarella, Swiss, and brick cheese liberally over sauce. Use toppings of your choice (pepperoni, green pepper, onions, mushrooms, ham, etc.). Sprinkle lightly with parsley and oregano and bake in 400⁰ preheated oven for 15-20 minutes, or until crusty.

Dearborn possesses a rich and productive history. The city first gained national note in the 19th century as the site of a major military garrison and later gained attention as the birthplace of Henry Ford, the world headquarters of Ford Motor Company, and the home of such attractions as Greenfield Village and the Henry Ford Museum.

White Chili

Mayor Richard L. Berkley
Kansas City, Missouri

1 lb. large white beans (soaked overnight in water and drained)
6 cups chicken broth
2 cloves garlic (minced)
2 medium onions (chopped)
1 tbsp. cooking oil
2 4 oz. cans chopped green chili peppers
2 tsp. cumin
1½ tsp. dried oregano
¼ tsp. ground cloves
¼ tsp. cayenne pepper
4 cups chicken breast (cooked and diced)
3 cups Monterey Jack cheese (grated)

8-10 servings

Combine beans, chicken broth, garlic, and ½ of the onions in large soup pot and bring to a boil. Reduce heat and simmer until beans are very soft,

3 hours or more. Add more chicken broth if necessary.

In a skillet, saute remaining onions in oil until tender. Add chili peppers and seasonings and mix thoroughly. Add to bean mixture. Add chicken and continue to simmer 1 hour.

Serve topped with grated cheese.

For a buffet, serve with some or all of the following condiments: chopped tomatoes, parsley, chopped ripe olives, guacamole, chopped scallions, sour cream, tortilla chips and salsa. Provide warm squares of hardy cornbread.

Kansas City, Missouri, is America's best kept secret. The home of the World Baseball Champion Kansas City Royals, the city is the "Heart of America," and the "City of Fountains," with more fountains than any other American city, ranking third in the world behind only Rome and Mexico City. Kansas City is renowned for its great jazz, beef and bar-b-que, and its parks and boulevards, which rival those in Paris.

CITY TRIVIA QUESTION #31

City in which the first commercially built horseless carriage was built by Elwood Haynes in 1894.

Answer on page 115.

ACCOMPANIMENTS

Broccoli Casserole

Mayor George V. Voinovich
Cleveland, Ohio

1 large bunch broccoli (cooked until tender, drained)
1 10 oz. can cream of mushroom soup
½ cup mayonnaise
2 eggs (slightly beaten)
1 cup (4 oz.) grated cheddar cheese
1 tbsp. dehydrated minced onion
1 4 oz. can mushrooms (drained) or 8 oz. fresh mushrooms (sliced and sauteed) (optional)
TOPPING:
3 oz. (32 crackers) Ritz crackers (crumbled)
¼ cup butter or margarine (melted)

6-8 servings

Cut broccoli into bite-size pieces. Place in greased 2 quart casserole. Mix remaining ingredients and pour over broccoli. Mix well. Mix cracker crumbs and butter or margarine and sprinkle over casserole. (Can be refrigerated up to 24 hours at this point if desired.)

Bake 350° for 35-45 minutes (or an hour, if chilled) until hot and bubbly and crust is browned.

Cleveland is the future home for the Rock-n-Roll Hall of Fame and Museum. For further information on Cleveland, turn to page 118.

Carrot Ring

Mayor Robert Buhai
Highland Park, Illinois

1 cup shortening (Crisco or Spry)	
½ cup brown sugar	
1 egg	
1 tbsp. water	1 tsp. baking powder
2 cups carrots (grated)	½ tsp. nutmeg
1½ cups flour	½ tsp. cinnamon
½ tsp. baking soda	½ tsp. salt

6-8 servings

Cream well together shortening and brown sugar. Add remaining ingredients and mix together. Place in greased mold.

Refrigerate 5-6 hours before baking 1 hour at 350°.

For additional color, fill center with green peas when serving.

May be prepared several weeks in advance and frozen before baking. May be used as vegetable and starch. Good side dish with beef or fowl. Great when reheated—crisp.

"Rich in tradition and culture, **Highland Park** is a sparkling example of the good life." These are the words that the *Chicago Tribune* used to describe the character of Highland Park, Illinois. Situated 28 miles north of Chicago along Lake Michigan, this vibrant North Shore community is home to 30,600 people. Highland Park lies in the heart of one of the most affluent areas in the nation. In terms of median family income, it ranks 4th in the U.S. More important, Highland Park is known for its high quality public services, active citizen participation, and progressive community development. These assets were recognized by the National Municipal League, which named Highland Park an "All America City." Other community awards include two national volunteerism awards for the senior and youth departments, a Presidential award for education, five Tree City USA Citations and Gold Medals for the Park District.

Festive Tapioca Fruit Salad

Mayor Kathryn C. Bloomberg
Brookfield, Wisconsin

1 small pkg. tapioca pudding
2 cups orange juice
1 can crushed pineapple (drained)
1 can mandarin oranges (drained)
Additional fruit of your choice*

8 servings

Heat pudding and orange juice over medium heat until boiling. Remove from heat and cool. Add drained fruit. Chill.

*The quantity depends on the type of fruit, but usually about 1 cup of additional fruit is used.

This salad is festive. I add cranberries at Thanksgiving, blueberries at the Fourth of July, and for children's parties I add miniature marshmallows. It is a versatile recipe because I add whatever fruit is in season and no matter what I add it always tastes great.

Solid, substantial things stand behind **Brookfield's** way of life; its excellent location is not the least of these. Residents enjoy convenient access to Milwaukee as well as the great variety of outdoor recreation pleasures offered within Waukesha County. Principal, however, are Brookfield's tranquil, open spaces, comfortable homes, superb schools, and unexcelled shopping, providing elements of pleasure and ease that enhance the community and make it a fine place to live.

Glamorized Wild Rice

Mayor Donald M. Fraser
Minneapolis, Minnesota

| 1 cup wild rice |
| 1 can condensed chicken broth |
| 1½ cups water |
| 1 tsp. dried onion flakes or 1 small onion (chopped) |
| ½ lb. mushrooms |
| 3 tbsp. butter |
| parsley as garnish |

4-6 servings

Cover cup of wild rice with can of condensed chicken broth and 1½ cans of water (3 cups of liquid in all) in saucepan and bring to boil. Simmer, covered, on lowest heat 45 minutes or until tender.

Drain and add mushrooms sauteed in 3 tablespoons butter with 1 teaspoon onion flakes or chopped small onion. Add salt and pepper to taste. Add slivered almonds or chopped apple for extra zest.

Wild rice is still harvested on Indian reservations in Minnesota in the old-fashioned way: using wooden paddles to beat rice into the bottoms of canoes guided through the tall stands of rice and grass edging Minnesota lakes. And it's still delicious!

People who live in this "City of Lakes" decided that the **Minneapolis** slogan should be "We Like It Here!" because we're the center for arts, finance, health care, telecommunications, high tech industry, and high fashion shopping for the Upper Midwest. We like our public-private partnerships, clean streets, clean politics, racial and ethnic integration, and wealth of community organizations.

Monkey Bread

Mayor Richard Gordon Hatcher
Gary, Indiana

| 4 tubes refrigerated biscuits (10 per tube) |
| ¾ cup butter |
| 1 cup sugar |
| 1½ tsp. cinnamon |

6 servings

Divide each tube of biscuits into four sections. Roll biscuits in ½ cup of the sugar mixed with 1 teaspoon of cinnamon. Place biscuits in greased angel food or bundt pan so the sides are touching. Form two layers. Boil ¾ cup butter, ½ cup sugar, and ½ teaspoon cinnamon together. Pour mixture over biscuits. Bake at 350⁰ for 45 minutes.

To serve, pull pieces apart.

"Great **Gary**!" is located on the southern shores of Lake Michigan with a beautiful expanse of beach, and it is the industrial hub of northwest Indiana. Indiana University Northwest, Indiana Vocational Tech, and the area's only school of visual and performing arts complement the fine public school system. A brand new transportation center and sports complex are major additions to its downtown redevelopment.

CITY TRIVIA QUESTION #32

International Business Machines (IBM) got its start in this city as the Bundy Time Company.

Answer on page 56.

Rice Pilaf

Mayor Michael B. Keys
Elyria, Ohio

1 tsp. salt
1 tbsp. butter
2 cups water
1 cup rice
soy sauce
¼-½ cup margarine or butter
½-1 cup mushrooms (sliced)
½ cup celery (chopped)
⅓-½ cup onion (chopped)

4-6 servings

Bring rice, butter, salt, and water to boil. Stir; turn heat down to simmer; cover and cook for 20 minutes. Melt margarine or butter. Saute mushrooms, celery, and onion. Add cooked rice. Add soy sauce to taste and heat through.

Good to serve with Marinated Flank Steak.

Elyria offers a vast array of benefits—reasonable taxes, cultural and performing arts, splendid recreation facilities, housing choices, excellent educational facilities, and more. Elyria also has a diversified industrial base with an emphasis on metal working and machine tool industries.

Seven Layer Salad

Mayor Carl E. Officer
East St. Louis, Illinois

1 large head lettuce
1 lb. raw spinach
1 can or 1 pkg. frozen sweet peas
1 bunch green onions
2 cups cheddar cheese (shredded)
6 eggs (hard-cooked and finely chopped)
1 cup bacon (crisp) or bacon bits
1 jar or pkg. of Original Ranch Salad Dressing

6 servings

Alternate layers of lettuce, spinach, peas, and green onions. On top of last layer, sprinkle eggs, then a layer of Ranch salad dressing. Top with cheddar cheese, then bacon or bacon bits. Chill and serve.

This recipe can be used with any meat complement.

East St. Louis, which sits astride ancient Indian mounds, serves as the center of commerce for the entire region. The center of a market for more than 2.5 million people in the local area and an additional 70 million within a few hundred miles, East St. Louis is a strategic location with abundant natural and human resources and solutions to complex industrial problems as exemplified by our current success in housing and business development. East St. Louis is the prototype city of the future.

CITY TRIVIA QUESTION #33
Virginia city that was the location of the first continuous English settlement in America.
Answer on page 64.

Spaghetti Salad

Mayor Peter Crivaro
Des Moines, Iowa

1 lb. thin spaghetti (broken in thirds)
1 large bottle Wishbone Italian dressing
1 bottle Schilling Salad Supreme
1 can black olives (pitted and sliced)
1 green pepper (chopped)
1 cucumber (chopped)
1 medium onion (chopped)
3 stalks celery (chopped)
2 tomatoes (chopped)

8 servings

Cook spaghetti. Drain and rinse. Add Italian dressing and Salad Supreme. Toss and chill. Add remaining ingredients and chill overnight. Stir before serving.

Des Moines' slogan is "The All-American City." Some of the special attractions of the city are the Des Moines Botanical Center, the new Des Moines Convention Center, and the annual 2 Rivers Festival. Des Moines is especially proud of its Living History Farms where visitors have an opportunity to see how our farms functioned before the introduction of modern equipment.

Spinach Casserole

Mayor Vincent C. Schoemehl, Jr.
St. Louis, Missouri

2 pkgs. frozen chopped spinach
1 8 oz. pkg. brick cheese (chopped)
1 8 oz. pkg. Swiss cheese (chopped)
12 oz. small curd cottage cheese
2 eggs (beaten)
2 tbsp. flour
2 tbsp. onion (minced)
salt and pepper to taste
1 stick butter (melted)

12 servings

Defrost spinach and drain well (squeeze dry). Add cheeses. Combine melted butter, eggs, flour, onion, salt, and pepper and pour over spinach and cheeses. Mix well. Pour into 8½"x13" pan and bake 1 hour at 350°.

St. Louis is a diversified and multi-faceted community; a meeting place, a fun place, and entertainment place. From a riverfront settlement in 1764, St. Louis has become the geographic and population hub of the U.S.—at the confluence of the Mississippi and Missouri rivers. The 1904 World's Fair in St. Louis created a number of firsts—the first hotdog, the first ice cream cone, and the first iced tea. St. Louis is home to a number of Fortune 500 companies, major universities, churches, and the Gateway Arch, the nation's tallest and most elegant memorial.

Spinach Salad with Dressing

Mayor Gerald E. Busch
Kettering, Ohio

1 lb. fresh spinach

4 hard-cooked eggs (chopped)

½ pkg. herb stuffing cubes

6 green onions (thinly sliced)

6 strips bacon (crisply fried)

dash pepper

DRESSING:

⅔ cup oil

⅔ cup sugar

⅓ cup wine vinegar

3 tsp. mustard

1 tsp. celery seed

8 servings

Wash spinach and remove stems; break into bite-size pieces. In a salad bowl, lightly toss with the next 5 ingredients. Refrigerate covered. Mix dressing ingredients together. Refrigerate.

To serve salad, pour dressing over it and toss to coat spinach well. Serve at once.

Kettering's success story is a story of many successes. Thriving, healthy businesses, both large and small...inviting neighborhoods and friendly neighbors...leisure activities to fit every lifestyle...involved people who spark excitement and community spirit...a bright future inspired by our tradition of invention and innovation. Kettering was named for one of its residents, Charles F. Kettering, world famous inventor and philanthropist.

Tabbouleh

Mayor James A. Maloof   *Peoria, Illinois*

1¾ cup fine bulgur (cracked wheat)

8 cups finely chopped parsley (about 3 large bunches)

½ cup green onions (chopped fine)

1 cup celery (chopped fine) (optional)

1 cup fresh mint (chopped fine) or 2 tbsp. dried mint

4 tomatoes (diced, about 3 cups)

1½ tsp. salt

¼ tsp. allspice

¼ tsp. black pepper	⅔ cup lemon juice (fresh)
7 cups boiling water	¼ cup olive or corn oil

8-10 servings

Put bulgur in bowl and add boiling water. Cover and let stand for 2 to 3 hours, until wheat has expanded and is light and fluffy.

Drain off excess water, transfer to sieve and shake until dry. In large bowl, add the chopped vegetables as they are cut. Sprinkle with seasonings and lemon juice and add bulgar and mix well. Chill.

Before serving, add oil and mix well. Serve with fresh small grape leaves and lettuce leaves to use as scoops. Adjust seasonings if desired.

Peoria, Illinois, is one of the oldest cities west of the Alleghenies, having been first inhabited in the mid-1600s. It is located on the Illinois River with its bluffs providing a unique vista that was described by President Theodore Roosevelt as "the world's most beautiful."

It is the home of Caterpillar, Inc. and has an economy that mixes both industry and agriculture functions as the economic hub of downstate Illinois.

Peoria's metropolitan population of 365,000 reflects the demographics of our nation useful not only as a test market, but also as a source of the thoughts and attitudes of America.

Yummy Zucchini Bake

Mayor Eugene B. Kunk
Springfield, Ohio

8-10 small zucchini
½ cup butter
½ cup onion (chopped)
1 cup cheddar cheese (grated)
½ cup gruyere cheese (grated)
1 cup sour cream
1 tsp. salt
½ tsp. paprika
1 cup bread crumbs
parmesan cheese to taste

6 servings

Wash and boil zucchini about 10 minutes. Cut off ends and halve lengthwise. Arrange in shallow, buttered casserole. Saute onion in butter; add remaining ingredients and spread over zucchini. Top with bread crumbs mixed with parmesan cheese. Bake at 350⁰ for 45 minutes.

Springfield—city of contrasts—has a four-season climate and an old and rich history combined with a promising future, and beckons the visitor to explore its many facets. Our 1,400 acres of public parklands invite you to kick off your shoes and relax. Another popular attraction is Buck Creek State Park and its 2,120 acre lake. George Rogers Clark Park, the site of the largest Revolutionary War battle west of the Alleghany Mountains, is now the site of the Clark Memorial and occasional battle reenactments. We invite you to visit us and discover for yourself why Springfield, Ohio, is Someplace Special!

DESSERTS

Apple Dumplings

Mayor Rodney D. Smith
Columbia, Missouri

SYRUP:	
1½ cups sugar	½ tsp. cinnamon
2 cups water	¼ cup butter or margarine
PASTRY:	
2 cups flour	⅓ cup evaporated milk
⅔ cup shortening	1 tsp. salt
FILLING:	
5 large or 7 medium tart cooking apples (peeled, cored, and sliced)	
1½ tsp. cinnamon	
6 tbsp. sugar	

6 servings

Make syrup: Cook sugar, water, and cinnamon for 5 minutes; add butter or margarine.

Make pastry: Mix all ingredients together thoroughly. Roll pastry out in a rectangle about 12"x18" and 1/8" thick; cut into 6" squares. Place one-sixth of apples in center of each square; sprinkle with sugar and cinnamon. Moisten edges of pastry, gather up and pinch together, sealing the apples in.

Transfer to baking dish and pour syrup over dumplings. Bake at 425⁰ for 20 minutes, then lower temperature to 350⁰ and bake for another 15 minutes. Serve warm with cream or a lemon sauce.

Columbia, situated in the center of Missouri's gentle hills and flanked by some of the finest apple orchards anywhere, has an ever-growing population of 65,895. Three colleges, six major hospitals, headquarters of several corporations, and 1600 acres of parks within the city limits, make Columbia "Ripe for the Picking" in education, medical care, employment, and recreation.

Black Forest Pie

Mayor Kathryn C. Bloomberg
Brookfield, Wisconsin

1 15 oz. pie crust mix or 1 homemade pie shell
¾ cup sugar
⅓ cup unsweetened cocoa
2 tbsp. flour
¼ cup margarine
⅓ cup milk
2 eggs (beaten)
1 21 oz. can cherry pie filling
1 9 oz. container whipped topping or sweetened whipped cream
1 1 oz. square unsweetened chocolate (coarsely grated)

8-10 servings

Prepare pie crust for filled 1-crust pie or make your own pie crust. Heat oven to 350⁰. In saucepan, combine sugar, cocoa, and 2 tablespoons flour; add margarine and milk. Cook until mixture begins to boil, stirring constantly; remove from heat. Add small amount of hot mixture to beaten eggs; return mixture to pan. Fold half can of pie filling into mixture. Pour into pie crust. Bake at 350⁰ 35-45 minutes or until center is set but still shiny. Cool. Chill one hour. Combine 2 cups topping or whipped cream and grated chocolate; spread over cooled pie. Top with remaining pie filling and topping. Chill 30 minutes.

Luscious recipe for chocolate lovers. Always the first to go at Pot Lucks.

Brookfield, located in Waukesha County has a great variety of recreational activities to offer. For further information on Brookfield, turn to page 124.

Bohemian Poppy Seed Cake

Mayor Anthony V. Dufek
Manitowoc, Wisconsin

⅓ cup poppy seeds
1 cup buttermilk
1 cup margarine
1½ cups sugar
4 eggs
grated rind of 1 orange
½ tsp. vanilla
½ tsp. salt
2½ cups flour (sifted)
2 tsp. baking powder
1 tsp. baking soda
2 tbsp. sugar blended with 2 tsp. cinnamon

12-18 servings

Soak poppy seeds in buttermilk overnight. Cream margarine and sugar together until smooth; beat in eggs one at a time. Stir in orange rind, vanilla, and salt. Sift together flour, baking powder, and soda; add alternately with poppy seeds in buttermilk. Mix to a smooth batter. Pour half the batter into a greased and floured 10" angel food or bundt pan. Sprinkle sugar-cinnamon mixture on batter, then add the rest of batter. Bake at 350⁰ for 35 minutes or until cake tests done.

Located on the shores of Lake Michigan, Manitowoc has a 150-year history of being a diversified manufacturing community. The city has been known as the "Aluminum Capital of the World." The city's maritime heritage is exemplified by a 1.5 mile waterfront development, which includes a public marina, a YMCA, a new hotel, a Maritime Museum, and a World War II submarine.

of our community—from its rural beginnings to its phenomenal growth, and its unique blend of industrial innovation, residential comfort, and educational and cultural opportunities. Warren is the home of the General Motors Technical Center and the U.S. Army Tank Automotive Command.

Cannoli Cake

Mayor Ronald L. Bonkowski
Warren, Michigan

1 box yellow cake mix
1 qt. half-and-half
1 cup cornstarch
1 cup sugar
cinnamon oil
1 large Hershey chocolate bar (grated)
½-¾ cup toasted sliced almonds
1 large container whipped topping
1-1½ cups cold milk

12 servings

Prepare cake mix as directed on box and bake in a 9" x 13" cake pan. Cool.

Dissolve sugar in half-and-half. Add cinnamon oil to taste. Heat until hot. Dissolve cornstarch with 1-1½ cups cold milk and add to hot milk mixture. Mix well. Continue heating, stirring until mixture thickens (should have the consistency of pudding). Cover immediately with waxed paper and refrigerate until cool.

Slice cake in half. Beat pudding with mixer until smooth; stir in grated chocolate. Spread on bottom layer of cake, sprinkle almonds on top. Put top on cake and frost with whipped topping. Garnish with sliced almonds or chocolate bits.

Warren is the "City of Progress!" Although it is thought of as a suburb of Detroit, Warren is the third largest city in Michigan, spanning 34.5 square miles with a population of 160,000. We are proud

Cheesecake Supreme

Mayor Terry J. McKane
Lansing, Michigan

CRUST: 1 cup flour
¼ cup sugar
1 tsp. lemon peel
½ cup butter
1 egg yolk (slightly beaten)
½ tsp. vanilla
FILLING:
5 8 oz. pkgs. cream cheese
¼ tsp. vanilla
¾-1 tsp. lemon peel
1¾ cup sugar
3 tbsp. flour
¼ tsp. salt
4-5 eggs (1 cup)
2 egg yolks
¼ cup whipping cream

16 servings

Crust: Combine first three ingredients. Cut in butter until crumbly; add egg yolk and vanilla. Blend thoroughly. Pat ⅓ dough on bottom of 9" springform pan (sides removed). Bake at 400° about 8 minutes; cool. Attach sides to bottom, butter, and pat remaining dough on sides to height of 1¾".

Filling: Let cream cheese stand at room temperature to soften, about 1-1½ hours. Beat until creamy. Add vanilla and lemon peel; mix next 3 ingredients and gradually blend into cheese. Add

continued

eggs and yolks one at a time, beating after each just to blend. Gently stir in whipping cream.

Turn into crust-lined pan. Bake at 450⁰ for 12 minutes. Reduce heat to 300⁰ and continue baking 55 minutes

---

Lansing, a community of some 130,000 residents, is situated in the lower part of Michigan halfway between Detroit and Grand Rapids. Lansing is known as Michigan's capital, with Oldsmobile and General Motors plants located here.

Cherry Cobbler

Mayor Cameron G. Priebe
Taylor, Michigan

1 large can cherry pie filling
1 20-oz. can crushed pineapple
1 box white cake mix
1½ sticks margarine
nuts (optional)

8-10 servings

Pour cherry pie filling in large 9″ x 13″ pyrex dish; add crushed pineapple (undrained). Top this with dry cake mix. Slice margarine into little pats and place over dry cake mix. (You may also add nuts if desired). Bake at 375⁰ for about 50 minutes, until golden brown.

It is very easy to make and always turns out great.

Taylor has a population of 77,568 and is a residential/commercial community consisting of 24 square miles located in south westerly Wayne County. Founded in 1968, Taylor is only 55 percent developed, and is known as "The City on the Grow."

Chilled Lemon Honey Cheese Pie

Mayor F. Joseph Sensenbrenner, Jr.
Madison, Wisconsin

16 graham crackers (crushed into crumbs)
6 tbsp. butter (melted)
¼ cup cold water
1 tbsp. unflavored gelatin
¾ cup boiling water
¾ cup mild flavored honey
½ cup fresh lemon juice
grated lemon rind
8 oz. Neutchatel cheese
½ cup whipping cream
1 tsp. vanilla

6-8 servings

Mix together graham crackers and melted butter for pie crust and press into 9″ buttered pan.

Sprinkle the gelatin over cold water and let set until absorbed. Add to the boiling water and stir until dissolved. Add honey, lemon juice, lemon rind. Chill until partially set. Whip the cream. With same beaters, cream the cheese and slowly add the chilled lemon mixture until well mixed. Add the vanilla and fold in the whipped cream. Pour into prepared crust. Chill until firm, at least 2 hours.

This recipe was one of the prize winners in Madison's and Dane County's 1986 Dairylicious Recipe Contest which is one portion of the celebration for Wisconsin's June Dairy Month. I sampled the pie at Madison's ''Cows on the Concourse'', an annual event for our city.

Madison is a gem in the Midwest—a cosmopolitan city with small town friendliness and big city ideas. Centered on a narrow isthmus among four scenic lakes, the city is a recreational paradise. Madison's waters are host to sailors and swimmers in the warm seasons, skaters and fishing enthusiasts when the 18,000 acres of lake surface freeze over. In the heart of Madison is the majestic State Capitol and the campus of the University of Wisconsin. A deep-seated community spirit and commitment make Madison one of the country's most satisfying places to live.

Chocolate Chip Cookies with a Flair

Mayor William H. Hudnut III
Indianapolis, Indiana

1 cup (2 sticks) unsalted butter
1½ cups light brown sugar (firmly packed)
1 egg (room temperature)
1 tsp. vanilla
2 cups unbleached all purpose flour
1 tsp. baking soda
1 tsp. cinnamon
1 tsp. ground ginger
½ tsp salt
1 12-oz. pkg. semisweet chocolate chips
1 cup chopped walnuts (pecans can be substituted)
1 cup powdered sugar

Makes 6 dozen

Cream butter using electric mixer. Beat in brown sugar, egg, and vanilla. Combine flour, baking soda, cinnamon, ginger, and salt. Blend into butter mixture. Fold in chocolate chips and walnuts. Refrigerate until firm. (Can be prepared 1 day ahead.)

Preheat oven to 375⁰. Lightly grease baking sheets. Break off small pieces of dough; roll between palms into 1" rounds. Dredge rounds in powdered sugar. Arrange rounds on prepared sheets, spacing at least 2" apart. Bake 10 minutes. Let cool 5 minutes on sheets. Transfer to racks and cool. Store in airtight container.

These cookies are great conversation pieces—people wonder what makes them taste "different" but so-o-o good!

Indianapolis is known as the "Crossroads of America" because more interstate highways intersect here than in any other city in the United States. For further information on Indianapolis.turn to page 110.

Coconut Balls

Mayor Barbara J. Potts
Independence, Missouri

1½ cups coconut
⅔ cup sweetened condensed milk
dash salt
1 tsp. vanilla
¼ tsp. almond extract

Makes about 18 balls

Combine ingredients and make into balls. Bake on greased sheet at 350⁰ for 15 minutes or until brown.

The recipe for Coconut Balls has been served by Mrs. Truman for White House Teas.

For more than 150 years, **Independence,** Missouri, has been making history. It was a starting point for pioneers headed west, a Civil War battleground, and best known as the hometown of President Harry S. Truman. Independence has been selected twice as All-American City, which speaks well for contemporary life in this city. We are always pleased to share our rich heritage with the 250,000 tourists who visit us each year. We hope to meet you soon!

Custard Bread Pudding

Mayor Walter Moore
Pontiac, Michigan

3 eggs
½ cup sugar
½ tsp. salt
3 cups milk (scalded and cooled slightly)
2 tsp. vanilla
1 qt. enriched bread crumbs
ground· cinnamon
raisins (optional)

6 servings

Beat eggs slightly. Stir in sugar and salt; add milk gradually. Add vanilla. Measure bread cubes and put into greased 1½ quart casserole dish. Pour egg and milk mixture over cubes. Sprinkle cinnamon over top. Bake slow oven (325⁰) 50-55 minutes. (Raisins can be added if desired.)

We call **Pontiac** "A City with a Proud Past and a Bright Future," and that statement is taking on more meaning every day, as city officials are attracting new commercial and residential developments. Pontiac is currently in contention for the first 1000-foot telecommunications tower in the United States. Efforts are being made to bring to Pontiac the 1991 Super Bowl. Pontiac still holds the distinction of being the only non-Sunbelt city to host a Super Bowl Game in its Silver Dome.

CITY TRIVIA QUESTION #34

This "City of Brotherly Love" will be the host city for the 200th celebration of the United States Constitution in 1987.

Answer on page 58.

Czech Fest Kolaches

Mayor Donald J. Canney
Cedar Rapids, Iowa

Any favorite fruit filling
DOUGH:
2 pkgs. of cakes yeast
1 cup warm water
½ cup sugar
½ tsp. salt
1 cup lard
1 cup cold water
2 eggs (beaten)
6 cups flour
melted butter (for brushing)

Makes 5 dozen

In large bowl, dissolve yeast in warm water and add sugar and salt. Melt lard and add cold water to it, then pour into yeast solution. Add beaten eggs and mix well. Stir in 2 cups flour and mix well. Beat in remaining flour 1 cup at a time. When dough becomes too thick to beat with a wooden spoon, turn out on floured board and knead until smooth and silky. Put in greased bowl and cover tightly. Refrigerate 4 or 5 hours or overnight.

Turn dough out onto lightly floured board and divide into 6 large pieces. Roll each of these large pieces into many walnut-sized balls. (Another method of forming kolaches is to roll out dough and cut using a 6-oz. size orange juice can.) Grease cookie sheet. Place dough portions on sheet 1½"-2" apart and brush each with butter. Let rise until doubled or warm and bouncy to touch.

Make an indentation in middle of each and fill with preferred fillings. Entire dough recipe requires about 2 pounds of filling. Let rise another 20 minutes. Bake at 425⁰ for 12 minutes or until golden brown. Brush kolaches with butter after you take them from the oven.

A Czech favorite. The Kolache Festival of St. Ludmila Paris in Cedar Rapids, Iowa, is held the second weekend in June and attracts more than 12,000 visitors annually. It is one of numerous festivals hosted in the Cedar Rapids area.

Named for the swirling rapids of the Cedar River, **Cedar Rapids** is surrounded by the rolling hills made famous by its native artist, Grant Wood. In the midst of rich Iowa farm land, the city is the state's leading center of agriculture, technology, and international trade. Quaker Oats, built in 1882, is the largest cereal manufacturer in the world today. Cedar Rapids prides itself on being a homogenous city with a proud past with its Eastern heritage reflected in Little Czech village, a neighborhood where Czech descendants still celebrate in "Old World" fashion each year during Czech days.

Double Chocolate Treat

Mayor Stephen J. Alfred
Shaker Heights, Ohio

⅔ cup butter
4 squares unsweetened chocolate
2 cups sugar
4 eggs (well beaten)
1⅓ cups flour
1 tsp. baking powder
½ tsp. salt
2 tsp. vanilla
2 cups whipping cream (garnish)
FILLING:
3 8-oz. boxes semisweet chocolate
½ cup strong coffee
3 eggs (separated)
½ cup coffee liqueur   ½ cup whipping cream

70 servings

Melt butter and chocolate in top of double boiler over hot water. Remove from heat; add sugar and eggs and mix well. Sift together flour, baking powder, and salt. Stir into chocolate mixture. Add vanilla. Pour into greased and floured 3-quart Pyrex pan. Bake at 350⁰ for 20 minutes. Cool; remove from brownie pan and cut into strips wide enough to fit 3 pans (each lined with foil) approximately 14" x 5" x ½". Cut each strip in half and line bottom and sides of pans with brownie layers.

For filling: melt chocolate with coffee in top of double boiler over hot water. Remove from heat. Beat egg yolks well and stir into chocolate. Add liqueur and allow to cool. Beat egg whites until stiff but not dry. Whip cream until stiff. Fold whites and cream into chocolate mixture.

Spoon filling into brownie-lined pans, wrap well, and chill overnight. To serve, gently lift foil lining from pan; unmold onto serving plate. Whip 2 cups whipping cream until stiff and cover top of cakes. Slice into ½"-¾" slices.

Extremely rich and delicious. The ideal dessert for the connoisseur, the chocoholic, and no one with hypoglycemia.

Shaker Heights was the first planned community in the United States. Best known for its beautiful homes and outstanding schools, it is the residence of many of Cleveland's business and professional leaders. It is one of few communities in the U.S. that has had successful, stable integration for almost 30 years. The Shaker School system has been rated as one of the top 10 in the country and the merit scholars from Shaker Heights High School usually exceed in number those of all other Ohio schools combined. Shaker Heights will be celebrating its 75th anniversary as an incorporated entity on February 13, 1987.

Fort Wayne Cheesecake

Mayor Win Moses, Jr.
Fort Wayne, Indiana

2 cups graham cracker crumbs
½ cup (1 stick) butter (melted)
1 cup sugar (divided)
2 lbs. cream cheese
2 large eggs (lightly beaten)
1 tsp. vanilla
1 cup sour cream

12 servings

Preheat oven to 450º. In a bowl, place graham cracker crumbs, butter, and 2 tablespoons sugar; blend well. Reserve 2 tablespoons for garnish (optional). Press remaining mixture onto bottom and sides of a greased 9" springform pan. Chill in freezer while preparing filling.

In mixer bowl, beat cream cheese and remaining sugar until smooth and light. Beat in eggs, vanilla, and cornstarch, just until blended. Stir in sour cream. Pour mixture into prepared crust and bake for 10 minutes. Reduce temperature to 200º and bake 45 minutes. Turn off oven; allow to cool with the door opened slightly for 3 hours. Remove sides from pan; sprinkle with reserved crumb mixture and chill.

Enjoy!

Fort Wayne is a midwestern city of approximately 180,000 and is known as "The City of Churches." Fort Wayne received the honor of "Most Livable City" in 1983 and the "All America City" award in 1982-83. It has had its problems...and came through with flying colors. In 1982, Fort Wayne was hit by a flood that could have caused much more damage than it did, but the youth in Fort Wayne banded together along with other citizens and sandbagged the dikes and low areas to save our city. They worked to such a degree that we were known nationally as "The City That Saved Itself."

Jackson Brownies

Mayor Richard Strunk
Jackson, Michigan

½ cup margarine
1 cup sugar
4 eggs
1 tsp. vanilla
1 can Hershey Chocolate Syrup
1 cup plus 2 tbsp. flour
¾ cup chopped walnuts (optional)
ICING:
6 tbsp. margarine
6 tbsp. milk
1½ cups sugar

8-10 servings

Mix cake ingredients together, adding eggs two at a time and beating well after each addition. Pour into large pan and bake at 350º for 20-25 minutes.

Combine icing ingredients; spread on brownies after they are baked and still warm.

Jackson is located in southern lower Michigan and was named an All-America City in 1986. Jackson has a Rose Festival in June of each year. The Republican Party had its beginning in Jackson on July 6, 1854.

> **CITY TRIVIA QUESTION #35**
>
> The city each year hosts the nation's largest hot air balloon festival and races with over 400 hot air balloons participating.
>
> Answer on page 169.

Johnny Appleseed Sour Cream Pie

Mayor Edward T. Meehan
Mansfield, Ohio

1-crust unbaked pie pastry
2 eggs
½ cup plus ⅓ cup sugar
½ cup plus 2 tbsp. all purpose flour
¼ tsp. salt
1 cup sour cream
1 tsp. lemon rind (grated)
1 tbsp. lemon juice
⅓ cup seedless raisins
2½ cups apples (sliced)
¼ tsp. grated nutmeg
3 tbsp. butter

6-8 servings

Preheat oven to 400⁰. Line a 9″ pie plate with the pastry.

Beat eggs and add ½ cup sugar, 2 tablespoons flour, salt, sour cream, lemon rind, and juice. Add raisins and apples; mix well. Pour into pastry-lined pie plate. Bake for 10 minutes.

Combine remaining flour and sugar and nutmeg. Cut in butter with 2 knives until mixture is crumbly. Sprinkle on the apple filling and continue baking 30-35 minutes, until crumbs are brown and filling is set. Chill.

Mansfield is Johnny Appleseed country, hence the apple pie recipe.

Mansfield, Ohio, is a community suspended gracefully between city and country. It is a city of more than 50,000 people with a rich vein of cultural and economic resources. Yet several moments east or west, the cityscape dissolves into jade-colored expanses of forest and farmland, sometimes punctuated by a horse-drawn Amish carriage.

Lemon Bars

Mayor Thomas M. McDermott
Hammond, Indiana

2 cups flour (sifted) plus 4 tbsp. flour
1 cup butter (melted)
½ cup powdered sugar
4 eggs (beaten)
2 cups sugar
1 tsp. baking powder
6 tbsp. lemon juice

Makes 12-15

Crust: Mix together 2 cups of flour, butter, powdered sugar; pat into a 10″ x 13″ pan. Bake for 20 minutes at 350⁰.

Filling: While crust is baking, mix eggs, sugar, 4 tablespoons flour, baking powder, and lemon juice. Pour over hot crust and bake 25 minutes at 350⁰. Sift powdered sugar on top; cool and cut into squares.

A quick dessert to make in a pinch; most of the ingredients you have on hand all the time!

An industrial city of 93,000, **Hammond** is located just 20 minutes from downtown Chicago, on the shore of Lake Michigan. It is the fifth largest city in the state of Indiana. Rebounding from the economic effects of the depressed steel industry, the city is attracting a variety of new businesses and industries, some related to steel and others that are water intensive.

Missouri Peach Custard Pie

Mayor Janet Majerus
University City, Missouri

| pastry for 9" pie pan |
| 1 cup sugar |
| 2 tbsp. flour |
| 1 egg |
| ½ pt. light cream |
| 5-6 peaches (sliced) |

6-8 servings

Make pastry for 9" pie pan. Line pastry-covered pie pan with sliced peaches. Mix sugar and flour; stir in egg. Add half the cream, mix, and pour over peaches. Pour rest of cream over. Bake 15 minutes at 400°. Reduce to 325° and bake an additional 30-35 minutes.

University City, the City of Lions, has a rich history dating from the 1904 St. Louis World's Fair with graceful tree-lined streets winding among early 20th century homes. As a center for the arts and education, it is a city that revels in its racial, cultural, and political diversity. It is a city that works because its people respect the past but look to the future.

Mocha Rum Mousse

Mayor William S. Moore
Newark, Ohio

| 1 6-oz. pkg. semi-sweet chocolate bits |
| 5 tbsp. hot coffee |
| 4 eggs (separated) |
| 2 tbsp. light rum |
| whipped cream |

6 servings

Place chocolate, coffee, egg yolks, and rum in blender. Cover and blend at high speed for about 1 minute (stop blender occasionally and scrape down sides with rubber spatula). Beat egg whites until stiff, but not dry. Slowly pour in the chocolate mixture; then with rubber scraper, fold until no egg white remains visible. Spoon into sherbet glasses. Refrigerate for 1 hour. If desired, top with whipped cream at serving time. (May be made ahead if carefully covered to keep airtight.)

Easy but very delicious.

Newark, Ohio, population 42,000, is called the Land of Legend. Two hundred years ago Newark's first settlers found a maze of strange earthworks. Artifacts from within these geometric mounds attest to a highly sophisticated early civilization. Today Newark is an industrial city. Educational opportunities, parks, museums, an art gallery, and an arboretum make Newark a desirable place to live.

CITY TRIVIA QUESTION #36

This Hampton Roads city is home base to one of the country's largest naval stations and the General Douglas MacArthur Memorial and Museum.

Answer on page 70.

Nut Rolls

Mayor Anthony J. Giunta
Euclid, Ohio

2½ cups flour
1 cake or pkg. yeast
3 egg yolks
½ lb. margarine (softened)
8 oz. sour cream
1 cup sugar
2 cups walnuts (ground)

Makes 50 pieces

Mix flour and yeast. Work in margarine (as for pie dough). Then add sour cream and egg yolks. Mix well with hands. Dough will be sticky, so use a little flour on your hands to make the dough dry. Pinch off dough to make balls about the size of half-dollars; dough will make about 50 balls. Put balls in a bowl, cover with waxed paper, and refrigerate overnight to chill.

Mix sugar and ground walnuts. Pat the balls in the sugar and walnuts on both sides and flatten to about 3" diameter. Roll and put onto greased cookie sheet. Bake at 350° for 20-25 minutes or until delicate brown. Cool cookies and sprinkle with powdered sugar.

Euclid enjoys an enviable location on Lake Erie, the nation's North Coast, adjacent to and part of metropolitan Cleveland. An ethnic community, Euclid is endowed with a fine transportation system, excellent schools, superb parks and recreational facilities, convenient shopping, and a solid industrial base. Recognized as a "City of Superior Services," Euclid residents are genuinely proud of their community.

Oatmeal Cake

Mayor Donald Canney
Cedar Rapids, Iowa

1¼ cups boiling water
1 cup quick Quaker Oats
½ cup shortening
1 cup white sugar
1 cup brown sugar
2 eggs
1½ cups flour
1 tsp. baking soda
½ tsp. salt
1 tsp. nutmeg
1 tsp. vanilla
TOPPING:
¼ cup butter or margarine
¾ cup brown sugar
3 tbsp. milk
½ cup nuts
½ cup coconut (shredded)

12 servings

Pour boiling water over oats; cover and let stand 20 minutes. Cream together shortening, sugars, and eggs and add to oatmeal; mix well. Add other dry ingredients and vanilla. Pour into greased and floured 9"x13" pan. Bake at 350° for 45-50 minutes. Remove and spread immediately with topping; brown in broiler for 1-2 minutes.

Topping: Mix all ingredients together until creamy. Spread on top of warm cake and broil 1-2 minutes.

"Heavy moist Iowa treat!"

Cedar Rapids is home to Quaker Oats, built in 1882, which is the largest cereal manufacturer in the world. See page 135 for additional information on Cedar Rapids.

Oatmeal Wafers

Mayor John F. McNamara
Rockford, Illinois

1 cup brown sugar
1 cup white sugar
1 cup margarine
2 eggs
1½ cups flour
1 tsp. baking soda
1 tsp. vanilla
½ tsp. salt
3 cups quick Quaker Oats

Makes 5 dozen

Mix all together in order given above. Drop by teaspoonfuls onto greased cookie sheet. Bake at 350⁰ for 10-15 minutes.

Rockford, Illinois' second city, was founded in 1834. A city of 140,000 that's also a place for people to come home to, Rockford is the home of everything from industries to peaceful parks and rivers, beautiful golf courses, rousing symphony performances and an internationally recognized theater. Come home to the real America . . . Rockford, Illinois.

Ozark Pudding

Mayor Barbara J. Potts
Independence, Missouri

1 egg	5 small apples (chopped)
¾ cup sugar	1/8 tsp. salt
2 tbsp. flour	½ cup chopped nuts
1¼ tsp. baking powder	1 tsp. vanilla

6 servings

Beat eggs; add sugar. Sift dry ingredients; add to eggs and sugar. Combine remaining ingredients and bake in a greased pan 35 minutes at 350⁰.

The Ozark Pudding is a very popular recipe made famous by Mrs. Bess Truman.

Independence was a starting point for pioneers heading out west. It was also a Civil War battleground, but is best known as the hometown of President Truman. For further information on Independence, turn to page 133.

Persimmon Pudding

Mayor Tomilea Allison
Bloomington, Indiana

3 eggs
2 cups flour
1 tsp. salt
¼ tsp. cloves
2 cups persimmon pulp
1 cup nut meats
2 tsp. soda
1¾ cup sugar
¼ tsp. ginger
1 cup milk
2 tsp. vanilla

12 servings

Add ingredients in order listed. Place in 9"x13" pan and bake in 350⁰ oven 1 hour or longer. When baked, make pattern of walnuts, coconut, cherries (red or green), powdered sugar on top of the pudding before it cools. Or leave plain and serve with lemon sauce, whipped cream, or hard sauce.

There are many persimmon festivals in Indiana. The persimmon tree is native to Indiana.

Bloomington is one of the four fastest growing cities in Indiana. In addition, Bloomington offers a rare combination of small town allure and big city advantages. With a diverse assortment of fine restaurants, the many cultural and special events at Indiana University, and an abundance of recreational facilities in and around Monroe County, we think we have something for everyone.

Pumpkin Pudding Cake

Mayor David L. Pierce
Aurora, Illinois

1 pkg. yellow cake mix
1 pkg. (4-serving size) butterscotch instant pudding mix
4 eggs
¼ cup water
¼ cup oil
1 cup pumpkin
2 tsp. pumpkin pie spice

8-10 servings

Combine all ingredients in large mixer bowl. Blend well, then beat at medium speed for 4 minutes. Pour into greased and floured 10" tube or bundt pan. Bake at 350⁰ for 50-55 minutes or until cake tests done in center and begins to pull away from sides of pan. Cool in pan 15 minutes. Remove from pan and finish cooling on rack. Spread glaze (recipe follows) over cake when cool.

Glaze: Gradually add 1 tablespoon hot milk and a few drops food coloring to 1 cup sifted confectioner's sugar in a bowl and blend well. Spread over cake.

The City of **Aurora**, Illinois (population 85,000), lies 40 miles west of Chicago. The Fox River passes through downtown Aurora, with entertainment and government offices located on Stolp Island. Lovely parks and bike trails along the Fox River provide recreational opportunities. We are in the process of creating our third Historic District and many buildings are designated national landmarks. A recent addition is the Illinois Math & Science Academy, the third such high school in the nation.

Rhubarb Cobbler

Mayor Bernard McKinley
Waterloo, Iowa

¾ cup sugar
3 tbsp. butter
½ cup milk
1 cup flour
1 tsp. baking powder
¼ tsp. salt
4 cups rhubarb (cut up)
TOPPING:
¾ cup sugar
1 tbsp. cornstarch
1 tsp. cinnamon
1 cup boiling water

8 servings

Cream together butter and sugar. Add milk, flour, baking powder, and salt; mix well. Lay rhubarb in bottom of an 8" square pan. Spread above mixture over fruit.

Topping: Combine dry ingredients; sprinkle over dough. Pour boiling water over all. Bake at 350⁰ for 1 hour.

Good served with cream or ice cream.

Waterloo, located in north central Iowa, has a lifestyle and economy that is a mixture of urban and rural. John Deere, the city's major employer, manufactures tractors. Waterloo was the home of the five Sullivan brothers who were all killed in

World War II when the ship they were on sank. Because of that tragedy, the Navy today does not allow members of the same family to serve on the same ship. The Navy also has commissioned a ship in their honor. Waterloo—A City of Changing Seasons and Possibilities.

Ricotta Cake

Mayor Thomas J. Longo
Garfield Heights, Ohio

1 box yellow cake mix (with pudding)	
CHEESE FILLING:	
1½ lb. ricotta cheese	
3 eggs	
½ cup milk	
½ cup sugar	
1 tsp. vanilla	

8-10 servings

Follow directions on cake mix and pour into 9"x13" glass baking dish. Beat remaining ingredients and pour over cake batter very carefully. Bake at 350⁰ for 50-60 minutes. Cake is done when it springs back. Let cool. Frost with whipped topping and top with any canned fruit filling or fresh strawberries in season.

Garfield Heights, Ohio, named after the 20th president of the U.S. (James A. Garfield), is known as "The City of Homes." The city is situated close enough to be able to enjoy downtown Cleveland, yet far enough away to allow us to continue to enjoy the heritage that bonds us together as a community. Garfield Park is the newest member of metroparks' Emerald Necklace park system.

Rum Cake

Mayor Mel Wetter
St. Charles, Missouri

1 cup pecans (chopped)	
1 box butter cake mix	
1 box French vanilla instant pudding	
½ cup water	
½ cup oil	5 eggs
½ cup white rum	
SAUCE:	
1 cup sugar	¼ cup water
¼ cup rum	1 stick butter

10-12 servings

Preheat oven to 300⁰. Oil and flour tube pan and cover bottom of pan with pecans. Combine cake mix, pudding, water, oil, rum, and eggs and mix for 2 minutes at high speed. Bake for 1 hour. While cake is baking, prepare sauce.

Sauce: Heat sugar, rum, and water together until sugar dissolves. Stir butter into sugar mixture; mix until it melts.

When cake is finished baking, remove from oven and poke holes in it. Pour sauce over cake immediately. Cake will fall a little after this. Let cake cool in pan for 40 minutes.

This is a yummy cake and very moist. Keep covered. I've taken this cake to a fund-raiser and everyone loved it — I brought home an empty cake plate.

St. Charles is located six miles from the St. Louis International Airport, along Interstate I-70. Some of the many attractions are the location of the beginning of the Lewis & Clark Expedition, historic South Main Street with its 100 shops and fine restaurants, Frenchtown antique shops, 160-year-old Lindenwood College, Sacred Heart Academy with the location of the first State Capitol of Missouri.

Scandinavian Rice Pudding

Mayor Herbert Mocol
Mankato, Minnesota

½ cup rice	
½ tsp. salt	
4 cups milk	
3 egg yolks	
⅔ cup sugar	
1 tsp. vanilla	
¼ cup raisins (optional)	
½ tsp. nutmeg (if desired)	
MERINGUE:	
3 egg whites	
6 tbsp. sugar	
½ tsp. vanilla	

8-10 servings

Cook rice, salt, and milk in a double boiler until rice is creamy, stirring frequently. Beat together egg yolks and sugar and add to first mixture gradually; cook until thick. Remove from heat and add vanilla, raisins, and nutmeg.

Meringue: Beat egg whites until stiff; gradually beat in sugar and vanilla. Spread over rice mixture and bake in 350⁰ oven until meringue is gold tipped. Cool.

Founded in 1850, **Mankato** is a progressive community located at the confluence of the Blue Earth and Minnesota rivers. Hub of commerce, education, health care, and government for Southern Minnesota, Mankato is one of the most beautiful regions in the Minnesota River Valley.

Seven Layer Bar Cookies

Mayor Richard L. Verbic
Elgin, Illinois

½ stick butter (melted)	
1 cup graham cracker crumbs	
1 cup Angel Flake coconut	
1 cup chocolate chips	
1 cup butterscotch chips	
1 cup chopped nuts	
1 cup Rice Krispies	
1 can condensed milk	

24 servings, more or less

Spread melted butter on a 10½"x15½" pan. Add the next 6 ingredients in order; drizzle milk over everything. Bake in 350⁰ oven for approximately 15-20 minutes. Watch carefully so it doesn't burn or overcook. Cut into squares while still warm.

Very quick and easy to prepare and everyone loves them. A tad messy at times if too warm. Even your children can be taught to prepare this in your absence. Yeah!

Elgin, situated on the Fox River, has protected its natural beauty with forest preserves and more than 1,000 acres of parkland. The original home of the Elgin Watch Company, the city recently celebrated its 150th birthday. Experiencing strong economic growth, Elgin offers the best of both rural and cosmopolitan life in the emerging high tech corridor of northern Illinois.

CITY TRIVIA QUESTION #37
Home of the "Big Apple."
Answer on page 42.

Strawberry Bread with Spread

Mayor Ronald L. Malone
Marion, Ohio

3 cups flour	2 cups sugar
1 tsp. baking soda	1 tsp. salt
1 tsp. cinnamon	1¼ cups vegetable oil
2 10 oz. pkgs. frozen strawberries (thawed and sliced, reserve juice for spread)	
4 eggs (well beaten)	
1 cup pecans (chopped)	
SPREAD:	
⅓ cup strawberry juice	
1 8 oz. pkg. cream cheese (softened)	

Makes 2 loaves

Mix all dry ingredients together. Make a hole in the center of mixture. Pour strawberries, oil, and eggs into the hole. Mix by hand until all ingredients are thoroughly combined. Stir in chopped pecans. Pour into 2 greased and floured 9"x5"x3" pans. Bake at 350⁰ for 40-60 minutes.

Spread: Place juice and cream cheese in blender. Process until spreading consistency. Spread on cold bread.

The bread can also be baked in five small (5"x2½"x2½") pans. When sliced and placed in a pretty basket with the pink cream cheese, it made a lovely addition to our buffet-type fundraisers!

Marion is an industrial and farming community. It is the home of Marion Power Shovel (now Presser Corporation), which built the machines that dug the Panama Canal and the Moon Station. It is the home of President Warren G. Harding, the United States Drum and Bugle Corps Open, and the Marion Popcorn Festival.

Strawberry Cake

Mayor Dana G. Rinehart
Columbus, Ohio

CAKE:
1 pkg. white cake mix
3 oz. pkg. strawberry gelatin
4 tbsp. flour
4 eggs
½ cup water
½ box (10 oz.) frozen, sliced strawberries
¾ cup cooking oil
FROSTING:
½ box (10 oz.) frozen, sliced strawberries
½ cup butter
1 lb. confectioner's sugar
½ tsp. vanilla

8-10 servings

Mix together cake mix, gelatin, flour, eggs, and water. Beat 2 minutes at medium speed. Add strawberries (including syrup) to batter. Beat 1 minute more. Add oil and beat 1 more minute. Pour into greased and floured 13"x9" pan or 2 9" round pans. Bake at 350⁰ for 35-40 minutes. Cool and frost.

Frosting: Beat butter until smooth. Add sugar alternately with berries and beat until smooth. Add vanilla. Frost cooled cake. Store in refrigerator.

As the only city in the northeast quadrant of the U.S. that has continued to grow since 1970, **Columbus** is a dynamic and vital community. Home of Ohio State University, "The Buckeyes," and a number of major corporations, our diverse and stable economy and our practical vision of the future will help Columbus lead America into the 21st century.

Wisconsin Cherry Pie

Mayor John Kannenberg
Wausau, Wisconsin

2 20 oz. pkgs. frozen cherries (thawed and drained)
1 cup sugar
3 tbsp. tapioca
¼ tsp. almond extract
¼ tsp. red food coloring
1 tsp. lemon juice
1 tbsp. melted butter
pastry for double crust pie

6 servings

Combine all ingredients and let stand for 15 minutes. Pour filling in 9" pastry-lined pie plate. Arrange lattice top. Bake on lower rack at 450⁰ for 15 minutes. Then reduce heat to 375⁰ and bake on raised rack for 30 more minutes.

Wausau comes alive when the winter winds blow in north central Wisconsin. Ice fishermen, in their quest for the perfect walleye, puncture the glacial covering on the many lakes surrounding the city. Snowmobiles and cross-country skiers crisscross Wausau's rolling hills, while downhill skiers from all over the Midwest trek here to challenge the slopes of Rib Mountain. When the sunshine melts the snow, sailboats drift on the lakes and freshwater fishermen search for a tranquil cove. A world-class kayak course along the Wisconsin River attracts an array of international paddlers and spectators, who can also enjoy the many fairs and festivals that celebrate Wausau's multi-ethnic heritage.

> **CITY TRIVIA QUESTION #38**
> Illinois city that is "Mr. Lincoln's Hometown."
> Answer on page 105.

Yum Yum Coffee Cake

Mayor Yvonne Petrigac
North Olmstead, Ohio

1½ sticks margarine	1 pt. sour cream
1½ cups sugar	1 tsp. vanilla
3 eggs	
3 cups flour	
1½ tsp. baking powder	
1½ tsp. baking soda	
1 tsp. salt	
FILLING:	
1 cup nuts (ground)	¼ cup sugar
1 tsp. cinnamon	½ cup brown sugar

10-15 servings

Combine margarine, sugar, and eggs and beat together. Sift flour, baking powder, baking soda, and salt and add to margarine mixture. Stir in sour cream and vanilla.

Prepare filling by combining all ingredients. Pour ⅓ of the batter into a greased bundt or angel food pan. Alternate with filling; repeat procedure until all ingredients have been used. Bake in 350⁰ oven for 1 hour or until cake tests done. Cool cake upright; allow to cool completely before removing from pan.

North Olmstead, Ohio, is an ideal location, just 15 minutes away from the shores of Lake Erie, 15 miles from downtown Cleveland, and 4 miles from Cleveland Hopkins Airport. It is a city of diversity and contrast that maintains a small-town charm unique to itself. Each fall, the city sponsors a" Homecoming Celebration." With resources such as involved people, healthy businesses, and a positive attitude that have residents, organizations, businesses, and government working together, North Olmstead looks forward to a future of continued progress and success.

ETC.

Holiday Hot Punch

Mayor David L. Pierce
Aurora, Illinois

3 qt. cranberry juice
4 qt. apple juice
1 cup brown sugar
½ tsp. (approximately) salt, or to taste
6-8 cinnamon sticks
1-1½ tsp. ground cloves

Makes 30 cups

In 30-cup coffee maker or percolator, pour cranberry juice and apple juice together. In coffee maker or basket, place brown sugar, salt, cinnamon sticks, and clove. Run coffee maker through the regular cycle (as if making coffee) or just once in percolator, according to how strong a spice taste you want. Recipe may be halved for smaller gatherings.

Aurora provides many recreational opportunities for its residents and visitors. For additional information on the city, see page 141.

Teriyaki Marinade

Mayor John A. Fedo
Duluth, Minnesota

2 cloves garlic (crushed)
½ cup soy sauce
¼ cup brown sugar
2 tbsp. olive or Wesson oil
¼ tsp. cracked pepper
2 small pieces fresh ginger root (diced)

Makes approximately 1 cup

Combine all ingredients in jar or bottle. Cover and shake well. Marinate meat or fish for 1 hour or more. Use with meat or fish, basting frequently, until cooked as desired.

Duluth rises steeply on a great hill at the western edge of Lake Superior and to the top of Spirit Mountain to the west, commanding a breathtaking view of the largest and clearest body of fresh water in the world.

It is a major shipping, manufacturing, commercial, and educational hub and a medical center for the Upper Midwest. It is a world port, the largest on the Great Lakes and the twelfth largest of all U.S. ports.

PLAINS

"Remember the pie alamo?"
Mayor Henry Cisneros
San Antonio, TX

*"Being mayor is icing on
the cake"*
Mayor Kathy Whitmire
Houston, TX

"Batter up"
Mayor Michael Boyle
Omaha, NE

Salina, Kansas, has a rich and varied heritage and counts itself as one of the most progressive small cities in the Midwest. Settled by pioneers and very proud of it, Salina recognizes its unique place in history and strives to insure that its past is very much a part of its history. Its location at the crossroads of two major interstate highways—I-70 and I-35— and very close to the geographical center of the continental U.S., gives Salina a distinct advantage in industry, business, and agriculture.

Beer Chili

Mayor Joe Ritter
Salina, Kansas

5 slices bacon
8 oz. hot bulk pork sausage
1½ lb. ground beef
1 cup onion (chopped)
½ cup green pepper (chopped)
1 clove garlic (crushed)
1 or 2 dried chili peppers (seeded and crumbled)
2 jalapeno peppers (seeded and diced)
1-1½ tsp. chili powder
¼ tsp. dried oregano
½ tsp. salt
2 12 oz. cans beer
1 12 oz. can tomato paste
1 16 oz. can pinto beans (drained)
shredded cheese   chopped onion

6-8 servings

Cook bacon until crisp; drain, crumble and set aside. Brown sausage; drain, reserving 2 tablespoons drippings. Set aside. In reserved drippings brown ground beef, onion, green pepper, and garlic. Add bacon, sausage, peppers, chili powder, oregano, and salt. Stir in beer and tomato paste. Bring to boiling; simmer, covered, 1½ hours. Add beans; simmer, covered, 30 minutes more. Serve with shredded cheese and chopped onion.

Chilis Rellenos

Mayor Jonathon W. Rogers
El Paso, Texas

6 long green chilis (California style)
1 lb. Monterey Jack cheese (grated)
3 eggs   dash salt   oil

6 servings

Roast chilis in 400° oven for about 20 minutes, until the skin puffs up or roast in an open flame. When chilis are cool, peel skin off and remove veins and seeds. Fill chilis with cheese.

Separate egg whites and yolks. Place egg whites in a large bowl and beat until stiff; then add yolks with a dash of salt.

In a large skillet, heat oil for deep frying. Dip chili into egg batter and deep fry until outside is medium brown.

El Paso is legendary; a history lesson hides on every rocky hillside. El Paso (The Pass) played host to Spanish explorers as early as the 1500s. In El Paso you will find evidence of three cultures—Indian, Mexican, and American—in our people, language, art, architecture, food, religion, and entertainment. The result is a city with great character. El Paso, with close to 500,000 residents, is a thriving center for commerce, manufacturing, tourism, clothing, electronics, and farming.

Mexican Dip

Mayor Frank C. Cooksey
Austin, Texas

1 can refried beans with green chilies
1 can hot sauce
4 green onions with tops (chopped)
1 small can black olives (chopped)
4 avocados (mashed with lemon juice and salt)
1 small carton sour cream
2 cups Monterey Jack or cheddar cheese (grated)

12 servings

Layer ingredients in the above order in a 9"x13" flat casserole or serving dish. Spread sour cream to edge to keep avocados green. Serve at room temperature with tortilla chips.

Austin is located in the hill country heart of the Lone Star State. Texas legends come to life in the Texas capital, a city steeped in the state's colorful past with the city being the home of the author O. Henry and the famous "Moonlights." You can kick up your heels on Old Pecan Street, a six-block strip of bars, restaurants, theaters, galleries, and specialty shops. Whether your tastes are for chicken crepes or chicken fried steaks, highbrow paintings or just painting the town, you'll find it right here in Austin.

CITY TRIVIA QUESTION #39

The world's largest collection of Indian Kachina dolls and the world's largest municipal park, South Mountain Park, can be found in this southwestern city. (Hint: The city rose from the ashes of an earlier Indian civilization.)

Answer on page 173.

Texas Cheese Straws

Mayor Ted B. Reed
Victoria, Texas

½ lb. margarine
1 cup sharp cheese (shredded)
1 cup American cheese (shredded)
2½ cups flour (sifted)
1 tsp. salt
¼ tsp. cayenne pepper
½ tsp. dry mustard

40-60 servings

Bring cheeses to room temperature and mix other ingredients. Press through star cookie press in strips on cookie sheet. With floured knife, cut into 4"-5" lengths. Bake at 350⁰ for 20 minutes.) When done, remove immediately to rack to cool. These will freeze well. (If you do not have a star cookie press, the mixture may be rolled into logs 2" in diameter, cut into ¼" wafers and baked for 8 minutes.)

Excellent—quick and easy—guests love 'em!

Victoria is a sampling of South Texas. Located inland on the Gulf Coast, Victoria lies between Houston and Corpus Christi. Rooted in Texas' history, the city offers a unique blend of modern medicine complexes and quiet, picturesque streets with turn-of-the-century homes. Area attractions include the Texas Zoo, horseracing, and the nearby world's longest fishing pier. Sample Victoria!

Tortilla Roll-Ups

Mayor John D. Dodd
Farmers Branch, Texas

2 8 oz. pkgs. cream cheese
8 oz. sour cream
juice of 1 lime
2 tbsp. picante sauce (salsa picante)
10 green onions with tops (chopped fine)
salt to taste
20 flour tortillas (slightly heated)

100 pieces

Mix all ingredients (except tortillas) and cream well. Spread generously over warn tortillas. Roll up tightly and chill 2-3 hours. Cut into bite-size pieces and serve with picante sauce for dipping.

The saga of **Farmers Branch** is long and colorful. We're in the center of everything simply because everything began here. We are the cradle of Dallas County! The first church and school in Dallas County were built here, and the first businesses sprang up here. We are a small city with big city opportunities.

CITY TRIVIA QUESTION #40

In the War of 1812, this Great Lakes city built the ships used by Commodore Oliver "Don't Give Up the Ship" Perry. (Hint: It is also where President William Taft, our largest president, once got stuck in a bathtub.)

Answer on page 46.

Warm Vegetable Dip

Mayor Jan Coggeshall
Galveston, Texas

8 oz. pkg. cream cheese (softened)
2 tbsp. milk
½ cup sour cream
2 tbsp. onion (chopped)
½ cup green pepper (chopped)
1 small jar of chipped beef (chopped)
½ cup chopped pecans (sauteed in butter)

Makes approximately 3 cups

Mix everything except pecans. Put in small baking/serving dish; top with pecans. Bake at 325⁰ for 30 minutes. Serve warm with raw vegetables.

Great with cold crab claws, cold boiled shrimp, and raw oysters, Galveston Island style.

Galveston is a 30-mile long resort an hour south of Houston. The home of the University of Texas Medical Branch, the Port of Galveston, and insurance industries, it attracts visitors year-round in hotels, beachfront homes, or condominiums. Picturesque and delicious shrimp, flounder, redfish, and many other Gulf treats are landed daily on Galveston Island docks and piers and served in wonderful seafood restaurants or in our own kitchens. Oysters are Texas braggin' size. A seaside resort, Galveston Island has historic homes and shopping areas on the Strand and beachfront as well as tours of the Tall Ship *Elissa* and paddlewheel boat rides on *The Colonel*, all in the port areas.

MAIN DISHES

Plano, Texas, in the southernmost corner of Collin County, is approximately 20 miles north of downtown Dallas. With a population of 120,000 in 64 square miles of land, Plano is the Hot Air Balloon Capital of Texas.

Apple-Glazed Brisket

Mayor Jack Harvard
Plano, Texas

1 4-4½ lb. brisket
1 small onion (quartered)
1 garlic clove (cut in half)
10 whole cloves
water
1 10-oz. jar apple jelly
⅓ cup dry white wine
3 tbsp. green onion (minced)
3 tbsp. prepared mustard
1½ tsp. salt
¾ tsp. curry powder
½ tsp. cracked pepper

6 servings

Put brisket, onion, cloves, and enough water to cover meat in large pot. Cover and simmer 2-3 hours.

One hour before serving mix apple jelly, white wine, green onions, mustard, salt, curry powder, and pepper. Baste meat with mixture while cooking on grill, 30-45 minutes.

Delicious! Tender and juicy! Easy to fix and great for dinner guests.

Arroz con Pollo (Rice with Chicken)

Mayor Tony Casado
Wichita, Kansas

1 cut-up frying chicken (or favorite pieces)
3 tbsp. fat
1 tsp. salt
¼ tsp. pepper
1½ cups green pepper (diced)
1½ cups onion (diced)
1½ cups peeled tomatoes (diced)
½ tsp. thyme
1 bay leaf
1 large clove garlic (diced)
1 tsp. oregano
½ tsp. paprika
½ tsp. saffron
2 cups rice
4 cups boiling water
2 tsp. salt
green peas
pimiento strips

6-8 servings

Brown chicken in fat. Remove. Stir in vegetables and spices in oil and cook for 5 minutes. Return chicken to pot and cook 20 minutes.

Add boiling water and 2 teaspoons salt and bring to a boil. Add rice, lower heat, and cook 30 minutes until rice absorbs water.

Garnish with green peas and pimiento strips. Serve with green salad and hot garlic bread.

My mother's favorite Sunday dinner in Cuba 40 years ago. Typical Cuban dish.

Wichita, the largest city in Kansas with a population of 290,000, is the "Airplane Capital of the World." Boeing, Beech, Cessna, and Learjet all have factories here.

Barbeque Beef

Mayor Douglas S. Wright
Topeka, Kansas

3-4 lb. chuck roast
½ cup of water
2 tbsp. vinegar
1 tbsp. Worcestershire sauce
¼ cup lemon juice
2 tbsp. brown sugar
1 cup chili sauce
½ tsp. salt
¼ tsp. paprika

10 servings

Cook chuck roast. Shred into sauce mixture and simmer 1 hour.

Best when served on hamburger buns.

Topeka, the capital of Kansas, is located on the banks of the Kansas River in northeast Kansas. A few of its popular attractions are the World Famous Topeka Zoo, Ward-Meade Historical Park, and the Kansas Museum of History. Many local festivals are held each year.

CITY TRIVIA QUESTION #41
What chicken appetizer is named after a city?
Answer on page 51.

Chicken Buffet Casserole

Mayor Ray Stephens
Denton, Texas

8 oz. medium noodles
4 tbsp. butter
4 tbsp. flour
2 tsp. salt
½ tsp. prepared mustard
½ tsp. pepper
4 cups milk
2 cups cheddar cheese (grated)
2 10-oz. pkgs. frozen broccoli (cooked)
4 cups chicken (cooked and cubed)
⅔ cup slivered almonds.

12 servings

Cook noodles according to directions on package.

Melt butter, blend in flour, salt, mustard and pepper. Add milk gradually. Cook until thickened, stirring constantly. Remove from heat, add cheese, blend until melted. Dice broccoli stems, leave flowerets whole. Arrange noodles, broccoli stems, and chicken in two 9" square baking dishes, top with cheese sauce. Arrange broccoli flowerets on top, pressing lightly into sauce; sprinkle with almonds. Bake at 350⁰ for 25-30 minutes. (May be frozen before cooking. If frozen, cook at 350⁰ for 40-45 minutes.)

Denton, a rapidly developing city atop the Golden Triangle of North Central Texas, combines the flavor of the Old South and the Great West. It is the home of two major state universities; a thriving economy based on education, industry, business, and agriculture; and a progressive-minded citizenry that truly lives up to the city's motto of "Growth with Grace." Three major lakes nearby and multiple recreational activities provide an abundance of leisure opportunities for this cosmopolitan community.

Chicken Enchilada Casserole

Mayor Jonathan W. Rogers
El Paso, Texas

1 chicken (cooked and cut up)
1 can cream of mushroom soup
1 can cream of chicken soup
1 cup sour cream
½ cup milk
1 medium onion (chopped)
3 tbsp. chicken broth
chopped green chilis to suit your taste (if desired)
1 lb. cheddar cheese (grated)
12 corn tortillas

12 servings

Combine chicken, mushroom soup, chicken soup, sour cream, milk, onion, chicken broth, and green chilis. Mix and refrigerate for 12 hours.

In a large casserole dish, layer tortillas, chili mixture, and cheese in 2 layers. (It is a good idea to put a *small* amount of the mixture under the first layer of tortillas in order to prevent tortillas from burning on the bottom.)Bake at 325⁰ for 1½-2 hours. Serve hot.

Excellent when served with tossed salad and pinto beans.

El Paso - meaning "The Pass" gets its name because it was the "gateway" to the West for Spanish explorers. For further information on El Paso, turn to page 148.

Chicken Tetrazzini

Mayor Andy Coats
Oklahoma City, Oklahoma

6 cups chicken (cooked and cut up)
8 oz. rich chicken broth
1 lb. Velveeta cheese (cut up)
2 onions (chopped)
2 green peppers (chopped)
1 pkg. thin spaghetti
2 tbsp. oil
2 small or 1 large jar of sliced mushrooms
3-4 oz. cheddar cheese (shredded)

8-12 servings

Chop onions and green peppers. Saute in hot oil until tender. Drain mushrooms and add to onions and green peppers.

Cook spaghetti according to package directions; drain. Heat chicken broth; add Velveeta cheese and melt in broth. Add all vegetables, cooked spaghetti, and chicken. Mix thoroughly. Cook over low heat for 10 minutes. Pour into 9" x 13" Pyrex dish. Sprinkle with cheddar cheese. Cover with foil. Bake covered at 350⁰ for 15 minutes. Uncover and bake until lightly brown.

This recipe has been in our family for over 20 years. My mother got it from a friend in her church and it has been a favorite of mine since then. I have used this recipe made with frozen vegetables and frozen diced cooked chicken and prepared it in 30 minutes. This recipe is simple and is delicious with a tossed salad with vinaigrette dressing and a pickled peach. White wine and rolls are suggested.

Located at the intersection of the major highways in the country, **Oklahoma City** is truly America's Crossroads. Oklahoma City was born in one day, April 22, 1889, with the famous

Oklahoma Land Run. We are a great place to live and work. The people of the city maintain the pioneer spirit of western hospitality and dedication to building a great city. The National Cowboy Hall of Fame and Western Heritage Center pays homage to three types of cowboys: the pioneers of yesterday and today, the movie and television actors and actresses, and the rodeo stars.

Chili Tulsa Style

Mayor Richard (Dick) C. Crawford
Tulsa, Oklahoma

2 lb. sausage
2 cans chili beans (in gravy)
1 1-lb. can tomatoes (chopped)
1 large can mushrooms (pieces and stems)
green pepper and celery (chopped)
bay leaf
tomato juice (optional)
chili powder (to taste)

6 servings

Cook and drain sausage (use hot if you like really spicy flavoring.) Add chili beans and gravy (put 1½ cans through processor if you don't like a lot of beans but need just the flavoring). Add tomatoes, mushrooms, green pepper and celery, and bay leaf. Use tomato juice for thinner consistency. Add chili powder to taste. Simmer 1 hour.

This recipe leaves a lot of room for personal creativity as pertains to individual tastes.

Tulsa is a city based on sound principles of God, family, and country. Often known as the "Oil Capital of the Nation," Tulsa today is diversifying its economy to include high technology and manufacturing. The Gilcrease Museum contains the largest collection of Remington western paintings and bronzes of any art museum. Tulsa is a wonderful place to live and work, as well as to commute to points of international interest and business.

Cornish Hens Stuffed with Wild Rice

Mayor John G. Lindgren
Fargo, North Dakota

4 1-lb. Cornish hens
¾ cup wild rice
2¼ cups water
2 tsp. chicken seasoned stock base
½ cup butter (melted)
½ tsp. basil leaves
¼ tsp. cinnamon
2 tsp. parsley flakes
3½ tsp. Bon Appetit
1 tbsp. instant minced onion
1 tsp. coarse grind black pepper
½ tsp. salt

4 servings

Wash and pat dry the Cornish hens; set aside. Wash rice; add water and seasoned stock base; cover and cook until tender and all water is absorbed, about 50 minutes. Add ¼ cup butter, basil leaves, cinnamon, parsley flakes, 2 teaspoons of Bon Appetit, onion, pepper and salt; mix well.

Fill cavities of hens with stuffing. Cover exposed stuffing with aluminum foil during the first 30 minutes of cooking time to prevent drying. Brush hens with a mixture of remaining ¼ cup butter and 1½ teaspoons Bon Appetit. Roast in 450⁰ oven 20 minutes; reduce temperature to 350⁰ and roast 45 minutes longer or until drumstick twists easily and birds are nicely browned. Baste several times with seasoned butter.

The subject of good food and **Fargo** go together very well. Fargo, North Dakota—a community of 66,000 with a trade area of 200,000 people—is int he great Red River Valley of the North. Fargo bills itself as the "Agricultural Capital of the World" with good reason. The soil of the valley is considered among the richest in the world and affords the area a diverse agricultural economy. This economy includes the growing and processing of sugar beets, potatoes, sunflowers, beans, wheat, barley and other small grains.Beyond this, Fargo enjoys a growing role as a regional center for the arts, communication, medicine, education, retailing, and manufacturing. With a well-deserved reputation for cold winters and exciting springs, lazy balmy summer days and beautiful, crisp fall months, Fargo enjoys a rich and diverse outdoor life that is the best kept secret of the region.

Dishwasher Shrimp or Shrimp Faux Pas

Mayor Luther Jones
Corpus Christi, Texas

20 jumbo shrimp
1 onion (sliced)
2 lemons (sliced)
1 tbsp. salt
1 tbsp freshly ground pepper
1 tbsp paprika
2 cloves garlic (chopped)

4 servings

Make sure your dishwasher is clean.

Prepare 4 double layers of heavy duty aluminum large enough to wrap shrimp and spices airtight. Arrange 2 slices of onion on each foil, then 5 shrimp. Distribute salt, pepper, paprika, and chopped garlic evenly among the 4 shrimp servings. Place 2 lemon slices on each serving and

distribute juice of second lemon evenly among the four servings. Wrap servings tightly, folding edges as you would a package. Load packages on top shelf of dishwasher. Run through rinse cycle. When the cycle is finished, you will have steamed shrimp and amazed guests.

This recipe is more than delicious. It is fun and it will amaze your guests. You can adapt the recipe, using white fish filets and various vegetables such as tomatoes and zucchini. Caution: Make certain foil packages are wrapped tightly and that your dishwasher is cleaned of soap residue.

Corpus Christi, Texas' Sparkling City by the Sea, is noted for its outstanding climate and natural beauty that attracts tourists and new residents each year. The city is the center for the agricultural, petroleum and shipping industries of South Texas. Corpus Christi Bay and the Gulf of Mexico offer unlimited recreational opportunities for beach lovers and for anglers, sailors, surfers, and board-sailors who come from all over the country to compete in tournaments and regattas held year-round.

CITY TRIVIA QUIZ

Scoring System

Throughout *The Mayors Cookbook* there are 62 City Trivia questions with 130 answers. Answer each question, follow the instructions to the page with the answer, and tally your results.

Correct Answers	Level of Knowledge
0—25	Municipal Rookie
26—50	City Gazer
51—75	Metropolitan Marvel
76—100	City Slicker
101 and up	Urbanologist

Fried Quail

Mayor Calvin Anthony
Stillwater, Oklahoma

milk
flour
2 tbsp. oil
salt and pepper to taste
water
12 cleaned quail

6 servings

Soak birds in milk for several hours before cooking. Flour birds and saute in oil in skillet. Add salt and pepper while browning.

When nicely browned, put birds in a heavy dutch oven, on a trivet or rack. Add several tablespoons water, and put in a 250^0 to 300^0 oven for 1 hour or so. Be sure lid is on tightly so birds will steam and get tender.

This is my favorite recipe for quail. Best served with cream gravy made from drippings, and buttermilk biscuits.

Located in North Central Oklahoma, **Stillwater** is the home of Oklahoma State University. With the fine university and a diversified economy, Stillwater enjoys a quality of life second to none in Oklahoma. All this plus the citizens' hospitality makes Stillwater the place to be.

CITY TRIVIA QUESTION #42

Residents in this state's largest city experience 19 hours and 28 minutes of darkness in the wintertime and a similar amount of daylight in the summertime.

Answer on page 197.

Hearty Hotdish

Mayor Marlan "Hawk" Haakenson
Bismarck, North Dakota

1½ lbs. lean ground beef
1 medium onion (chopped)
8 oz. sliced mushrooms
1 packet taco seasoning mix
2 cups tomato sauce
1 16-oz. can green beans (drained)
1 16-oz. can kidney beans (drained)
12 oz. cheddar cheese (shredded)
salt and pepper to taste
sliced black olives

6 servings

Brown ground beef; add onion and mushrooms and cook until tender. Drain. Mix in taco seasoning according to package directions and simmer until well blended. In 9" x 12" baking dish combine meat mixture, beans, tomato sauce, and salt and pepper. Cover with cheese and sprinkle with sliced olives. Bake at 350^0 for approximately 30 minutes or until cheese is bubbly.

Bismarck, the state capital, is located in Central North Dakota among rolling hills, and is on a green belt along the half-mile wide Missouri River. The river fishing for walleye, salmon and northern pike is among the world's best and recreation areas with campsites are plentiful. The Dakota Zoo—with the world's largest Kodiak Bear in captivity—the Heritage Center, Fort Lincoln, General Custer's home (under reconstruction), plus many other interesting things to do and see, blended with good old western hospitality and friendliness, can make your day when you visit us.

Huevos con Chorizo (Eggs with Sausage)

Mayor Kathryn J. Whitmire
Houston, Texas

½ lb. chorizo Mexicano (Mexican pork sausage) or American pork sausage (crumbled and fried with salsa picante)
6 eggs (beaten)
6 flour tortillas
salsa picante (preferably brand made in Texas) (optional)
guacamole (optional)
sour cream (optional)

4 servings

Wrap tortillas in foil and heat in oven. Fry chorizo (or substitute) in large skillet. Drain off grease if desired. Add beaten eggs to sausage in skillet and scramble, mixing with sausage. Remove tortillas from oven, and spread scrambled egg and sausage mixture on each. Add dollop of guacamole, sour cream and/or salsa picante (Mexican hot sauce) to taste. Serve immediately with slices of tomato, avocado, guacamole, or refried beans on the side.

Visitors to **Houston** are pleasantly surprised to find that we are truly an international city—something that Houston residents have known and been proud of for many years. Each spring, during the Houston Festival, we celebrate our ethnic diversity by honoring our diplomatic corps, representing 55 foreign governments, and by enjoying the foods, arts, and performances of our many different cultural groups. With a reputation as the energy capital of the world, Houston also claims the Johnson Space Center, the Texas Medical Center, the Port of Houston, the third largest in the country, and the Astrodome. Houston enjoys a blending of economic interests, cultural, and recreation opportunities. Our ethnic diversity affords us a rich and exciting heritage in this city on the nation's third coast and makes us "Houston Proud."

Neches Shrimp

Mayor Maury Meyers
Beaumont, Texas

3 lb. jumbo shrimp
½ cup flour
2 tbsp. red pepper
4 tbsp. thyme
2 tbsp. butter
2 tbsp. oil
½ cup vermouth (dry)
½ cup onion (chopped)
2 cups chicken stock from bouillon
RICE BED:
1 cup long-grain white rice (uncooked)
2½ cups chicken stock from bouillon
2 tomatoes (peeled, seeded, and chopped)
1/8 tsp. saffron
1 tbsp. oil

6 servings

Clean and devein shrimp, leaving tail section intact. Wash and drain shrimp; pat dry with paper toweling. Sprinkle with red pepper and thyme and pat into shrimp. Dust shrimp with flour.

Melt butter in oil in large saute pan over moderately high heat. When hot, place shrimp in pan without crowding. Lightly brown on each side, about 2 minutes each. Remove from oil and place on broiler pan. When all shrimp have been browned set pan aside reserving all juices.

Set oven on broil. When hot place broiler pan with shrimp in oven with heat source about 18 inches from pan. Broil 2-3 minutes or until tender.

While shrimp are broiling reheat pan with juices over moderately high heat. Add onion to pan juices, stir for 1 minute, add vermouth to deglaze pan, and add stock. Simmer 2-3 minutes.

Arrange shrimp over rice (see recipe below) and pour gravy over all.

Rice Bed: Heat oil in saucepan over moderately high heat. Add tomatoes and stir 2-3 minutes. Add rice and stir to coat 1 minute. Add chicken stock and saffron; stir briefly and bring to a boil. Reduce heat to moderately low and cook covered for 20 minutes or until all liquid is absorbed. Remove from heat, stir, cover pan, and let stand 2 minutes.

In **Beaumont**, Texas, on January 10, 1901, at 10:30 a.m. the Anthony F. Lucas oil well at Spindletop blew in from a depth of 1,020 feet with oil shooting 200 feet in the air. It made Beaumont the birthplace of the modern oil industry. A center of commerce in the Sabine-Neches area of Texas, Beaumont is an important part on a 50-mile-long waterway connecting to the Gulf of Mexico. It is rich in the romance of colonial Spanish, French, and early Texas days. Our inland city began on the Neches River miles from the sea. Eventually we brought the sea to us, and our port is the second largest in Texas. Our historic past blends with the region's energetic present and diversified future to form a rich tapestry of cultural themes. When you add it all up, Beaumont is a great place to live, work, and raise your family.

Red River Chili

Mayor Charles Harper
Wichita Falls, Texas

5 lbs. chili meat (not ground meat) (cut up)
2 onions (chopped)
2 cloves garlic
1 tbsp. salt
¾ bottle chili powder
1 tbsp. paprika

7 tbsp. cumin
2 tbsp oregano
2 tbsp. red pepper
½ cup masa harina

15 servings

Put chili meat in 1-gallon cast iron pot (with lid). Sear meat until grayish in color. Add two cups water and boil 15 minutes. Add onions and garlic and simmer for 30 minutes. Add remaining ingredients, except masa harina. Simmer 1½ hours or until meat is cooked thoroughly.

Dip out 1 cup of liquid; add masa harina. Stir and add to chili, stirring until thickened. Serve immediately. May garnish with jalapeno.

Chili is good year-round, especially in the Fall and Winter. Serve with large onions, crackers or cornbread, and a large glass of cold beer. Not for the timid. The amount of red pepper makes it hot, so vary to taste.

Wichita Falls has a population of more than 100,000 and is located in the northwestern part of Texas. It is the heart of the "cow country," and the independent oil capital of the world.

Shrimp Gumbo

Mayor Emmett O. Hutto
Baytown, Texas

2 lbs. shrimp (fresh or frozen)
2 cups onions (chopped)
1 gallon warm water
1½ cups cooking oil
½ cup onion tops and parsley (chopped)
4 cloves garlic (minced)
1½ cups all purpose flour
salt, black peppr and cayenne red pepper (to taste)

6 servings

If using fresh shrimp, peel them and season

generously with salt, black pepper, and cayenne. Set aside.

Make Roux: Put oil in heavy iron pot over medium heat; when hot, stir flour in gradually. Lower heat, stirring constantly. After all the flour is combined with the oil, turn fire down low and cook until golden brown, stirring constantly. Pour excess oil off. Add onions and garlic into roux and cook slowly until onions are wilted. Add water and boil slowly in uncovered pot for 45 minutes to 1 hour. Add shrimp and cook over medium heat in uncovered pot for 20 minutes. Add onion tops and parsley. Serve in soup plates over desired amount of cooked rice.

This dish was originated by the Cajuns of Southern Louisiana who settled there as immigrants from Nova Scotia.

Baytown developed due to the oil boom of the 1900s, which drew people to the region from various parts of the country. Located 35 miles east of Houston, the area played a significant role in the battle for Texas independence from Mexico. Baytown is located on several bays and the Houston Ship Channel, which accounts for the many industries located here. Humble Oil and Refining Company (Exxon Company U.S.A.) began with a refinery in Baytown.

Shrimp and Peppers

Mayor Andy Coats
Oklahoma City, Oklahoma

1 lb. shrimp (shelled and cleaned)
1 green pepper (sliced)
1 red pepper (sliced)
1 yellow pepper (sliced)
1 tbsp. olive oil
2 tbsp. onion (chopped)
1 tsp. garlic (minced)
¼ cup white wine
2 tbsp. lemon juice
butter, salt, pepper to taste

2 servings

Heat oil in large frying pan. Saute onions for 3 minutes, until soft but not brown. Add shrimp and saute until pink on both sides. Add peppers. Cover and saute until peppers are slightly cooked but still crisp. Add garlic and wine. Mix thoroughly and cook for another minute or two. Serve with white rice seasoned with salt, pepper, butter and lemon juice.

This makes a very pretty dish which is very tasty as well as low in fat and calories.

Oklahoma City is home to the National Cowboy Hall of Fame and Western Heritage Center. For further information on Oklahoma City, turn to pages 153 and 154.

Shrimp Saute

Mayor R.P. Rick Klein
Amarillo, Texas

2 lbs. raw shrimp (shelled and deveined)
½ tsp. salt
¼ tsp. pepper
2 cups chicken broth
2 cups cooked rice
½ cup butter or margarine
½ cup green onion (chopped)
½ cup celery (chopped)
½ cup green pepper (chopped)
2 tbsp. ketchup
½ cup dry white wine (optional)
½ cup fresh parsley (chopped)
shake of Worcestershire sauce
½ tsp. garlic powder

4-6 servings

continued

Melt margarine in heavy skillet over high heat; add onions, celery, and green pepper. Stir and cook 1 minute; then add ketchup, Worcestershire sauce, salt and pepper, and garlic powder. Cook for 3 minutes. Add shrimp, wine (optional), and chicken broth. Cook until shrimp loses its transparency. Stir in parsley. Simmer about 1 hour.

To serve, put shrimp mixture over rice. Good served with Caesar salad, hot French bread, and Chinese pea pods.

This is a great company dish. It is nice because it is a one dish supper.

Amarillo is the community, cultural, and recreational center of the vast plain of the Texas Panhandle. Only 30 minutes from beautiful Palo Duro Canyon, Amarillo has several lakes close by for great fishing and waterskiing activities. The city is also the leading helium producer and has the largest livestock auction in the nation.

Shrimp Victoria

Mayor Jan Coggeshall
Galveston, Texas

| 1 lb. raw shrimp (peeled and deveined) |
| 1 cup sour cream |
| 1 small onion (chopped) |
| ¼ cup margarine or butter |
| 1 6-oz. can mushroom pieces |
| 1 tbsp. flour |
| salt and cayenne pepper to taste |

4 servings

Saute shrimp and onion in margarine for 10 minutes or until pink. Add mushrooms and cook 5 minutes more. Sprinkle in flour, salt, and pepper. Stir in sour cream and simmer for 10 minutes, not allowing to boil.

Serve over rice. I have made this with 10 pounds of shrimp for 40 people. It can be made a half hour in

advance and kept in a double boiler.

Galveston called the "Wall Street of the Southwest" in the 1800s, is again thriving. For further information on Galveston, turn to page 150.

Tuna Salad

Mayor Lou Galasy
Longview, Texas

| 1 pkg. plain gelatin |
| 1 chicken bouillion cube |
| 1 cup sour cream or plain yogurt |
| ¾ cup mayonnaise |
| juice of half a lemon |
| dash Worcestershire sauce |
| 1 tsp. sugar |
| salt and pepper to taste |
| ⅓ cup sweet pickle relish |
| 1 cup water chestnuts (sliced) |
| 6-8 olives with pimento (sliced) |
| 2 6.5-oz cans tuna (drained) |

6 servings

Dissolve gelatin in ¼ cup cold water. Add ¾ cup boiling water and bouillion. With wire whisk, blend in sour cream and mayonnaise. Add seasonings, pickle relish, water chestnuts, olives, and tuna. Chill in oiled 6" x 10" Pyrex dish. Serve on bed of lettuce, garnish with asparagus, hard-cooked eggs, marinated artichoke hearts, and either carrots or tomato wedges. (Can substitute chicken for tuna.)

Longview, located in East Texas is in the center of oil country. During World War II, 70% of Texas oil used for the military flowed through the "Big Inch" pipeline located in Longview. Today, a nearby oil museum describes the history of East Texas and the oil boom. Longview, a city where the quality of life is excellent and the people are friendly.

ACCOMPANIMENTS

Cinnamon Salad

Mayor David Stubbeman
Abilene, Texas

2 2-lb. cans crushed pineapple with juice
1 6¾-oz. pkg. cinnamon candies
4 cups miniature marshmallows
1 5½-oz. pgk. instant vanilla pudding mix
1 10-oz. carton Cool Whip

6-8 servings

Mix pineapple and juice, cinnamon candies, and marshmallows together. Let stand overnight in a closed Tupperware bowl. Before serving, add the instant vanilla pudding and Cool Whip. Chill 2 hours before serving.

Abilene, part of the "Big Country," is located in Central West Texas. The city, through Dyess Air Force Base, serves as home to the B1-B Bomber, the most sophisticated, yet sleek, of the United States Air Fleet. Abilene also places a high priority on higher education by supporting three private universities. Abilene hosts numerous annual events such as the Southwest LaJet Classic, PGA Golf Tournament, and the Western Heritage Festival, which relives the days of old West Texas. Abilene is a very diversified community clinging to the Western Heritage of the past while ushering in the new technologies of the '80s.

East Texas Corn Casserole

Mayor Emmet F. Lowry
Texas City, Texas

2 cans cream style corn
1 pkg. cornbread mix
2 eggs
6 tbsp. margarine
1 tsp. garlic powder
1 can green chilis
2 cups cheddar cheese (grated)

8-10 servings

Mix first 5 ingredients well; pour half of batter in casserole dish. Over this spread green chilis and grated cheddar cheese. Pour remaining batter over cheese and chilis and bake at 350⁰ for 30 minutes.

Texas City, the center of a huge petrochemical complex located between Houston and Galveston, has a population of about 45,000. Texas City has one of the lowest tax rates in the State of Texas, a good climate, and many recreational activities.

CITY TRIVIA QUESTION #43

Match the city slogan with the city:

____Savings Bond Capital   A. St. Petersburg, FL
____Beertown, USA   B. Memphis, TN
____City of Lakes   C. Billings, MT
____Sunshine City   D. New Bedford, MA
____Capital City   E. Miami, FL
____America's Distribution City   F. Tuscon, AZ
____Old Pueblo   G. Birmingham, AL
____Come See It Like A Native   H. Milwaukee, WI
____Vulcan City   I. Minneapolis, MN
____Magic City in Big Sky Country   J. Washington, DC
____Whaling City   K. Parkersburg, WV

Answers on pages 90, 115, 125, 87, 45, 86, 175, 62, 81, 168, 33.

Eggplant Dressing

Mayor John Ray Harrison
Pasadena, Texas

1 medium to large eggplant (peeled and diced)
1 large onion (chopped)
1 green pepper (chopped)
1 small hot pepper
1 lb. ground meat
¼ cup cooking oil
½ tsp. salt
½ cup uncooked rice
½ cup water
1 small can stewed tomatoes (optional)

6 servings

Heat oil; add onion and peppers and cook until soft. Add ground meat and brown lightly. Add eggplant, rice, salt, ½ cup of water, and tomatoes. Bring to boil. Cover and simmer, stirring occasionally, until everything is done. If you don't want to serve it right away, put in flat Pyrex dish and heat in oven. (If it gets too dry, add a little more water.)

Pasadena, the birthplace of Free Texas, has 120,000 friendly people. A warm Texas welcome is the trademark of this Industrial Center of the South. Pasadena lies in one of the most historic areas in Texas history. The 18-minute battle of San Jacinto opened the U.S. to the great southwestward expansion experienced following the Texas Revolution. The significance of the Texas independence is what makes Pasadena the city of today: Pasadena—People, Pride, Progress!

Lone Star Broccoli Casserole

Mayor Jerry V. Debo, III
Grand Prairie, Texas

2 boxes frozen broccoli (chopped)
1 can cream of celery soup
1 cup white rice
1 small jar Cheez Whiz (larger size may be used for more cheese taste)
dash salt (optional)

6-8 servings

Preheat oven to 350⁰. Thaw frozen broccoli by following directions on box label. Cook 1 cup rice in 3 cups water and dash of salt. While rice is cooking and broccoli is thawing, pour cream of celery soup and Cheez Whiz into large bowl. When rice is cooked, fold broccoli and rice into soup and cheese; heat of the rice will melt cheese. Mix. Pour into casserole dish and bake about 5-10 minutes. (Recipe may be cut in half by using half of listed ingredients. Use more Cheez Whiz for cheesier taste.)

Grand Prairie has it all, the atmosphere of a small town and the benefits of a large city. With more than 1400 acres of parks, ten area lakes, five major tourist attractions, easy access to Dallas and Fort Worth cultural and recreational activities, and more, Grand Prairie is simply a great place to live.

CITY TRIVIA QUESTION #44

This California city was the site of Father Junipero Serra's first mission (Hint: Orky, the world's largest mammal can be found at this city's world famous zoo.)

Answer on page 217.

Nebraska Cabbage Salad

Mayor Roland A. Luedtke
Lincoln, Nebraska

1 medium to large cabbage (shredded)
1 onion (minced)
2 carrots (chopped or grated)
1 green pepper (chopped)
¾ cup sugar
1 cup white vinegar
1 tsp. sugar
1 tsp. prepared mustard
1 tsp. celery seed
1½ tsp. salt
1 cup salad oil

16-18 servings

Layer vegetables in large bowl and sprinkle with ¾ cup sugar. Put remaining ingredients (except salad oil) in pot and bring to hard boil. Stir in salad oil and return to boil. Pour hot over vegetables. Do not stir.

Refrigerate for several hours or overnight (better if made a day ahead). Mix well and drain before serving. Reserve dressing to pour on leftover salad. Keeps well refrigerated.

Lincoln is the state capital of Nebraska and our skyline is dominated by the impressive State Capitol Building, acclaimed as one of the ten architectural wonders of the world. Lincoln is a friendly, hospitable city of over 180,000 people—a good-sized city with a small-town atmosphere. Lincoln's diversity and our emphasis on a high quality of life provide a strong base for future growth and development.

Summer Salad with Pine Nuts

Mayor Henry G. Cisneros
San Antonio, Texas

2 heads butter lettuce
¾ cup pine nuts (lightly toasted)
1 cup peanut oil
3 tbsp. balsamic vinegar
½ tsp. brown sugar
¼ cup blue cheese
¼ tsp. white pepper
1½ tbsp. lemon juice

8 servings

Wash lettuce and let it dry; toast nuts and crumble cheese. Mix remaining ingredients and season to taste. Combine lettuce, nuts, and crumbled cheese; pour dressing over the salad and let set before serving

This is a very healthy salad that can serve as a light meal.

Since its founding in 1691 by Spanish missionaries, **San Antonio** has grown from a sleepy little Texas town into a large and dynamic city. It is now the tenth largest city in the nation and is blessed with a grand historical past, including the Alamo, our famed Riverwalk, promises of a bright and prosperous future, and an extraordinary cooperative spirit.

CITY TRIVIA QUESTION #45

This Iowa community has the largest cereal plant in the world and produces a hot cereal known to millions of school children and adults.

Answer on page 135.

Texas Deli Slaw

Mayor Ted B. Reed
Victoria, Texas

2 medium heads cabbage (shredded)
6 carrots (shredded)
6 stalks celery (cut up)
½ cup honey
⅓ cup oil
1 cup vinegar
¼ cup sugar
½ tsp. salt

8-12 servings

Bring the last five ingredients to a rolling boil. Pour over vegetables and let cool to room temperature; then cover and refrigerate. Let stand for 12 hours before serving. This will keep for 2-3 weeks and gets better.

If you like slaw you'll love this dish!

Victoria, located inland on the Gulf Coast lies between Houston and Corpus Christi. For further information on Victoria, turn to page 149.

For further information on Victoria, turn to page 149.

DESSERTS

Dewberry Cobbler

Mayor Larry J. Ringer
College Station, Texas

1 cup flour
1 cup sugar
1 tbsp. baking powder
⅔ cup milk
1 stick butter (melted)
2 cups dewberries (or other fruit)

8 servings

Mix first four ingredients in round baking dish. Pour melted butter over the mixture. Sweeten the fruit to taste and put on top of batter and add butter; do not stir. Bake at 375⁰ for 45 minutes. The fruit sinks and a cake is formed on top. Excellent with ice cream, cream, or milk. (Recipe can be doubled.)

College Station was incorporated in 1938 and now has a population of more than 50,000. Located in Brazos County, College Station is the home of Texas A&M University. Located not far from the major urban areas of Texas, College Station offers the friendliness of a smaller community and the advantages of a larger city. College Station is minutes away from many of the sites associated with the rich heritage and history of Texas.

Easy Brownies

Mayor Michael Boyle
Omaha, Nebraska

2 sticks margarine	2 cups sugar
4 eggs	1½ cups flour
2 tsp. vanilla	¾ cup cocoa
½ cup walnuts (chopped) (optional)	

12-15 servings

Melt margarine in pan. Add sugar and cocoa; mix well. Stir in eggs, vanilla, flour, and nuts. Pour into cake pan and bake at 350⁰ for 20 minutes. Dust with powdered sugar or frost. Cut and serve.

This is one of my family's favorite snacks, because it is so good and easy to make.

Omaha is a "city on the move" with a great deal to offer its citizens and its guests. The Henry Doorly Zoo, Rosenblatt Stadium, shops and fine dining facilities provide a full array of business and pleasure activities. But our city's most important resource is our people. The Omaha Playhouse Theater was where the Fondas, Henry, Jane, and Peter, all got their start. We pride ourselves on traditional Midwestern friendliness and hospitality. We invite all of you cooks to visit Omaha and see for yourselves what our city has to offer!

Forgotten Cookies

Mayor Bill Tomlinson
Garland, Texas

1 tsp. vanilla	2 egg whites
1 6-oz. pkg. chocolate chips	salt
1 cup pecans (chopped)	¾ cup sugar

Makes 36

Preheat oven to 350⁰. Beat egg whites until foamy, add a sprinkle of salt. Gradually add sugar, one teaspoon at a time, beating until stiff peaks form. Fold in vanilla, chocolate chips, and pecans. Drop by spoonfuls onto cookie sheets that have been lined with aluminum foil. Place in oven and immediately turn it off. Do not open oven for at least 8 hours. Remove cookies from foil carefully.

Garland is the second biggest city in Dallas County. We offer citizens unparalleled avenues of recreation such as Surf and Swim; the only municipally-owned wave action pool in Texas; the Jerry Carter Softball Complex, which hosts national tournaments; and our new Firewheel Golf Park. Tourists admire the historical and cultural activities that make Garland exciting. Garland's Performing Arts Center and the Historical Park sit just across from City Hall. Garland truly is City for All Seasons...and People.

Mom's Apple Crunch Pie

Mayor Henry G. Cisneros
San Antonio, Texas

10 tart apples (thinly sliced) or 1 can sliced apples	
⅔ cup granulated sugar	
dash nutmeg	¼ lb. butter
1 cup brown sugar	1 cup flour

6-8 servings

Place apples in pie pan; mix granulated sugar into apples; add dash or nutmeg. Cream brown sugar and butter together, mix in flour; spread this mixture on top of apples. Bake at 350⁰ until well browned or about 45 minutes. Serve warm or cold; delicious when served with vanilla ice cream.

San Antonio, home of the Alamo, was founded in 1691 by Spanish missionaries. For further information on San Antonio, turn to page 163.

Mt. Oread Mocha Pie

Mayor Sandra K. Praeger
Lawrence, Kansas

1 9" chocolate pie shell
2 qts. vanilla ice cream (softened)
1 qt. chocolate ice cream (softened)
3 tbsp. instant coffee
½ cup hot water
½ cup pecans (chopped)
12 maraschino cherries
½ cup coffee liqueur
16 oz. whipping cream (whipped)
¼ cup hot fudge topping

12 servings

Dissolve instant coffee in *hot* water and liqueur. Add to 1 quart vanilla ice cream. Mix until well incorporated; pour into pie shell and freeze 2-3 hours or until ice cream has hardened. Remove from freezer and spread chocolate ice cream on top of the mocha ice cream. Take remaining vanilla ice cream and spread on top of chocolate ice cream. Top pie with pecans. Place a cherry on for each piece of pie and freeze until hard.

To serve, use a hot, wet knife to slice pie. Top each slice with whipping cream and hot fudge immediately.

Founded by educated New Englanders and rich in history, **Lawrence** was the catalyst that brought Kansas into the Union as a free state. The ultimate university community, Lawrence combines a vibrant downtown of renovated storefronts, a respected university atop Mr. Oread, lovely neighborhoods of brick-paved streets and 19th Century homes, and "more culture per capita than any other city under 100,000," according to Rand McNally.

Strawberry Ice Box Pie

Mayor Bob Bolen
Fort Worth, Texas

9" pie shell (prebaked)
½ cup granulated sugar
1 envelope unflavored gelatin
½ cup water
1 10-oz. pkg. frozen strawberries
juice of ½ lemon
1/8 tsp. vanilla
1 cup heavy cream (whipped)

6-8 servings

In saucepan, stir sugar with gelatin. Stir in water, then cook over low heat, stirring until just below boiling point. Remove from heat. Add unthawed strawberries, lemon juice, vanilla. Stir, breaking up berries with fork, until fruit thaws and mixture thickens. Then fold in whipped cream. Pour filling into pie crust shell. Refrigerate until set, about 1 hour.

Fort Worth combines the excietment of a vibrant, diverse metropolitan area with its western heritage to make it one of the most unique communities in the United States. Found in 1849 as a U.S. Army outpost, Fort Worth was the last major stopover on the Chisholm Trail to the Kansas City railhead. The North Side Stockyards keep the western heritage alive. The West Side Cultural District not only commemorates the western heritage of the city, but it also is a world-class showcase for art.

CITY TRIVIA QUESTION #47

The Civil War began in this city in 1861 with the firing upon Fort Sumter.

Answer on page 69.

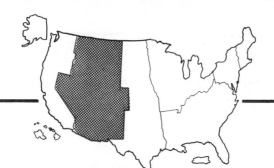

MOUNTAIN

"Chuckwagon Don"
Mayor Don Erickson
Cheyenne, WY

"Up from the ashes"
Mayor Terry Goddard
Phoenix, AZ

*"Hungry Mr. Caterpillar
and friends"*
Mayor Federico Peña
Denver, CO

167

STARTERS

Cream of Almond Soup

Mayor Peter J. Sferrazza
Reno, Nevada

1 cup blanched almonds
3 cups chicken broth
½ onion (sliced)
1 bay leaf
1 cup milk
2 tbsp. butter or margarine
2 tbsp. flour
½ cup heavy cream
pinch ground cardamon (optional)

4 servings

Grind almonds a few at a time in blender. Add 1 cup broth and onion and blend until onion is minced. Combine almond mixture, remaining broth, and bay leaf in saucepan. Cover and simmer 30 minutes. Remove bay leaf. Without washing blender, combine milk, butter, flour, cream, and cardamon and blend until smooth. Stir into hot soup and cook, stirring until slightly thickened. Serve hot or chilled.

Reno, "The Biggest Little City in the World," has two different and distinct appeals, both friendly. One is its attraction as a glittering entertainment center and the other is its setting in natural scenic beauty, making Reno a haven for many outdoor sports and recreation enthusiasts.

Oxtail Soup

Mayor Jim Van Arsdale
Billings, Montana

fat for browning
1½ lb. oxtail (cut into 2" pieces)
1½ qts. water
1 tbsp. salt
½ cup onion (diced)
¾ cup carrot (diced)
½ cup celery (diced)
2 tbsp. white rice
1 cup tomatoes (cooked)

6 servings

Brown oxtail in fat. Add water and salt; simmer, covered, about 3¾ hours. Remove meat from bones and return to liquid. Add onions, carrots, celery, and white rice. Simmer, covered, for 30 minutes. Skim fat; add cooked tomatoes. Heat and serve.

Billings is the largest city in Montana and became known as the "Magic City" soon after its founding in 1882; magic because its growth was immediate and phenomonel. With an area in excess of 125,000 square miles, the city's primary trade territory is one of the largest in the U.S. Billings is also a regional center for eduation, medicine, the energy industry, and a wide range of agriculturally-related businesses. The recreational advantages are hard to praise too much—each of the four seasons offers something different but there are two constants, Yellowstone National Park in our background, and all of the scenic and recreational wonders of Montana. There is much to discover: an unlimited number of uncrowded activities available year-around. Come see us!

Summer Party Pleasers

Mayor Ken Schultz
Albuquerque, New Mexico

1¾ lb. ground chuck
¼ lb. ground mild Italian sausage
1 medium onion (finely chopped)
¼ cup green pepper (finely chopped)
1 cup fine rye bread crumbs
1 egg
¼ tsp. each chili powder, oregano, dry mustard, black pepper
½ tsp. each seasoned salt and garlic salt
2 tsp. Accent
3 tbsp. burgundy
1 tbsp. Worcestershire sauce
½ cup evaporated milk
1 tbsp. Parmesan cheese (grated)
1 tbsp. blue cheese (finely crumbled)
¼ cup butter
1 cup barbeque sauce
¼ cup burgundy

Makes 60 meatballs

Mix meat, onion, green pepper, bread crumbs, egg, seasonings, 3 tablespoons burgundy, Worcestershire sauce, milk, and cheese thoroughly. Form into balls, about 1" diameter. Brown all sides in butter; mix barbecue sauce and ¼ cup wine. Pour over balls, simmer for 30 minutes.

Albuquerque, New Mexico, the City of Friendship, was founded in 1706 and has become the multicultural center of the U.S. Surrounded by mountains, desert, and Indian pueblos, Albuquerque is one of our nation's most vital scientific centers. As the nation's highest elevated city, Albuquerque is also the host to the nation's largest hot air balloon festival with over 400 hot air balloons participating annually.

MAIN DISHES

Arroz a la Valenciana (Paella)

Mayor Federico Pena
Denver, Colorado

2 fryers (cut up and boned)
6 pork chops or ½ lb. pork (cut into 1" cubes)
¼ lb. sausage (sliced)
6 tbsp. oil
1 lb. shrimp (or lobster)
1 can clams
8 clams in shell for decorating top (optional)
3 canned artichokes (more if you like)
1 small can sweet peas
1 lb. Uncle Ben's converted rice
1 lb tomatoes (peeled)
1 small onion (minced)
1 clove garlic (minced)
½ tsp. each: saffron, salt, pepper, allspice
small jar pimientos (sliced)

6 servings

Heat oil; fry chicken, pork, and sausage. Cover chicken, pork, and sausage, and cook 45 minutes. Remove meats and set aside. Boil shrimp—leave in water until ready to use. Fry rice in same skillet as chicken—add onion and garlic—saute and add tomatoes and seasonings. When rice has changed color, cook a few minutes longer and add chicken, pork, and sausage. Add 2½ cups liquid (chicken broth and clam juice; if not enough, you

continued

can use some of the shrimp water). Cover and cook approximately 30 minutes. Add shrimp, clams, and artichokes. Decorate with pimiento, peas, and clams in shell. Cover again and cook a few minutes longer.

This is a favorite recipe of Mayor Pena's. His mother is the originator.

Mile-high **Denver** is one of the country's most diversified cities, economically and culturally. Denver is the home of wonderful museums, theaters, and pedestrian malls, as well as some of the most livable neighborhoods in the country, surrounded by open spaces and parks. The population is energetic, highly educated, and committed to its community's improvement. For millions of tourists each year, Denver serves as gateway to the Colorado Rockies—with its famous skiing in the winter and hiking, river rafting, and fishing in the summer. Surprising to some, the city maintains an agreeable climate, with an average of more than 300 days of sunshine a year. Most winters are mild as the nearby mountains absorb much of the winter storms.

Baked Salmon with Sour Cream Stuffing
Mayor Dirk Kempthorne
Boise, Idaho

4-6 lbs. dressed salmon (fresh or frozen)
1½ tsp. salt
2 tbsp. melted fat or oil
1½ tsp. salt
STUFFING:
¾ cup celery (chopped)
½ cup onion (chopped)
¼ cup fat (melted)
1 tsp salt
½ cup sour cream
¼ cup lemon (peeled and diced)
2 tbsp. lemon rind (grated)
1 tsp. paprika
1 qt. dry bread crumbs

6-8 servings

Cook celery and onion in fat until tender. Combine all stuffing ingredients and mix thoroughly.

Thaw frozen salmon. Clean, wash, and dry fish; sprinkle inside and out with salt. Stuff fish loosely. Close opening with small skewers or toothpicks. Place fish in well greased baking pan; brush with fat. Bake at 350° for approximately 1 hour or until fish flakes easily when tested with a fork. Baste occasionally.

This recipe came from the butcher's shop at our grocery store. We have made it several times. It is easy and very attractive for a buffet.

Boise, the capital of Idaho, has 107,000 enthusiastic residents. We are the world headquarters for major corporations such as Boise Cascade, Morrison-Knudsen, Simplot and we are enriched with a variety of cultural activities including a philharmonic, museum, art gallery, zoo, and a performing arts center which is state of the arts accoustics, and a trout stream that runs through the City of Trees.

CITY TRIVIA QUESTION #48

The first professional basketball game was played in this city and a manufacturing plant here supplied the cable used in the building of the Brooklyn and Golden Gate bridges.

Answer on page 38.

Boulder Baked Trout

Mayor Linda S. Jourgensen
Boulder, Colorado

3 tbsp. butter (melted)	
2 tsp. parsley	
1 tsp. yellow onion (diced)	
3 cloves garlic (minced)	
3-4 tbsp. mushrooms (chopped)	
6 medium Boulder Trout	
1 tsp. mixed salt and pepper	
4 egg yolks	
3 tbsp. brandy	
6 tbsp. bread crumbs	
5 tbsp. Parmesan cheese	
paprika to taste	

6 servings

Butter a baking dish thoroughly. Sprinkle in mixture of parsley, onion, and garlic. Sprinkle mushrooms over this and place trout on top (season trout beforehand with salt and pepper). Pour melted butter over the trout and cook at 400° for 10-12 minutes. Meanwhile, beat egg yolks and add brandy. Pour mixture over the trout and sprinkle with bread crumbs, cheese, and paprika.

The Boulder Baked Trout is a favorite of mine and is representative of our community dedication to outdoor life. Like any good recipe, this one is a little borrowed, a little begged and yet has more than a pinch of my own designing.

Boulder combines the excitement of high-technology development with the historical legacy of the Old West. Tucked away in a protected valley, the community enjoys a spectacular backdrop of the Rocky Mountains. The city has developed one of the most extensive Greenbelt and Open Space programs in the nation and is well known for its progressive comprehensive growth plan. Among other activities, Boulder hosts the annual colorado Shakespeare Festival, the Coors Bicycle Classic,and the popular Kinetics Conveyance Race.

Cashew Chicken

Mayor Dennis Champine
Aurora, Colorado

1 can bamboo shoots	
½ lb. mushrooms (sliced)	
3 whole chicken breasts (boned and skinned)	
⅔ cup chicken stock	
¼ cup soy sauce	
2 tbsp. cornstarch	
½ tsp. sugar	
1 tbsp. vegetable oil	
1 6-oz. pkg. frozen Chinese pea pods	
4 green onions	
1 cup cashews (chopped)	
dash each of salt, pepper, ground ginger	

6-8 servings

Combine bamboo shoots and mushrooms and cover bottom of large earthenware baking dish. Cut chicken into 1" cubes and place on top of mushrooms and bamboo shoots. Mix cornstarch and chicken stock. Add soy sauce, salt, pepper, ginger, and sugar; pour mixture over chicken.

Bake at 400°, covered, for about 40 minutes, or until chicken is done. Stir two or three times during baking. Chop green onions including tops. Add onions and pea pods to chicken mixture. Return to oven. Turn off oven and let dish remain there about 10 minutes or until pea pods are tender. Meanwhile, brown cashew nuts in 1 tbsp. vegetable oil. Remove chicken dish from oven, stir in browned cashews.

continued

Aurora—Gateway to the Rockies! Aurora, one of the fastest-growing mid-sized cities in America, lying about 25 miles east of the majestic Rocky Mountains, began as a farming community in the late 1800s and has grown to become the third largest city in Colorado.

Cheyenne Cream Can Supper

Mayor Don Erickson
Cheyenne, Wyoming

---

25 ears fresh corn (most of husks and silks removed; just leave a few around corn)

25 medium red potatoes (well scrubbed)

5 lb. onions (peeled and halved)

6 lb. carrots (well scrubbed)

6 heads cabbage (washed and quartered)

Italian, Polish, and German sausage (enough to cut into 50 pieces, each 4" long; cut *after* cooking)

½ gal. beer

½ gal. water

---

25 servings

Use a leak-proof, well scrubbed old cream can or a new galvanized large garbage can. Poke a few holes in the lid to allow steam to escape. Place corn in bottom of can, then layer other ingredients. Cover with beer and water. Cook over open wood fire until steam comes through holes in lid. (You can use a wheelbarrow to build the wood fire in—just use large cement blocks to set the can on inside the wheelbarrow.) Continue cooking for 2½-3 hours.

Serve using mitt and long-handled barbeque spoon and ladle. Remove contents from can and place on trays or in separate dishes.

A little Cheyenne, Wyoming, culinary secret ingredient would be to substitute a genuine fresh jack-a-lope (cross between an antelope and jackrabbit) in place of sausage to give the dish that unique country-western flavor. There is however one problem—jack-a-lopes are very rare and hard to catch. In fact, the only way to catch them is to stomp on the ground three times and yell "Mayor Erickson rides sidesaddle!" This recipe has been exceptionally successful in Wyoming for raising campaign money to re-elect dastardly mayors, back-shooting sheriffs, and hang 'em high judges.

Cheyenne is known as the "Magic City of the Plains" and is the home of Cheyenne Frontier Days, the world's largest outdoor rodeo, an annual event held the last full week of July celebrating our Old West heritage. We call it the "Daddy of 'Em All."

Chicken Asado

Mayor Terry Goddard
Phoenix, Arizona

---

2 frying chickens (cut in quarters)

2 cups olive oil

2 cups vinegar

1 cup dry white wine

1 tbsp. salt

1 tsp. red pepper flakes

2 tsp. oregano

1 tsp. thyme

1 tbsp. parsley

1 clove garlic (minced)

---

4 servings

Make marinade by mixing together all ingredients except chicken; heat to boiling. Coat chicken quarters with marinade and leave overnight in refrigerator. Place chicken on charcoal grill and baste with marinade often. Grill for 1 hour, turning frequently.

Asado is the Spanish term for a style of cooking marinated food over the charcoal grill. Chicken Asado is a very popular dish for cooking on the patio because it's quick, easy and delicious. It's a meal that fits easily into the outdoor style of life and which reflects our Hispanic heritage.

Phoenix is the nation's ninth largest city and one of the fastest-growing metropolitan areas. It is the state capital and the center of business, finance, government, and leisure activities for the State of Arizona. The resort-like climate attracts a steady flow of new residents and visitors to its many internationally known resorts. Phoenix has a distinctly Southwestern flavor and the influence of the Hispanic and Indian cultures can be seen in local food, architecture, and at the Heard and Pueblo Grande Museums which contain the world's largest collections of Indian Kachina dolls. Phoenix boasts the largest municipal park in the world in the Mountain Preserves.

Green Chicken Enchiladas
Mayor David M. Steinborn
Las Cruces, New Mexico

| 2 cans cream of chicken soup |
| 1 medium onion (chopped) |
| 1 cup Longhorn cheese (shredded) |
| 1 cup chicken (cooked and diced) |
| 1 soup can milk |
| 1 4 oz. can chopped green chiles |
| 1 pkg. taco shells |

4-6 servings

Mix soup, milk, onion, chicken; heat in pan until onions are tender. Remove from stove and add chile to mixture. Crush 4 taco shells and place in bottom of casserole dish. Spoon ⅓ mixture over shells, sprinkle with salt and pepper, and top with cheese. Repeat two more times. Bake at 350⁰ for 30 minutes.

Las Cruces is a beautiful, rapidly growing city located in the South Central portion of New Mexico. The city is quite diversified, ranging from rugged mountain peaks to green, cool valleys with pecan trees and chile to desert landscaping. One of the unique events at Las Cruces is the Whole Enchilada Festival, held the first weekend in October. Hot air balloon races precede this festival. The three-day event is punctuated with games, taste-tempting food booths of local New Mexico recipes, street dances, and the cooking of the giant enchilada.

Old West Spaghetti Sauce
Mayor Herbert Drinkwater
Scottsdale, Arizona

| 3 onions (sliced extremely thin) |
| 12 medium size fresh mushrooms |
| 3 cloves garlic (mashed) |
| ½ cup olive oil (top grade) |
| 2 lb. lean ground chuck for meatballs (use your favorite meatball recipe) |
| 2 lb. fresh Italian hot sausage |
| 2½ cups Mr. and Mrs. T Bloody Mary Mix |
| 1½ cups tomato puree |
| 1 cup Italian tomato paste |
| 1 large can Italian whole tomatoes |
| 4 jalapeno chili peppers |
| 1 tsp. salt |
| ½ tsp. pepper |
| 1 tsp. sugar |
| 18 king-size stuffed pimiento olives |

Makes approximately 3 quarts

Put olive oil in large pot over medium heat. Saute onions, garlic, and mushrooms. Remove from pot and set aside. Take the meatballs (which must be made with extremely lean meat) and the Italian hot sausage and cook until they are approximately half done. Add the onions, garlic, mushrooms, Bloody Mary mix, tomato puree, tomato paste, whole tomatoes, salt, pepper, and sugar to the meat. Take the 4 jalapeno peppers and put them in the sauce whole. Simmer sauce for approximately 4 hours. Remove peppers and discard them. Slice olives in thin slices and add to the sauce. Simmer for another 30 minutes.

Scottsdale, located in Arizona's Valley of the Sun, has grown from a tiny farming cluster of 2,000 occupying one square mile in 1951, to a vibrant community of 115,000 occupying 183 square miles in 1985. Founded by U.S. Army Chaplain Winfield Scott in 1888, Scottsdale, long known as the "West's Most Western Town," has matured into a "World Class City." Scottsdale's quality lifestyle includes well planned living, working, and shopping areas and pleasant neighborhoods and residential areaas protected from traffic and noise. The city's emphasis on mountain conservation and protection of its rich desert areas is known nationally. The ambiance of Scottsdale reflects a unique blend of traditional Western and modern living.

One Pot Chicken and Dumplings

Mayor Michael Occhiato
Pueblo, Colorado

medium-size chicken
1 cup carrots (diced)
¼ cup celery (diced)
¼ cup onion (diced)
3 cups water
3 cans cream of chicken soup
DUMPLINGS:
1½ cups flour
¾ tsp. salt
2 tsp. baking powder
¾ cup milk.

4-6 servings

Brown chicken over medium heat (or in the oven). Add carrots, celery, onions, and water. Bring to boil, add soup. Heat for 1¾ hours (or longer if desired). Combine ingredients for dumplings, mixing thoroughly and quickly. Drop spoonfuls into boiling chicken soup. Cook 20 minutes uncovered and an additional 20 minutes covered.

After bringing the soup to a boil, make sure you heat it for the one hour and 45 minutes at a medium setting to avoid too much burning on bottom of pot. The dumplings will soak up a lot of the soup mixture. If you wish, check the dumplings before serving by cutting one in half. If it appears it has not soaked up soup through the middle, let it cook a little longer for better taste.

Pueblo, with a population of approximately 100,000, is located east of the Rocky Mountains in the middle of beautiful country. Pueblo is an ideal area for economic development, the cost of living is low, and the people are great.

Pollo Vaquero

Mayor Dan Flammer
Carson City, Nevada

2 large frying or stewing chickens	
2 cans golden mushroom soup	
¼ lb. sliced mushrooms	
½ pt. heavy cream	
½ cup white wine	
1 tbsp. pimientos (sliced)	
1 12 oz. pkg. boiled noodles	
⅓ cup celery (chopped)	

6 servings

Boil chicken until done. Cool and tear the chicken off bones, into large strips, using only the choice pieces.

In a large saucepan add golden mushroom soup and whipping cream; bring to boil, then turn down and simmer. Add mushrooms, white wine, sliced pimientos, and celery. Cook until mushrooms are tender.

In a 3 quart casserole dish, spoon in one layer of sauce, then a thin layer of noodles, then a thin layer of chicken. Continue layering this way until you fill the casserole dish. Bake at 350⁰ for 1 hour.

Carson City, in the heart of the Old West, is the capital of Nevada. It is the home of the Virginia and Truckee Railroad and the Carson City Mint, which is rated as one of the top 10 museums in the Western Region. Carson City is known for its Majestic Mountains on one side and its desert on the other side.

Southwestern Fried Chicken

Mayor Lewis Murphy
Tucson, Arizona

1½ cups flour	1 cup cooking oil
seasoning to taste	1 whole chicken (cut up)
½ cup white wine	

6-8 servings

Shake chicken pieces in bag of flour. Pan fry in hot oil just long enough to brown both sides. Season to taste. Bake in 300⁰ oven, covered, for 1 hour; basting with wine. Remove cover and bake for another hour.

Any klutz can do this recipe for a Sunday brunch and become an instant hero at home.

Tucson is probably the oldest continuous community in the country, inhabited since the first century. More recently, it has had five flags fly over it, from that of Spain brought by the Conquistadores to the present American flag restored during the Civil War. Reminders of this unique past are abundant. Within the environs also, we have an entire movie set with sound stage; the internationally acclaimed Arizona-Sonora Desert Museum; the University of Arizona, built on land provided by local gamblers a century ago; a ski area within an hour's drive; and San Xavier mission, which has served the Tohono O'Odham Indians since the 18th century, founded by Father Eusebio Kino. We Tucsonians bask in our year-round sunny weather, and our laid-back lifestyle. We cherish and protect our community—the historic "Old Pueblo."

CITY TRIVIA QUESTION #50

The French for "Red Stick" is the name for this Louisiana city.

Answer on page 67.

ACCOMPANIMENTS

Mountain Top Baked Beans

Mayor Kelly Ohlson
Fort Collins, Colorado

4 16 oz. cans pork and beans in tomato sauce
½ cup sorghum
3 tbsp. brown sugar
4 tbsp. ketchup
1 tsp. liquid smoke
8-10 strips bacon

8-10 servings

Mix ingredients well in 13"x9" pan. Cover with bacon. Bake at 325⁰ for 2½-3 hours. Cool in pan 5-10 minutes.

Fort Collins is nestled at the foothills of the Rocky Mountains. Founded in 1844 by French trapper Antoine Janis, Fort Collins is rich with history, natural resources, and recreational opportunities. A strong, diversified economy and a deep concern for the environment and overall quality of life combine to make Fort Collins the "Choice City."

Sopaipillas de Lev Adura Quimica (Baking Powder Puffed Bread)

Mayor W. Samuel Pick
Santa Fe, New Mexico

4 cups flour
2 tsp. baking powder
1 tsp. salt
4 tbsp. shortening
1½ cups warm water
shortening

Makes 4 dozen

Combine dry ingredients in a medium-size mixing bowl and cut in shortening. Make a well in the center and add water to dry ingredients; work into a dough. Knead dough until smooth; cover and set aside for 20 minutes.

Heat 2 inches of shortening in a heavy pan at medium-high heat. Roll dough to a 1/8-inch thickness on a lightly floured board. Cut dough into 4-inch squares and fry until golden on both sides, turning once. (If shortening is sufficiently hot, the sopaipillas will puff and become hollow shortly after being placed in the shortening.) Drain sopaipillas on absorbent towels.

Sopaipillas may be served as a bread with any New Mexican menu. They may be served with honey, dusted with a sugar-cinnamon mixture, and served as a dessert, or may be filled.

Bienvenidos a La Villa Real de **Santa Fe**!—the oldest capital city in the United States of America. Enjoy our Indian summer weather, clear skies, the smell of pinon burning from our fireplaces, beautiful mountains that offer skiing, and the beautiful aspens and clean air, all minutes from the central downtown area. Our city, the nation's second largest art community, offers you 190 galleries in which to shop and enjoy our art, the Santa Fe Opera, historical sites such as the oldest church and the oldest house, and the miraculous winding staircase at the Loretto Chapel. We have many eating establishments offering you comfort and delicious native American foods. In addition, each year the city of Santa Fe sponsors a national awards program to recognize cities' safety belt educational programs. Join us in our tri-cultural city where our hospitality is yours.

Summer Squash New Mexico

Mayor Thomas C. Taylor
Farmington, New Mexico

2 straight neck yellow squash (sliced)
8 oz. green chiles (chopped)
1 lb. cheddar cheese
6 tbsp. butter
salt

6 servings

Butter the bottom of a 9"x12" casserole and cover with a layer of squash. Sprinkle with chopped green chiles; cover with grated cheese. Repeat three times. Bake at 350⁰ for 30 minutes.

Don't eat it all, because it's even better reheated for the second time!

Farmington, New Mexico, in the Four Corners region, is not only well known for its fascinating Indian Ruins, spectacular Mesa Verde, and beautiful Chaco Canyon, but also because it boasts the best trout fishing in the U.S. in the fresh, clean Quality Waters of the San Juan River! If you don't believe us, come out and visit our lovely city with its hauntingly beautiful sunsets, sandstone mesas, and vast horizons.

Swiss Cheese Loaves

Mayor Peter J. Sferrazza
Reno, Nevada

1 pkg. dry yeast
¼ cup hottest tap water
2⅓ cups flour
2 tbsp. sugar
1 tsp. salt
¼ tsp. soda
1 cup sour cream
1 egg
1 cup Swiss cheese (shredded)
sesame seeds

Makes 2 loaves

Grease 2 loaf pans. In large mixer bowl, dissolve yeast in hot water. Add 1⅓ cups flour, sugar, salt, soda, sour cream, and egg. Blend ½ minute on low speed, scraping bowl constantly. Beat 2 minutes on high speed, scraping bowl occasionally. Stir in remaining flour and cheese thoroughly. Divide batter evenly between pans; sprinkle with sesame seed. Let rise in warm place 50 minutes. (Batter will rise slightly but will not double.) Bake in 350⁰ oven 25-30 minutes or until golden brown. Remove from pans immediately. Serve warm.

Reno is the "Biggest Little City in the World." For further information on Reno, turn to page 168.

For further information on Reno, turn to page 168.

CITY TRIVIA QUESTION #51

The nation's oldest continuously operating amusement park in America with the oldest operating carousel can be found in this northeastern city.

Answer on page 24.

DESSERTS

Chocolate Luck

Mayor Thomas V. Campbell
Idaho Falls, Idaho

2 cups flour
1 cup margarine
½ cup walnuts (chopped)
8 oz. cream cheese (softened)
1 cup powdered sugar
1 cup whipped cream or 8 oz. Cool Whip
2 small pkgs. instant chocolate pudding
3 cups milk

20 servings

Mix flour, margarine, and chopped walnuts with a fork. Press into bottom of 9"x13" pan and bake at 350⁰ for 20 minutes. Cool.

Mix cream cheese, powdered sugar, and whipped cream or Cool Whip and spread over baked crust.

Mix pudding and milk and pour over cream cheese mixture. Top with more whipped cream or Cool Whip and chopped walnuts. Refrigerate 30 minutes to an hour.

You can use any flavor of pudding for different taste. You can use 1 large package of instant pudding with ½ cup milk less than recipe calls for.

Idaho Falls is the third largest city in Idaho. Located in a wide valley formed by the Snake River, the city lies halfway between Jackson Hole, Wyoming, and Sun Valley, Idaho. To the east, the wooded foothills lead one's eye to the majestic Teton Mountains, which are visible from just outside the city. To the west lie the vast lava deposits of a prehistoric volcano. Agriculture is still the leading industry, although nuclear research facilities of the Department of Energy employ about 7,000 of our residents. The Snake River flows through the city and is laced with greenery and beauty.

Chocolate Mousse

Mayor Palmer A. DePaulis
Salt Lake City, Utah

12 oz. chocolate chips
1½ tbsp. water
4 eggs (separated)
pinch salt
1 cup nuts (chopped)(optional)
1 pt. heavy cream (whipped)
½ cup sugar
1 tsp. vanilla

12 servings

Melt chocolate chips with water in double boiler over hot, not boiling, water. Add 1 egg yolk at a time to hot chocolate mixture, stirring well after each addition. Beat whites until stiff. Add sugar and salt; beat 5 minutes longer. Fold egg whites into chocolate. Whip cream and add vanilla; fold into chocolate mixture. Add nuts if desired. Refrigerate 12 hours or more. Serve in individual dishes or mold.

This is one of the easiest Chocolate Mousse recipes around. This recipe was used in the Mayor's annual 12 days of Christmas social for the Mayor's office.

Beautiful **Salt Lake City** is located at the crossroads of the intermountain west. Its proximity to the mountains and lakes affords easy access to skiing, hiking, camping, and other recreational activities. Downtown is highlighted by the lovely Mormon Temple Square. Symphony Hall elegantly houses the acclaimed Utah Symphony. Salt Lake City is also the home of Ballet West and the Utah Opera Company. Our many parks and friendly people make Salt Lake a wonderful city to live in or visit.

Cold Oven Pound Cake

Mayor Al Brooks   *Mesa, Arizona*

½ lb. butter	3 cups cake flour (sifted)
½ cup Crisco	½ tsp. baking powder
3 cups sugar	1 cup milk
5 large eggs	1 tsp. lemon juice
1 tsp. vanilla	

10-12 servings

Cream butter, Crisco, and sugar. Add eggs one at a time, beat until light and fluffy. Add dry ingredients alternately with milk, vanilla, and lemon juice. Beat for 20-25 minutes. (This is the secret of this cake.)

Pour into greased tube or bundt pan. Put in COLD oven; turn heat to 350°. Bake 1 hour 15 minutes. Cool on rack; remove from pan.

This is a wonderful dense pound cake. Can slice thin and serve with fresh fruit, ice cream and sauce, or anything else.

Mesa, "where the sun spends the winter," is the third largest city in Arizona, with a population of 242,000. The climate is excellent, offering 4,000 hours of sunshine per year and clean, warm, dry air. Mesa is the winter home of the Chicago Cubs and the California Angels.

"Let Them Eat Cake" Cake and "Cover Your Assets" Frosting

Mayor Harry E. Mitchell
Tempe, Arizona

CAKE:
fine, dry bread crumbs
¼ cup unsweetened cocoa (strained)
1 lb. (4½ cups) walnuts (finely ground)
12 eggs (separated)
2 cups sugar
¼ tsp. salt

FROSTING:
6 egg yolks
½ cup sugar
3 tbsp. instant coffee
½ cup boiling water
1 lb. (2 cups) butter
1 tsp. vanilla
3 tbsp. dark rum or cognac
additional rum, cognac, or creme de cacao

12-14 servings

Preheat oven to 350°. The three layers for this torte should not be baked too high or too low in the oven or they will burn. Adjust two racks to divide the oven in equal thirds. Butter 3 9" round layer cake pans (not the kind with loose bottoms). Line the bottoms with paper. Butter the paper. Dust all over lightly with fine, dry bread crumbs.

Add the cocoa to the walnuts and stir with a fork to mix. Set aside.

In small bowl of electric mixer, at high speed, beat yolks about 3 minutes until thick and pale lemon-colored. Reduce the speed and gradually add sugar. Increase speed to high again and continue to beat for 5 minutes more, until very thick. Remove from mixer and transfer to a very large bowl.

continued

In the large bowl of an electric mixer (with clean beaters) beat egg whites and salt until stiff but not dry. Remove from mixer. Fold half of the nut mixture into the yolks and then, in the following order, fold in one-third of the whites, the remaining half of the nut mixture, half of the remaining whites, and then the balance of the whites. Divide the batter among the prepared pans. Spread tops level.

Bake 45-50 minutes or until tops spring back when lightly touched and layers come slightly away from sides of the pans. (During baking the layers will rise and then sink.)

Remove pans from oven. Cover with racks and invert but do not remove pans until they are cool enough to handle. If necessary, cut around edges to release, invert, remove pans and papers, cover with racks, and invert again to finish cooling right side up.

Frosting: Place yolks in top of small double boiler. Beat a little, just to blend, with a small wire whisk. Gradually stir in the sugar. Dissolve instant coffee in boiling water. Very gradually whisk coffee into the yolk mixture. Place over hot water on moderate heat. (Water must not touch top of double boiler and it must not boil, or the mixture will curdle.) Cook over moderately low heat, stirring and scraping pot constantly until mixture takes on a soft custard consistency, about 170° to 175° on a candy thermometer. Remove from heat. Place the custard mixture over ice water. Stir occasionally until mixture is cool.

Beat butter in small bowl of electric mixer to cream it slightly. Very gradually add the custard mixture, vanilla, and 3 tablespoons rum or cognac, beat until smooth. (If necessary, refrigerate mixture to firm it, and then beat again.)

Place four strips of wax paper around the edges of the cake plate. Place the first layer on the plate right side up. Optional, additional rum, cognac, or creme de cacao may be sprinkled over each layer before spreading with the buttercream. (The filling must be spread thin or you won't have enough to cover the top and sides.) Continue stacking layers (right side up) and buttercream. Cover

sides and then top with the buttercream, spreading it smoothly.

If you wish, reserve some of the buttercream and with a pastry bag fitted with a small star tube, form a ruffled border on the top rim of the cake and another around the base.

Remove wax paper strips, sliding each one out by a narrow end. Refrigerate and serve cold.

Optional: Decorate top with 12 walnut halves and, if you wish, coat the sides with rather finely chopped walnuts, applying them with the palm of your hand and your fingers before removing the wax paper strips.

Tempe is currently the fourth largest city in Arizona with a population of 135,000. Though quickly becoming the hub of the rapidly growing Phoenix Metro area, Tempe maintains a small town charm and neighborliness. Tempe is especially proud of its recent designation as an "All America City," awarded for citizen involvement in the local government process. Home of Arizona State University, Tempe has one of the most highly educated populations in the state, with 72% of its residents college-educated.

CITY TRIVIA QUESTION #52

Match the sports event/place with the city:

____Soap Box Derby	A. Minneapolis, MN
____1986 Super Bowl Champions	B. Cherry Hill, NJ
____Astrodome	C. Los Angeles, CA
____Kentucky Derby	D. Pontiac, MI
____1986 NBA Champions	E. Arcadia, CA
____Santa Anita Racetrack	F. Boston, MA
____Silverdome	G. Louisville, KY
____1984 Summer Olympics	H. Houston, TX
____Garden State Racetrack	I. Inglewood, CA
____Metrodome	J. Hot Springs, AR
____Arkansas Derby	K. Chicago, IL
____The Forum	L. Akron, OH

Answers on pages 120, 110, 157, 93, 18, 211, 134, 198, 41, 125, 82, 215.

Two Layer Pound Cake

Mayor J. Steven Newton
Sandy City, Utah

1 cup margarine (not shortening)
2 eggs
2 cups sugar
1 tsp. baking powder
½ tsp. salt
1 cup sour cream
½ tsp. vanilla
2 cups flour plus ¼ scant cup
TOPPING:
½ cup pecans or walnuts (chopped)
2-3 tbsp. brown sugar
1 tsp. cinnamon

12-15 servings

Blend cake ingredients into a batter, being careful not to overbeat (cake will be dry if overbeaten). Spoon half the batter into greased and floured tube or bundt pan. Cover with half of topping over this layer. Repeat to make second layer. Bake at 350⁰ for 55-60 minutes. Remove from pan when almost cool and sprinkle with powdered sugar. (Cake may be frozen; warm slices in 200⁰ oven.)

Sandy City is located 15 miles from Salt Lake City and was incorporated in 1893. Sandy is listed as one of the fastest growing suburban communities in the nation, with an increase in population from 6,438 in 1970 to almost 70,000 in 1986. Some other interesting facts: Sandy is the "Youngest Community in the Nation." The median age is 20.2 years. Sandy is the "Most Married Community in the U.S." 92 percent of adults are married. Sandy is a "Motorized Community": 88 percent of the wage earners drive their own cars to work.

Whole Wheat Brownies

Mayor Dean S. Stahle
Bountiful, Utah

1½ cups whole wheat flour
2 tsp. baking powder
2 tsp. salt
2 cups raw sugar
4 eggs
2 squares semisweet chocolate (melted)
1 cup salad oil
2 tsp. vanilla
chopped nuts

12-15 servings

Sift whole wheat flour, baking powder, and salt. Mix raw sugar and eggs; combine with flour mixture and add vanilla, chopped nuts, melted chocolate, and oil. Spread in square cake pan; sprinkle more nuts on top and bake in 375⁰ oven for 20 minutes. (Watch brownies carefully and remove from oven while they are still slightly underdone.)

Bountiful is an affluent community nestled in the foothills of the Wasatch Mountains overlooking the Great Salt Lake. Known as the "City of Beautiful Homes and Gardens," Bountiful has ten park facilities, an olympic recreation center that assisted in hosting the 1984 Winter National Ice Skating Competition, and a championship 18-hole golf course.

WEST COAST

"Double, double, toil and trouble"
Mayor Peggy Mensinger
Modesto, CA

"Sorry Charlie!"
Mayor Tony Knowles
Anchorage, AK

"Hold the pickle, hold the lettuce, special orders don't upset us!
Mayor Charles Royer
Seattle, WA

"A way to a mayor's heart is through his stomach"
Mayor Nao Takasugi
Oxnard, CA

STARTERS

Asparagus Roll-Ups

Mayor Barbara Fass
Stockton, California

12 slender asparagus spears
salted·water
¼ lb. sharp cheddar cheese
12 slices sandwich bread
½ cup butter (softened)
1 tbsp. parsley (chopped)
½ tbsp. green onion (minced)
salt and pepper
½ tsp. dill weed

Makes 36

After discarding white fibrous ends from asparagus, rinse spears. Bring about 1" water to boil in a wide shallow pan; drop in asparagus and boil, uncovered, until just tender when pierced, 4-7 minutes. Drain well. Or, cook spears in microwave until tender.

Cut asparagus spears into thirds. Trim crusts from 12 slices of bread, cut into thirds, and *flatten each slice slightly with a rolling pin.*

Cut cheese into lengths 1"x¼". Combine ¼ cup butter, parsley, dill, green onion, and salt and pepper to taste; spread evenly on bread slices to edges, and top each with and asparagus spear and a cheese stick.

Roll tightly and arrange on a baking sheet. Melt remaining ¼ cup butter; brush evenly over rolls. Broil, about 5" from heat, until golden, 3-5 minutes.

This winning appetizer recipe was submitted by Sue Wilcox of Stockton.

Stockton is located at the confluence of the San Joaquin and Calaveras Rivers and is surrounded by rich agricultural land where tomatoes, asparagus, corn, fruits, nuts, etc. are grown. A unique mix of the traditional and modern is but one way in which Stockton exhibits its most fascinating characteristic—diversity! A modern city in the lush agricultural lands of San Joaquin Valley, Stockton has been called the "food basket of the nation." For this cookbook, residents of Stockton were asked to submit their favorite recipes using one of the major crops of the valley. The winning recipes are included in this cookbook.

Artichoke Appetizer

Mayor Carol Beswick
Redlands, California

2 cans artichoke hearts (not packed in oil) (chopped) or 1 pkg. frozen (S&W brand) artichoke hearts (parbroiled, cooled, chopped)
½ cup mayonnaise
½ cup Parmesan cheese (grated)
½ tsp. garlic powder

6-12 servings

Mix ingredients; place in small casserole dish. Bake at 350⁰ for 25 minutes. Serve on not too salty crackers or cut up pita bread triangles or toast rounds.

A different and tasty dish when one is asked to "bring your favorite" recipe.

Redlands, California, is located near Riverside and has a population of 51,567. Redlands has the largest inventory of historic homes and turn-of-the-century housing in Southern California and an aggressive historic preservation program. The first bed and breakfast inn (Morey Mansion) is located in Redlands. One of the finest and most attractive colleges, the University of Redlands, is located here. The city is currently undergoing an aggressive downtown revitalization program.

Chicken Soup

Mayor Dale Doig
Fresno, California

1 chicken (cut up)
garlic powder to taste (any seasoning may be added to suit your fancy)
salt and pepper to taste
10 oz. pkg. frozen spinach (cut up) (when in season, fresh spinach may be substituted)
½ head cabbage (cut up)
4-5 carrots (cut up)
4 medium-sized potatoes (cut up)
2 large onions (cut up)

10-12 servings

Place cut up chicken in large pot, and cover with water 1" above chicken. Bring to a boil; reduce heat to low. Add cut up vegetables to chicken; add more water to cover vegetables. Season with garlic powder, salt, and pepper to taste. Stir periodically to make sure chicken does not stick to the bottom of the pot. Cook until chicken falls off bones; remove the bones. Poultry seasoning is optional and may be added if desired. (It should be noted that the above listed vegetables are only recommendations. Any vegetables that are favorites of yours or that suit your fancy may be used. The amounts of vegetables and chicken used can vary according to the taste of the preparer.)

Advantages of this "gourmet" meal: (1) Extremely economical. (2) If chicken is skinned, very low in calories. (3) It is assumed by Ersatz medical practitioners to be equivalent to Jewish Penicillin and of great medicinal and healing values. (4) Although there is no definitive proof, this "culinary delight" could be on a par with ginseng and possibly have unique aphrodisiacal qualities. (5) This hearty meal is not recommended for Quiche eaters. (6) "Adult Mayors" should add Louisiana Tabasco Sauce to enhance the ecstasy from eating this soup/meal.

Fresno, the heart of and eighth largest city in California, has an annual growth rate of 4.4 percent and is the raisin capital of the nation. It seems that more and more people are coming to delight in the opportunities Fresno has to offer. Being at the center of this great state, Fresno is a mere one to three hours away from areas as diverse as desert and snow, ocean and mountains. And when you come back home our own parks, theaters, restaurants, and college sports can keep even the most active of us busy for a good, long time.

Corn-Oyster Chowder

Mayor Ab Brown
Riverside, California

1 onion (chopped)
1 stalk celery (chopped)
¼ cup butter
3 cups water
¼ cup fresh parsley (chopped)
1 carrot (thinly sliced)
1 tsp. sugar
¼ tsp. salt
¼ tsp. pepper
dash tabasco
1 lb. potatoes (diced)
1 lb. canned cream corn
2 cups milk
4 oz. can pimientos (chopped)
1 pt. oysters with liquid

6-8 servings

Saute onion and celery in butter. Add water, parsley, carrots, sugar, salt, tabasco. Cook until carrots are soft. Add potatoes; cook until tender. (Potatoes can be cooked separately and added later before serving.) Add corn, milk, and pimientos. Cook 5 minutes; add oysters and liquid. Cook 5 minutes more. Never boil.

I serve this soup at my Christmas holiday soup parties.

Riverside, a city of 174,000 located in southern California, is famous for the Mission Inn and orange industry. In 1873 L.C. and Eliza Tibbets planted the first Washington navel orange trees from which California's $100 million citrus industry grew. Those trees still produce fruit today. Riverside offers a lifestyle that is close to the beach, mountains, and desert areas. The city has one of the most beautiful city entrances in America with some of the earliest tree-lined boulevards in the state. Riverside—a nice surprise!

Crab Dip

Mayor Jonathon H. Cannon
Garden Grove, California

8 oz. cream cheese (softened)
1 cup mayonnaise
4 stalks celery (diced)
4-6 green onions (diced)
1 can cream of mushroom soup
1 pkg. imitation crabmeat or 1 can crabmeat
1 pkg. unflavored gelatin
3 tbsp. water

Makes approximately 5 cups

Warm soup, water, and gelatin. Blend cream cheese and mayonnaise; add warmed ingredients. Blend well, then add celery, onions, and crab. Mix together and pour into serving dish. Refrigerate at least 12 hours. Serve as spread for crackers.

Great for any kind of function. Easy to take for potluck, etc. The mixture of ingredients sounds strange, but it tastes delicious.

Garden Grove, a community of 126,000 is located in the heart of Orange County. It is home to the world famous Crystal Cathedral, Reverend Robert Schuller's church. Our motto, "City of Youth and Ambition," signifies the relatively young age of our community and our efforts to meet the challenges that face us today.

Crabmeat Potpourri Jelle

Mayor Daniel E. Griset
Santa Ana, California

6 oz. can crabmeat
1 can cream of mushroom soup
1 cup mayonnaise
½ cup celery (chopped)
½ cup onion (chopped)
3 oz. cream cheese (whipped)
1 packet unflavored gelatin

20 servings

Mix everything together except gelatin. Mix 2-3 tablespoons water in with gelatin and add to crabmeat mixture; stir well. Pour into greased mold and refrigerate until firm.

Eat with your favorite crackers.

Being the second largest city in one of the fastest-growing counties in California doesn't keep **Santa Ana** from remembering the basic need to have fun. More than half of its 225,000 residents are Hispanic, adding a colorful Latin flair to cultural offerings. Its artful harmony between brown and

continued

white, basic business sense and high technology, past and future accentuates the charm of this lively southern California city.

Lentil Soup

Mayor Doug Sutherland
Tacoma, Washington

2 cups dry lentils
1 qt. water
2 qts. beef soup stock
1 potato (peeled and diced)
2 carrots (grated)
3 tbsp. white vinegar
1/8 tsp. ground cloves
salt to taste
Parmesan cheese (for garnish)

8 servings

Soak the lentils in water for 2 hours. Place lentils and water into a soup pot, and add the soup stock, potato, carrots, vinegar, salt, and cloves. Cook over low heat for 3 hours. Serve with Parmesan cheese in a bowl.

Tacoma—its vitality and growth is nothing short of a renaissance. The Tacoma Dome...a revitalized downtown...a deep-water port teeming with activity...a waterfront alive with restaurants. They all add up to a city with a bright future, thanks to a special partnership. Representatives from the community, government, and private business rolled up their sleeves and worked as partners to make Tacoma something special. So special, that in 1984 Tacoma was named one of nine "All America Cities."

Meat Minestrone Soup

Mayor Ab Brown
Riverside, California

½ cup dried kidney beans
¼ lb. sweet Italian sausage
¼ lb. each bacon and ham (diced)
1 onion (sliced)
2 cloves garlic (crushed)
2 stalks celery (diced)
1 zucchini (sliced)
1 leek (sliced)
salt and pepper to taste
2 qts. beef soup stock
2 cups cabbage (shredded)
1 cup chianti dry red wine
1 lb. tomatoes (diced)
½ cup small elbow macaroni
fresh or dried basil to taste
Romano cheese (freshly grated)

6-8 servings

Soak beans 12-24 hours. Cook bacon, ham, and sausage together until brown. Add garlic, celery, zucchini, onion; cook until tender. Lay out thick section of newspaper, line heavily with paper towels. Use to drain grease. Heat beef stock with beans, cabbage, and wine; cook until tender. Add cooked vegetables, tomatoes, macaroni, basil. Cook until it tastes good. Serve with freshly grated Romano cheese.

This soup is one of six soups that I prepare for my Christmas parties.

In **Riverside**, in 1873, the Tibbets planted the first Washington navel orange trees from which California's $100 million citrus industry grew. For more information on Riverside, turn to page 184 and 185.

Pennsylvania Dutch Corn Soup

Mayor George F. Ziegler
Placentia, California

1 stewing hen (about 4 lb.)	
4 qts. water	
1 onion (chopped)	
10 ears of corn	
½ cup celery (chopped with leaves)	
2 eggs (hard-cooked and chopped)	
salt and pepper	
RIVELS:	
1 cup flour	pinch of salt
1 egg	milk

6-8 servings

Put cut-up chicken and onion into the water and cook slowly until tender; add salt. Remove chicken, cut the meat into 1" pieces and return to broth, together with corn kernels (which have been cut from cob), celery, and seasoning. Continue to simmer. Make rivels by combining 1 cup flour, pinch of salt, 1 egg, and a little milk. Mix well with fork or fingers to form small crumbs. Drop these into the soup; add hard-cooked eggs. Boil for 15 minutes or longer.

Placentia is located in northeast Orange County, 24 miles southeast of Los Angeles. Orange growing and packaging are an important part of the city's history and economy. It has received recognition as an "All American City."

CITY TRIVIA QUESTION #53

The Fondas—Henry, Jane and Peter—all got their start at a community playhouse theater in this city.

Answer on page 165.

Potage Fraise d'Anjou

Mayor Nao Takasugi
Oxnard, California

4 cups strawberries (hulled, washed, drained)
1 tbsp. mint leaves (chopped)
2 tbsp. cornstarch
1/8 tsp. salt
⅔ cup sugar (divided)
14 tbsp. water
2 cups d'Anjou (Rose) wine
2 oz. plain yogurt
6 whole strawberries for garnish (optional)
fresh mint sprigs for garnish (optional)

6 servings

Chill six soup or dessert bowls. Place the strawberries and mint leaves in a blender and puree. Press the mixture through a sieve. Discard the seeds and pulp.

Place cornstarch, salt, and sugar (minus 3 tablespoons to be used later with the yogurt) in a saucepan. Stir in 2 tablespoons of water into the cornstarch mixture, cooking over low heat. Add the remaining water, stirring to prevent lumping. Stir in strawberry puree, and d'Anjou wine, until thoroughly combined. Refrigerate until well chilled.

Add reserved 3 tablespoons of sugar to the yogurt, stirring well. Place the mixture into a squeeze bottle, with a fine tip.

When ready to serve, equally distribute the chilled soup among the chilled bowls. With the "yogurt" bottle, draw three circles of graduating sizes within each other. With a butter knife, draw 8 spokes through the circles, starting just beyond the outside of the circle and ending in the center of the smallest circle. (This will create a scalloped edge.) Garnish the center with a sprig of mint and whole strawberry (optional).

This recipe was the 1985 Strawberry Festival winner submitted by Debbie Sheesley of Sacramento, California.

continued

Oxnard lies along Southern California's famous Gold Coast. Spectacular sunsets, uncrowded beaches, and the Channel Islands Harbor attract thousands of visitors each year. The city's rich cultural heritage is balanced with its diversified industry, business and agriculture. As the Strawberry Capital of California, Oxnard is host to the Annual California Strawberry Festival.

Salmon Mousse

Mayor Lionel J. Wilson
Oakland, California

1 large can red Sockeye salmon
1 envelope unflavored gelatin
¼ cup cold water
½ cup dry white wine
¼ cup mayonnaise
¼ cup sour cream
1 tbsp. white wine vinegar
1 tbsp. lemon juice
1 tsp. salt
¼ tsp. paprika
¼ tsp. tarragon
1 tsp. dill weed
dash white pepper

15-20 servings

Soften gelatin in cold water in a bowl. Bring wine to boil; remove from heat and add to gelatin. Flake fish (remove bones); add gelatin mixture and all additional ingredients. Mix thoroughly; taste for seasoning and moisture. (This can be made in a food processor or blender.) Pack mixture into oiled mold. Refrigerate about 24 hours. Unmold, sprinkle with chopped parsley, and garnish with lemon slices.

Serve with crackers or baguettes.

Oakland is without question the best kept secret in the Bay Area. Not only can we boast a number one national ranking for our outstanding climate, and the second largest container port in the country, but we also have "California's best airport." Oakland is also proud of its designation as the "most integrated U.S. city" because of our diverse ethnic population and rich variety of cultural attractions. We are continuing our dream as the renaissance city of America and an urban model for our nation.

Shrimp and Scallop Seviche

Mayor Lawrence E. Mulryan
San Rafael, California

3 lb. medium shrimp (cooked and peeled)
2 lb. raw bay scallops (thinly sliced) (use sea scallops if bay scallops are unavailable)
2 cups fresh lime juice (about 12 limes)
9 tbsp. red onion (finely chopped)
6 tbsp. fresh parsley (chopped)
2 tbsp. green pepper (finely chopped)
1 cup olive oil
1 tsp. Italian seasoning
2 dashes tabasco
1 tsp. garlic powder
1½ tsp. salt
freshly ground pepper
4 avocados (peeled and sliced)
3 tomatoes (thinly sliced)

8-10 servings

Cut shrimp in thirds and mix with sliced scallops in a bowl. Add lime juice to marinate the mixture. Do this 3-4 hours stirring once or twice (marinating should always be done at room temperature for the most flavor). Drain and discard the juice. Add remaining ingredients (except avocados and tomatoes), to seafood and toss lightly. Chill 1 hour. Arrange on plate with avocado and tomato slices. Scallop shells make a particularly attractive plate for this appetizer.

San Rafael is the oldest city in Marin County and is home of the Mission San Rafael Archangel (twentieth of the 21 missions in California), which was founded in 1817.

Stuffed Mushrooms

Mayor Gregory R. Cox
Chula Vista, California

24 large mushrooms
½ cup bread crumbs
½ cup Parmesan cheese
1 tbsp. parsley flakes
½ tbsp. onion flakes
1 tbsp. butter (melted)

24 mushrooms

Wash mushrooms thoroughly; remove stems (set caps aside). Chop stems; combine in mixing bowl stems and all other ingredients except butter. Mix, then stuff mushrooms. Drizzle with melted butter. Bake 350⁰ for 10-15 minutes.

Chula Vista is situated on the shores of San Diego Bay seven miles north of the International Border and seven miles south of downtown San Diego. This city of 116,000 prides itself on an ideal climate, excellent recreational opportunities, a responsive municipal government, and a constituency that truly cares about its community. Incorporated in 1911, the city celebrated its 75th Diamond Anniversary in October 1986.

Tostado Dip

Mayor Paul A. Netzel
Culver City, California

34 oz. spicy refried beans
1 can bean dip
8 oz. sour cream
1 pkg. dry taco mix
2 avocados
6 oz. Monterey Jack cheese (grated)
6 oz. cheddar cheese
2 tomatoes
4-6 green onions
1 small can chopped black olives

10-15 servings

Mix and spread refried beans and bean dip on platter. Mix and spread sour cream and taco mix onto bean mixture. Mash and spread avocados over sour cream mixture. Sprinkle Monterey Jack cheese over mixture; sprinkle cheddar cheese over that. Remove the seeds from tomatoes; chop and sprinkle over cheddar cheese. Sprinkle chopped black olives and then chopped green onions. Can be refrigerated 4-5 hours. Serve with tortilla chips.

Great for campaign meetings—especially victory parties. Fills everyone up.

Culver City, just two miles from the Pacific Ocean on the west side of Los Angeles, is called the "Heart of Screenland." Home of MGM, Lorimar-Telepictures, and other major motion picture, television, and radio production companies, Culver City has served as the center of this industry for 70 years. With a moderate year-round climate, its convenient location to most major points of interest in Southern California, and its warm hospitality, Culver City is a popular place both for visitors to stay and corporations to locate.

Walnut Spread

Mayor Barbara Fass
Stockton, California

1 slice French bread (crust removed)
¼ cup milk
1 cup walnuts
½ cup parsley (cut up)
2 cloves garlic
4 tbsp. butter
¼ tsp. salt
½ cup olive oil
⅓ cup cream

10-12 servings

Soak bread in milk for about 15 minutes. Combine walnuts, parsley, and garlic and process in food processor. Squeeze the bread well and discard milk. Add the bread, butter, salt, and, while the processor is running, gradually add oil and then cream. Process until smooth. Decorate with almonds or walnut halves.

Spread on rounds of toasted bread or crackers.

This recipe may also be used as a sauce on all cooked pasta. Just add a little more cream to the sauce. Stockton resident Ina Lucchetti submitted this winning recipe for the contest.

Stockton, a modern city in the lush agricultural lands of the San Joaquin Valley, has been called the "food basket of the nation." For more information on Stockton, turn to page 183.

MAIN DISHES

Chicken a la Hawaiian

Mayor Frank F. Fasi
Honolulu, Hawaii

2 pkgs. chicken pieces
½ cup flour
1 tsp. salt
½ tsp. celery salt
¼ tsp. garlic salt
½ tsp. nutmeg
1 medium can pineapple juice
½ cup shoyu
2 tbsp. sugar

4 servings

Dust chicken with flour, salt, celery salt, garlic salt, and nutmeg and brown in melted butter. Combine pineapple juice, shoyu, and sugar; pour over chicken, cover, and simmer until tender.

Honolulu (meaning "peaceful haven") is a truly cosmopolitan city and county where no ethnic group is in the majority and where exotic cooking is an everyday happening. Whatever your taste buds crave, you can find it easily here on the 610-square-mile Island of Oahu. Located in the subtropics, Honolulu enjoys temperatures usually associated with late spring and early summer, making outdoor activities popular the year-round. As the financial, commercial, and governmental center of the mid-Pacific, Honolulu prides itself on being the major link between East and West. Honolulu is the only city in the United States today which has a Royal Palace (Iolani).

Chicken Breasts in Parmesan Cream

Mayor Dianne Feinstein
San Francisco, California

6 split chicken breasts (3 whole) (skinned and boned)
5 stalks celery (chopped)
3 medium or 4 small tomatoes (chopped)
1 tsp. tarragon
salt and pepper to taste
⅔ cup Parmesan cheese (freshly grated)
2 cups heavy cream
¼ tsp. paprika

6 servings

Place chicken in large baking pan. Sprinkle with half the cheese, surround chicken with celery and tomato, and sprinkle with seasonings. Pour cream over; sprinkle with remaining cheese. Bake in preheated oven at 350° about 50 minutes.

San Francisco is routinely called "everybody's favorite city". It is home to our world famous trolley cars, the Golden Gate bridge, fishing and amusement piers, restaurants, and Alcatraz Island. It is the commercial and cultural capital of northern California, as well as the largest urban area, with a population of more than 700,000. San Francisco is the economic dynamo for the 7,000-square mile, Bay area, and the nation's fifth largest metropolitan area.

Chicken Roll-Ups

Mayor Donald L. Dear
Gardena, California

6 chicken breasts (skinned and boned)
6 thin slices boiled ham
3 slices of mozzarella cheese (halved)
2 medium tomatoes (seeded and chopped)
¾ tsp. sage (crushed)
¾ tsp. thyme (crushed)
1 cup dried bread crumbs
4 tbsp. Parmesan cheese (grated)
2 tsp. snipped parsley
6 tbsp. butter or margarine (melted)
1 can Hollandaise Sauce

6 servings

Place chicken, boned side up, on cutting board. Place piece of waxed paper over and pound lightly with meat mallet. Removed wrap; place a ham slice and a half cheese slice on chicken. Top with tomatoes and dash each of sage and thyme. Roll up jelly-roll style and secure with toothpicks. Repeat with each breast. Combine bread crumbs, Parmesan cheese, and parsley. Dip chicken roll-ups in butter or margarine, then roll in crumbs. Place in shallow baking pan; bake at 350° for 45 minutes. Top with heated hollandaise sauce before serving.

Gardena, an All American city, is located in southern California. Its slogan, "Freeway City," was chosen by city officials because of Gardena's central location and proximity to constructed and planned freeways of the area. The city has also received national recognition for its beautification program and its program for helping children and strengthening families.

Chicken Salad with Roast Garlic Vinaigrette

Mayor Stephen Schulte
West Hollywood, California

1 chicken
1 grapefruit
¼ head Napa or chinese cabbage (slivered)
¼ lb. snow peas (slivered and blanched)
8 cloves elephant garlic (peeled)*
4 oz. fresh pasta or eggroll skins (sliced in ¼" strips)
1 qt. chicken stock, or enough to cover chicken
½ cup chicken stock to roast garlic
2 cups salad oil (enough to fry pasta)
¼ cup salad oil to roast garlic
2 cups grapefruit juice
¼ cup soy sauce
¼ cup salad oil
¼ cup sesame oil
2 tbsp. ginger (chopped)
2 tbsp. cilantro (chopped)
2 tbsp. mint (chopped)

*Elephant garlic is larger and milder than regular garlic. If you substitute regular garlic, use 4 cloves, halve them, and remove the bitter center.

4-6 servings

Heat ¼ cup salad oil in small skillet, and saute the garlic until golden. Add ½ cup stock, bring to boil, and place in 325⁰ preheated oven. Roast until garlic is soft, about 20 minutes. Remove garlic from stock; set both aside.

Heat the oil to 325⁰ in a 5-6" deep pot. Fry ¼ of pasta at a time until golden and crisp. Remove to paper towels and set aside.

Boil chicken stock; add the chicken when stock is boiling, and cook until done, about 30 minutes. Stock should be boiling to keep flavor in bird. When it's done, remove the chicken, chill it, skin it. Remove meat and cut into slivers.

Take liquid from roasted garlic, add enough stock to make 2 cups, mix in grapefruit juice, and boil until liquid is reduced by ¾. Add soy sauce and chill. When cool, mix in salad oil and sesame oil.

Peel and section grapefruit. Toss together with chicken, cabbage, peas, pasta, ginger, mint, cilantro, and ½ of dressing. Dopn't worry if the pasta breaks. Arrange on plates, garnish with roast garlic, and spoon rest of the dressing over the garlic.

West Hollywood, incorporated in 1984, is the newest city in Los Angeles County. A young and thriving city, West Hollywood's success is in large part attributable to the design industry, centered around the famous Pacific Design Center. Fashion design, the fine arts, and the musicd and movie industes are also preeminent here. To feed the fertile imaginations of these industries, West Hollywood has a collection of world famous restaurants. As the home of these innovative and trend-setting endeavors, West Hollywood well deserves its nickname, "The Creative City." This commitment to creativity would matter little, however, without the city's deep commitment to public service. One way West Hollywood celebrates its creativity while promoting the public good is by hosting the opening event of the annual Los Angeles Garlic Festival. Garlic lovers from all over enjoy this gastronomic extravaganza, which benefits the Community Emergency Relief Fund of the Los Angeles Chapter of the American Red Cross. The event features culinary treats prepared by the Los Angeles area's finest chefs, with musical entertainment by renowned jazz musicians. The accompanying recipe, from acclaimed chef Michael Roberts of Trumps, provides a healthy taste of the festival's garlicky attractions.

CITY TRIVIA QUESTION #54

Florida city that served as the headquarters for Teddy Roosevelt and his Rough Riders before the Spanish-American War.

Answer on page 74.

Chicken Sauteed with Cognac and Wild Mushrooms

Mayor Bonnel F. Pryor
Visalia, California

2 chickens	1 cup heavy cream
3 tbsp. oil	½ lb. mushrooms
salt, pepper	juice of ½ lemon
¼ cup cognac	2 tbsp. butter
1 cup chicken stock	fresh basil

6-8 servings

Bone chickens, reserving the bones for stock. Season with salt and pepper. Heat oil until very hot and place chicken in, skin side down. Saute until brown, about 8 minutes; turn chicken over and brown 2 more minutes. Remove chicken from pan and keep warm. To pan add mushrooms and saute until soft; add cognac and chicken stock and reduce to ½. Add cream; reduce again until slightly thickened. Swirl in the butter, juice of ½ lemon; taste for salt and pepper and serve.

Visalia is known as Tree City, USA, in recognition of its efforts to preserve the endangered Valley Oak Trees. Nestled among the fertile fields of California's San Joaquin Valley, Visalia offers a diversified range of business, industrial, and agricultural opportunities—all in a hometown atmosphere that makes everyone feel welcome.

CITY TRIVIA QUESTION #55

The "Longest Main Street" in the country running from the Atlantic Ocean to the Gulf of Mexico can be found in this city.

Answer on page 63.

Chicken Tortilla Casserole

Mayor Kenneth R. Prestesater
Glendora, California

6 chicken breasts
12 corn tortillas (cut in 1" squares)
1 can cream of mushroom soup
1 can cream of chicken soup
1 tsp. chicken concentrate
1 cup milk
1 can green chile salsa
1 onion (grated)
1 lb. cheddar cheese (grated)

8 servings

Wrap chicken breasts in foil and bake 1 hour at 450⁰. When baked and cooled, cut in pieces about 1" square. Save juices. Mix soups, milk, onion, and salsa. Butter large shallow baking dish and pour juice from baked chicken on bottom of dish. Place layer of tortillas on bottom, then a layer of chicken, then soup; sprinkle with grated cheese. Continue with layers, end with soup on top, then add remaining cheese on top. Make this casserole 24 hours ahead of serving. Keep in refrigerator, remove an hour before baking. Bake at 350⁰ for 1 hour.

This is a great hot dish to serve at dinner parties, buffets, and potlucks. Since it is made the day before, the host or hostess is free to enjoy his or her guests.

Glendora, "Pride of the Foothills," is a beautiful town nestled at the base of the San Gabriel Mountain Range, 27 miles east of Los Angeles. Glendora is a family-oriented community with outstanding schools, library, parks, and recreational facilities, and a business district with a unique village atmosphere. The citizens of Glendora are looking forward to a gala Centennial Celebration to honor the town's founding, 1887-1987.

Crepes a la Stockton with San Joaquin Sauce

Mayor Barbara Fass
Stockton, California

BATTER:
2 eggs
4 tbsp. Wondra flour
6 tbsp. milk
pinch salt
pinch cayenne pepper
SAUCE:
13 oz. light cream
2 tsp. cornstarch
1 egg yolk
½ cup Monterey Jack cheese (shredded)
½ cup sharp cheddar cheese (shredded)
FILLING:
1 lb. Stockton asparagus (cleaned, steamed until fork tender)
6 slices ham
2 tomatoes (sliced)

4-6 servings

Coat small skillet lightly with oil. Whip batter ingredients in small bowl with whisk until smooth. Preheat skillet over medium heat; pour in only enough batter to cover bottom of skillet. When surface of crepe appears bubbly, lift crepe and flip it over. Brown other side. Can fill or freeze for later use.

Combine all sauce ingredients in a saucepan. Cook, stirring, over low heat until mixture is thick and well blended. Do not boil.

Spoon a little sauce on each crepe. Place a ham slice and 2-3 asparagus stalks on crepe. Roll and place in buttered 9" x 13" pan. Complete all crepes. Spoon sauce over each crepe in pan; garnish with sliced tomatoes and additional asparagus. Bake 20 minutes at 325⁰.

This winning recipe was submitted by Stockton resident, Diane Lowery.

Stockton, a modern city in the lush agricultural lands of the San Joaquin Valley has been called the "food basket of the nation." For further information on Stockton, turn to page 183.

Crock Pot Chicken Tortillas

Mayor Herb. A Hennes, Jr.
Huntington Park, California

4 cups chicken or turkey (cooked)
1 10-oz. can cream of chicken soup (undiluted)
½ cup fresh tomatoes
½ cup canned Ortega chiles (diced)
6-8 flour tortillas (broken into pieces)
1 medium onion (chopped)
2 tbsp. flour
2 cups cheddar cheese (grated)

4 servings

Cut chicken or turkey into bite-size pieces. Mix well with soup, tomatoes, chiles, and flour. Line bottom of crock pot with a layer of tortillas. Add ⅓ of chicken and soup mixture and sprinkle with onions and cheese. Repeat 2 more times. Cover and cook on low 6 hours or high 3 hours.

This is a very simple and carefree recipe. It needs no watching, stirring or tasting. After it is put together forget about it until it's time to eat. It also makes a great hot dish for a buffet.

Founded in 1906, **Huntington Park** today is a vibrant multiracial, multiethnic communtiy of 50,763, housed in three square miles. Unprecedented redevelopment activity caused an increase in building activities from $1.7 million in 1976 to $18 million in 1985. Called the "City of Perfect

Balance," Huntington Park harmonizes its growth in industrial, commercial, and residential areas.

Curried Peanut Chicken

Mayor Charles Royer
Seattle, Washington

1 tsp. curry powder (or more)
1 red pepper (sliced in strips)
1 green pepper (sliced in strips)
1 large white onion (sliced)
2 fresh tomatoes (peeled) or canned whole tomatoes
1 clove garlic (minced)
1 cut-up frying chicken (or breasts)
½ cup chunky peanut butter
1 cup water
1 tbsp. olive or vegetable oil
½ lb. fresh mushrooms (optional)
salt and pepper to taste

6 servings

Saute minced garlic in oil in large, heavy pot; remove. Brown chicken, then remove from pot. Stir curry powder into oil over medium heat, saving remaining chicken bits. Add vegetables, except mushrooms; cover and cook for a few minutes. Put reserved chicken pieces in with vegetables, cover, and cook until chicken is done and a good sauce develops. Just before serving, remove chicken parts. Mix peanut butter with water; add to sauce and stir over high heat for a few minutes. Reduce to simmer, replace chicken parts, add mushrooms, and simmer for at least 10 minutes.

Serve over rice. Noodles are ok, too. Regular peanut butter with unsalted peanuts may be substituted for chunky peanut butter.

Seattle has many attractions that make it special and unique such as the Space Needle. Our strong ethnic and cultural diversity is reflected in our neighborhoods: the Asian International District, Scandinavian Ballard and "trendy Broadway," Pike Place Market, our historic Pioneer Square District, and the bustling waterfront attract many visitors as well as locals. Seattle's physical surroundings are spectacular. With the majestic Cascade and Olympic mountains to the east and west and bounded by the sparkling waters of Puget Sound and Lake Washington, its beauty is unmatched.

Easy Beef Stew

Mayor Gus Morrison
Fremont, California

3 lb. stew beef
vegetable oil
flour
salt
pepper
2 medium onions (quartered)
750 ml. inexpensive red wine
1 bunch celery (cut in 1″-2″ lengths)
1 15-oz. can tomatoes
2 pkgs. beef stew seasoning
¼ cup A-1 Steak Sauce
2 lb. frozen baby carrots
1 15-oz. can white hominy
3 cans whole new potatoes

8 servings

Dredge beef in four with salt and pepper. Brown floured beef in vegetable oil in large pot. When meat is browned, add wine, onions, celery, tomatoes, seasoning, and A-1 Sauce. Add salt and pepper to taste. If there appears to be insufficient liquid, add water to cover meat.

continued

Simmer until meat begins to become tender. Add remaining ingredients. Serve when carrots and beef are tender. As the pot boils, be sure you keep enough liquid present. (Bisquick dumplings are a good addition.)

This is a tasty stew but one should be careful to select the right wine. It must be the cheapest bottle of red wine available and it must have a screw top. Corks only ruin the flavor of the stew.

Fremont, California, is a city of 153,000 people on 96 square miles on the Southeast shore of San Francisco Bay. The city is framed by an impressive set of open hills to the east and the San Francisco Bay National Wildlife Refuge to the west. Fremont has combined the advantages of a modern city with the maintenance of its historical roots, Mission San Jose and Niles, the original Hollywood. It is the home of the California Schools for the Deaf and Blind, the new United Motors manufacturing plant (the joint venture between General Motors and Toyota), and is presently attracting large numbers of high technology firms.

Goose Hollow Inn Reuben Sandwich

Mayor J.E. "Bud" Clark
Portland, Oregon

| Russian rye bread |
| Russian dressing (made of ⅓ chili sauce and ⅔ mayonnaise) |
| sauerkraut |
| natural Swiss cheese (sliced) |
| corned brisket of beef |
| garlic |
| bay leaf |

Makes 1 sandwich

Cook corned beef brisket in water with garlic cloves and bay leaf. Cook until tender, so all of the fat is cooked out, leaving only the rich flavor. Use Russian rye, since it is a heavy bread with no seeds in it, and Russian dressing (which is Thousand Island without the pickles). Put dressing on each piece of bread. Put sauerkraut on one piece of bread and top with natural Swiss. On the other piece, put slices of corned beef brisket. Toast sandwich in a pizza oven, or on the lower half of regular oven preheated to 500°, until cheese is completely melted.

This sandwich is popular at Goose Hollow Inn, the restaurant/tavern which I have run for a number of years.

Picturesque **Portland** is nestled under Mt. Hood, at the confluence of the spectacular Columbia and Willamette rivers. It is an eminently livable city of quiet neighborhoods, good restaurants, and abundant parks. Known as the City of Roses because of Washington Park's famous Rose Test Gardens, Portland has the largest wilderness park totally within the limits of an American city. The bustling downtown area, traversed by the Transit Mall and served by the brand new Banfield Light Rail system, is crowned with the newly erected 6½-ton copper statue of Portlandia, who kneels on a portico of the city's municipal building designed by architect Michael Graves. She is a symbol of the city—a burnished gold statue of a woman holding a trident high in one outstretched hand while the other beckons a friendly welcome to tourists and businesses alike.

CITY TRIVIA QUESTION #56

The poet, Henry Wadsworth Longfellow, grew up in this northeastern city and mentions his boyhood city in his collection of works about the sea.

Answer on page 25.

Grilled King Salmon

Mayor Tony Knowles
Anchorage, Alaska

6 salmon steaks (about 1" thick)	
MARINADE:	
3 tbsp. butter (melted)	¼ cup lemon juice
1 cup mayonnaise	½ tsp. dry mustard
2 cloves garlic (crushed)	

6 servings

Mix marinade ingredients and brush generously on steaks. Refrigerate for 2 hours. Prepare grill by oiling it to prevent fish from sticking. At medium height over a bed of coals, cook until browned (about 5 minutes) and turn, basting all the while with marinade. Grill until fish is flaky and cooked through. Serve hot.

Many people who don't generally like fish, love this recipe. This is best, of course, done next to the river right after the salmon has been caught, but store bought fish will work too.

Anchorage, Alaska's largest community, was selected as an All American City in 1956, 1965, and 1985 and is America's choice for hosting the 1992 Winter Olympic Games. Mount McKinley, in Denali State Park, is 150 miles north of town. Being visible from Anchorage on many clear days, it's not uncommon, but still a treat to hear people say "McKinley's Out!" One of Anchorage's most unusual features is the amount of daylight. On June 21st residents and visitors alike enjoy 19 hours and 28 minutes of daylight. On December 21st people live with 19 hours and 28 minutes of darkness and look forward to June. Anchorage is a cultural and recreational bonanza with its own dance, theater, and music companies and more than 220 miles of bike trails that stretch throughout the municipality.

Gumbo

Mayor Eugene "Gus" Newport
Berkeley, California

⅔ cup flour
⅔ cup vegetable oil
1 3-3½ lb. fryer (cut up)
1 lb. Polish sausage
½ lb. ham (cut in cubes)
12-15 crab claws (if unavailable, substitute 1 or 2 pkgs. frozen crabmeat)
2 cups onion (chopped)
2 tbsp parsley (finely minced)
1 pt. raw oysters
1 lb. shrimp
½ tsp. cayenne
1½ tsp. black pepper
½ cup green onions
3-4 cups water or water and chicken broth
2 tbsp. garlic (finely minced)
3 bay leaves
1 cup celery (chopped)
1 tsp. dried thyme
3 tbsp. file powder
salt

6-8 servings

Use about a 6-quart pot. In about ⅔ cup vegetable oil, brown chicken (optional: lightly flour chicken and season it with Creole seasoning before browning). After chicken is brown, remove it and add about ⅔ cup flour to the oil to make roux. Cook over low flame, stirring constantly until roux is dark brown. Turn off fire and quickly add sausage, ham, onion, parsley, celery, and garlic. Continue cooking over low flame for 10 minutes, stirring constantly. Add about 1-1½ cups liquid (1 cup chicken broth, ½ cup water), the browned chicken parts and all other ingredients except the shrimp, oysters, and file powder. Mix gently but

continued

thoroughly; bring to boil. When boiling, reduce heat, simmer until chicken is tender.

About 5-10 minutes before serving, add shrimp, then oysters. When they have cooked, turn off the fire. Mix the file powder in a little water, and add it to the Gumbo. Let gumbo stand about 5 minutes before serving. While cooking the Gumbo, add a little water now and then to get the consistency you like. Serve over steamed rice. (Remember, gumbo spoils easily, do not let it sit out too long. Refrigerate it if it has to stand more than an hour or two.)

Berkeley is located approximately 20 minutes away from San Francisco and is the home of the University of California. A city of more than 100,000, Berkeley often has a small town feel, proud of its tradition of cultural diversity and alternative lifestyles that coexist with a fast-growing high tech industrial center. Its many fine and diversified restaurants, including Chez Panisse, the originator of "California Cuisine," add to the richness of Berkeley's city life.

Leg of Lamb

Mayor Don Roth
Anaheim, California

leg of lamb (no larger than 6 lbs.)
garlic
pepper
salt
lemon
butter (softened)
bread crumbs
olive oil

6-8 servings

Cut several slits in lamb; fill with pieces of garlic. Spread butter over entire top of lamb. Salt and pepper all over. Cover with aluminum foil and bake at 425⁰. For well done lamb, cook 2½ hours; for rare, 1½ hours.

Unwrap lamb 15 minutes before meat is done and cut thin slice down top. Cover top with bread crumbs that have been mixed with softened butter and a little olive oil. Place lamb back in oven for last 15-20 minutes to brown.

Just before serving squeeze a little lemon juice over top of lamb. Place whole lamb on tray that has been covered with nice size green lettuce leaves and slice at table.

Anaheim, home of the California Angels, Los Angeles Rams, and the one and only original Disneyland, is known as "The Hub of Happiness." We are located in beautiful Orange County, California and we have some of the finest restaurants and hotel accommodations anywhere, plus outstanding convention facilities.

Lemon Chicken

Mayor Tom Bradley
Los Angeles, California

1 whole chicken (quartered)
¼ cup lemon pepper
1 lemon (sliced)
parsley

4 servings

Clean chicken thoroughly. Season with lemon pepper; top with lemon slices and place in covered baking dish. Bake in 375⁰ oven until done (approximately 45 minutes). Garnish with parsley.

Los Angeles, the second largest city in the nation, is a leader and innovator in California. As the host site for the successful 1984 Olympic Summer Games, Los Angeles was in the international spotlight and could boast its rich cultural diversity.

With residents from every nation in the world, Los Angeles has the influential position of leading the state in international trade with the Pacific rim. From the beaming high-rise buildings downtown to the incredible variety of bustling ethnic neighborhoods, from the lights and action of a Hollywood sound stage, to the crashing waves of the Pacific Ocean, Los Angeles is a diverse and always-changing city.

ed in green parkways, scenic waterways, and stately oaks. In addition, Sacramento is host to many of California's historic sites, including the restored State Capitol, Sutter's Fort, and Old Sacramento. Sacramento's setting at the confluence of two rivers makes it an excellent choice for boating, waterskiing, fishing, rafting, and other sports. Our annual Dixieland Jazz Festival and Camellia Festival are world famous.

Middle Eastern Chicken

Mayor Anne Rudin
Sacramento, California

2 tbsp. lemon juice
2 whole chicken breasts (boned and halved)
2 cloves garlic
1 tsp. salt
¼ tsp. ground pepper
1 tbsp. fresh mint (chopped)
1 cup plain yogurt

4 servings

Sprinkle lemon juice over chicken in glass baking dish; let stand for 10 minutes, turning once. Chop garlic with salt and mash together. Mix with pepper, mint, and yogurt in small bowl. Spread mixture over chicken, spooning any excess lemon juice over chicken. Marinate 1 hour at room temperature. Place chicken on broiler pan rack, skin side down. Set pan so that chicken is about 7" from heat. Broil 8-10 minutes on each side.

This is a quick and elegant dish that I have made many times, always successfully. It is so easy that even a mayor's husband can make it. Serve with bulghur.

Sacramento is a growing, vibrant city located in one of the world's most fertile valleys. It is nestled between the American and the Sacramento rivers and is blessed with a natural beauty express-

Pizza with Stewed Whole Garlic

Mayor Eugene "Gus" Newport
Berkeley, California

DOUGH: ¼ cup rye flour
1¾ cups bleached all purpose flour
2 tbsp. olive oil
1 tbsp milk
2 tsp. active dry yeast
¾ cup lukewarm water
½ tsp. salt
TOPPING (optional):
several heads of garlic
olive oil
1 red onion (sliced)
strips of anchovy filets (chopped)
fresh basil (chopped)
black pepper

4-6 servings

Pizza Dough:
Make a sponge by mixing together ¼ cup lukewarm water, 2 tsp. active dry yeast, and ¼ cup rye flour. Let it rise 20-30 minutes, then add ½ cup lukewarm water, 1 tbsp. milk, 2 tbsp. olive oil, ½ tsp. salt, and 1¾ cups unbleached all purpose flour. Mix the dough with a wooden spoon, then knead on a floured board. It will be soft and a little sticky. Use quick light motions with your

hands so the dough doesn't stick. Add more flour to the board as you knead but no more than is absolutely necessary. A soft, moist dough makes a light and very crispy crust. Knead for 10-15 minutes to develop strength and elasticity in the dough. Put it in a bowl rubbed with olive oil, and oil the surface of the dough to prevent a crust from forming. Cover the bowl with a towel and put it in a warm place, approximately 90^0 to 110^0. (An oven heated just by its pilot light is a good spot.) Let the dough rise to double its size, about 2 hours, then punch it down. Let it rise about 40 minutes more, then shape and bake it. This recipe makes one 12" to 14" pizza or several small ones.

One of the very best ways to bake a pizza is directly on the floor of a wood-fired brick or stone oven. The intense heat of a wood fire can drive the temperature to 500^0 or more, and it gives the dough a smoky flavor. When the dough slides onto the hot bricks it reacts instantly: both top and bottom of the pizza cook at once. Not too many households have a brick oven to bake in, but the effect can be approximated by putting a layer of unglazed ceramic tiles on a rack in your oven. Preheat the oven to 450^0-500^0. Use a wooden paddle made especially for the purpose, or the back of a baking sheet, to put the pizza in and remove it from the oven.

Flatten the dough on a heavily floured board. Use a rolling piin to roll the dough to roughly 12"-14" in diameter. The dough should be 1/8"-1/4" thick. Transfer the dough to a paddle or baking sheet, also heavily floured. Have your toppings ready, at room temperature, and work quickly putting them on the pizza. After a minute or so it will begin to stick, and will be impossible to slide off the paddle. When garnishing the pizza, anticipate flavor and balance. A light hand with weighty ingredients such as cheese, tomatoes, sausage, and so on, and bold amounts of fresh herbs, garlic, anchovies, flavored oils, and the like, works best. It is better to err on the side of too little flavor. Tomatoes and other wet foods should be drained of excess liquid. Too much weight or moisture on the dough makes it difficult for it to rise and cook well on the bottom. Whatever is on top must be able to cook in 15 minutes, or should have had some partial cooking beforehand. Beware of spilling anything wet or oily between the dough and paddle, as that too will prevent it from sliding. Give the paddle a few shakes back and forth to make sure the dough is loose. Slide the pizza from the paddle onto the hot tiles in the oven with abrupt jerking motions of your wrist. This takes a certain knack but comes easily after a few tries. The pizza will be browned and cooked in 12-15 minutes.

When you roll and shape the dough, feel free to make it any shape you wish. Large flat pizzas with uneven bubbly edges have a rustic appeal. Small individual-sized pizzas, served as a savory accompaniment to a meal, instead of bread, are very satisfying.

If your oven cannot maintain an intense heat of 450-500^0, then the dough will perform better if rolled a little on the thick side, $\frac{1}{4}$" or more. When the dough is rolled thin and requires 20 to 25 minutes to cook at some temperature less than 450^0, it tends to have a cracker-like texture. A thicker dough allows for a bready interior and a crusty exterior. When you are deciding if the pizza is cooked, check the bottom to make sure it is quite crisp. The crust always softens a bit when it cools down. The real purpose of the tiles is to make a good texture on the bottom of the pizza.

Stewed whole garlic topping:

Peel cloves of several heads of garlic and stew them slowly in olive oil, stirring constantly, until soft and beginning to carmelize, about 15-20 minutes. Soften a sliced red onion in olive oil. Spread these over the dough and bake it. When it comes from the oven, drizzle with olive oil and garnish with strips of anchovy filets, chopped basil, and black pepper.

Berkeley, home to many fine restaurants, including Chez Panisse, the originator of "California Cuisine." For further information on Berkeley turn to pages 197 and 198.

Pollo Tortilla

Mayor Brian O'Toole
Sunnyvale, California

4 whole chicken breasts
1 dozen corn tortillas
1 can cream of chicken soup
½ cup chopped black olives
1 can cream of mushroom soup
1 cup milk
1 onion (grated)
1 clove garlic
1 can green chili salsa
1 lb sharp cheddar cheese (grated)

8 servings

Bake breasts in foil at 400⁰ for 1 hour. Bone chicken and cut into large pieces; reserve any juices. Cut tortillas into strips or squares. Mix soups, milk, onion, salsa, and chicken juices.

Butter large shallow baking dish. Place layer of tortillas in dish, then chicken, then soup mixture. Continue layers until all ingredients are used, ending with soup mixture. Top with cheese and olives. Refrigerate 24 hours.

Bake at 300⁰ for 1-1½ hours.

Sunnyvale, located in the "Heart of Silicon Valley" prides itself on its solid management practices. An "All America City," Sunnyvale has a low crime rate, good community involvement, and a high quality of lifestyle.

CITY TRIVIA QUESTION #57

This midwestern city is often used as a test market for national products. (Hint: If it "plays here, it will play anywhere.")

Answer on page 128.

Pork/Chicken Monterey

Mayor G. Monty Manibog
Monterey Park, California

1½ lb. pork boneless shoulder
1½ lb. chicken legs or thighs
½ cup water
1 cup white wine vinegar
6 cloves garlic (chopped)
2 tbsp. soy sauce
1 tsp. garlic salt
¼ tsp. pepper
2 tbsp. vegetable oil
hot cooked rice

8 servings

Trim fat from pork; cut pork into 1" cubes. Heat pork, chicken, water, vinegar, garlic, soy sauce, salt and pepper to boiling in Dutch oven; reduce heat. Cover and simmer until pork and chicken are done, 45-55 minutes.

Remove pork and chicken from Dutch oven. Skim fat from broth if necessary. Cook broth uncovered until reduced to about 1 cup. Heat oil in 10" skillet until hot. Cook chicken in oil over medium heat until brown on all sides. Add pork; cook and stir until brown. Serve pork, chicken, and broth over rice. Garnish with snipped parsley and tomato wedges if desired.

This dish reflects an exotic blending of the Filipino, Chinese and Spanish influence and is a spicy treat to the western taste buds.

Monterey Park, selected as an "All American City" in 1985 by the National Municipal League, lies immediately east of Los Angeles. First settled by Gabrielino Indians, then colonized by Spain and Mexico, it is now home to 60,000 happy residents of diverse ethnic and cultural backgrounds, essentially Asian, Latino, and Anglo (including many recent immigrants), living and working together harmoniously. As a host city to the 1984 World Olympic Games and known for its outreach, people programs, Monterey Park is an upper middle class community that enjoys the reputation as "The Olympic City with a Heart."

Portuguese Stew

Mayor Hannibal Tavares
Maui, Hawaii

| regular stew fixings |
| Portuguese sausage (linquesa) |

Cook regular stew—any kind—but add generous amount of linquesa for special flavor!

This stew was a popular entry in St. Francis Hospital's 1985 ''beef stew cook-off'' in Honolulu, Hawaii, and took second place honors.

The County of **Maui** comprises a group of what may easily be claimed as the most beautiful, God-blessed islands in the world. Located in the middle of Hawaii, the islands of Maui County (Lanai, Molokai, Maui, and Kahoolawe), glisten like jewels in the Pacific pendant that is Hawaii, our nation's 50th and youngest state. Maui's exotic vistas, balmy weather, friendly and charming people who represent a mix of so many different nationalities have made it a unique and highly desirable place to live or visit. Today, it is one of the world's most popular vacation spots, and

through careful planning, it has lived up to its slogan, established in the days of ancient Hawaii when the islands of Maui were proudly lauded as "Maui No Ka Oi," Hawaiian for "Maui is the Best."

Sarrma (Pig in a Blanket)

Mayor Joseph E. Cvetko
Bellflower, California

| 1 medium head cabbage |
| 1 large can sauerkraut |
| 4-5 strips of bacon |
| 1 small can tomato suace |
| 2 lb. ground beef |
| ½ cup onion (chopped) |
| 2 eggs |
| 1 tsp. salt |
| ½ cup Minute Rice |

5-6 servings

Soften cabbage head in hot water until leaves can be taken off whole. Mix together ground beef, onion, eggs, salt, and rice. Take small amount of ground beef mix and roll up in one softened cabbage leaf. Layer rolls in pan on top of half the sauerkraut. Add remaining sauerkraut, tomato sauce, and bacon strips. Add water to almost cover "pigs." Cook on low heat two hours, or longer.

Serve "Pigs" with mashed potatoes. "Pigs" are just as good the next day and several days later.

Bellflower, situated 12 miles from the Pacific Ocean, is an all American city of 57,000 people of many nationalities and races blending together to show why we have as our slogan, "The Friendly City." That spirit is shown in our city seal, which depicts two hands reaching out together in friendship. A bedroom community where people live and work elsewhere, Bellflower is a city of many fine churches, schools, shopping centers, and parks and recreation facilities for all our residents.

CITY TRIVIA QUESTION #58

Terminus, was the former city name of this Georgia city which is also the home of Coca Cola.

Answer on page 77.

Sauteed Fish and Bell Pepper

Mayor Sheila Lodge
Santa Barbara, California

2 large cooking onions (sliced thin)
2 red bell peppers (sliced thin)
2 tbsp. lightly flavored olive oil or cooking oil
1 lb. fresh ling cod, white sea bass, sheepshead, or other firm fish (fileted and sliced thin)
2 tbsp. dry vermouth

4-5 servings

Saute onion and bell pepper in oil in a large frying pan until tender. Add fish and vermouth. Stir fry just until the fish is cooked. Serve with herb rice (see Accompaniments section).

15% of the boats in Santa Barbara's harbor are commercial fishing boats. They bring in a variety of seafood including red snapper, lobster, shrimp, halibut, crab and abalone along with the varieties in the recipe. Santa Barbara may be the largest sea urchin port in the world. Most of the sea urchin roe—a sushi delicacy—is shipped to Japan. The rest is consumed in sushi bars in the U.S.

Santa Barbara lies between mountains rising to 4,000 feet on one side and more than six miles of public beaches on the other. The city's racially, ethnically, and economically diverse population enjoys a beautiful natural setting and a very temperate climate as well as excellent art, natural history, and history museums; a Botanic Garden of California native plants; and preservation of Santa Barbara's historic tradition in its Hispanic architecture. During President Reagan's visits to his ranch, Santa Barbara serves as the "Western White House" to staff and reporters.

Tortilla Salad

Mayor Gil De La Rosa
Pico Rivera, California

1 onion
4 tomatoes
1 head lettuce
1 bag tortilla chips
1 lb. ground round
1 avacado
8 oz. 1000 Island dressing
4 oz. cheddar cheese (grated)
1 can kidney beans
hot sauce to taste

6 servings

Chop onion, tomatoes, and lettuce. Toss with cheese, 1000 Island dressing, and hot sauce. Crunch tortilla chips and add them, slice avocado and add it. Brown ground round with drained beans, simmer. Mix into chilled salad.

Makes an ordinary meal a real festive affair! Serve with a cold pitcher of Margaritas.

Pico Rivera, located ten miles southeast of Los Angeles, is very close to both ocean and mountains. It is close to Orange County attractions, a perfect bedroom community with no local taxes.

CITY TRIVIA QUESTION #59

Texas city that was the last major stopover on the Chisholm Trail. Its famous stockyards keep the western heritage alive today.

Answer on page 166.

Zucchini Pesto Quiche

Mayor Alex Giuliani
Hayward, California

1 9" prebaked pastry shell
3 small to medium zucchini (halved and cut in ¼" slices)
2 tbsp. pesto (recipe below)
2 cups Swiss cheese (grated)
1¼ cups Jack cheese (grated)
2 cloves garlic (minced)
½ tsp. white pepper
¼ tsp. cayenne pepper
¼ cup red bell pepper (chopped)
3 eggs
1 cup half-and-half
EASY PESTO:
1 cup chopped basil leaves (cleaned and dried)
3 cloves garlic
½ cup pine nuts or walnuts
½ cup Parmesan cheese (grated)
½ cup good quality olive oil

8 servings

Precook zucchini (saute in butter or microwave 5 minutes). Cool and drain off excess moisture. In mixing bowl, combine zucchini, pesto, cheeses, seasonings, and pepper. Mound filling in pastry shell. Whisk eggs and half-and-half until smooth. Pour over filling. Bake in preheated 375⁰ oven for 30 minutes or until done. If top begins to brown too fast, cover with foil. Quiche is done when knife inserted in center comes out clean. Allow to stand on wire rack 5-10 minutes before cutting. Serve hot. Quiche may be reheated. (Great with sour cream.)

Easy Pesto: In a blender, combine basil, garlic, nuts, and cheese. Slowly add oil while blender is running. Makes about 1½ cups.

This recipe won first prize in our Annual Zucchini Cooking Contest, one of the events preceding our City's Zucchini Festival held in August. It is absolutely delicious as well as nutritious.

Hayward is the hub of the San Francisco Bay Area, with a population of more than 100,000. It is a very diversified city with many residential areas, industrial parks, its own airport, housing over 500 private and business-owned planes, a state college, a community college, and excellent park and recreational facilities.

ACCOMPANIMENTS

Artichoke Casserole

Mayor Anthony A. Giammona
Daly City, California

3 boxes frozen artichokes (cooked as directed on pkg.)
1 chopped onion
1-2 cloves garlic
¼ cup chopped parsley
2-3 tbsp. olive oil
6 eggs (slightly beaten)
2 slices white bread (crumbled in ½ cup milk)
¾ cup grated Parmesan cheese
¼ tsp. each salt and pepper
1 tsp. Italian Seasoning
paprika

6-8 servings

Chop artichokes when cool. Saute onion, garlic and parsley in olive oil, add to slightly beaten eggs. Add all of the rest of ingredients. Pour into a 9" x 13" x 2" lightly greased baking dish. Sprinkle with paprika. Bake ½ hour in 350⁰ oven. Cut into squares.

Can be served as a side vegetable hot or can be served in smaller pieces for a cold appetizer.

Daly City is proudly celebrating its 75th anniversary since its incorporation on March 22, 1911. Daly City is located south and adjacent to San Francisco in San Mateo County. It has a population of nearly 83,000 people, and it is rich in ethnic and racial influence. Like many cities across the country, we have grown and changed to keep up with the needs and times of our citizens. Housing continues to be the cornerstone of our community. However, over the years, Daly City has become a noted regional center for shopping, entertainment, and transportation. Daly City is proud of its accomplishments and growth during the past 75 years, and is looking to a bright and expanding future.

Better Bagels

Mayor Howard J. Snider
Ontario, California

100 lb. high gluten flour	
25 lb. coarse ground whole wheat flour	
10 lb. cracked wheat	
60 oz. malt	
32 oz. salt	
16 oz. S.A.F. yeast	
5 lb. dehydrated apple bits	
15 lb. raisins	
10 lb. honey	
67 lb. water	

Makes 900-1000

Mix dry ingredients. Add honey and water and mix for 8-10 minutes in a 300-pound mixer. Mix in raisins and apples. Roll 4-ounce pieces of dough between hands to form fat snakes; join ends together. Bake 10-12 minutes at 500⁰. After first 15 seconds inject steam into oven.

This recipe comes straight from my Better Baked Bagel Bakery.

Ontario, California, located 40 miles east of Los Angeles, is a community with an international image. Flights arrive and depart daily from the new international airport. A World Fest is now in the planning stages for next year to recognize the many cultures and foods that make Ontario a special place to live.

Blueberry Salad

Mayor Ernie Kell
Long Beach, California

1 pkg. unflavored gelatin	½ cup hot water
¼ cup cold water	1 cup sugar
1 pkg. raspberry gelatin	1 cup table cream
1 cup hot water	1 pt. sour cream
1 can blueberries (undrained)	pinch of salt

6 servings

Combine unflavored gelatin with ¼ cup cold water and ½ cup hot water; set aside. Combine sugar, cream, sour cream, salt; add gelatin mixture and refrigerate until firm. In the meantime, mix raspberry gelatin with 1 cup hot water. Add blueberries and their juice. Pour over top of first mixture after that mixture is firmly set.

Good for buffet—very pretty looking.

Long Beach, California, has a population of approximately 400,000. It has several miles of beachfront, and one of the largest ports in the country. It is the home of the *Queen Mary* and *Spruce Goose*, and is soon to have a large world trade center.

Curry Rice Salad

Mayor Thomas McEnery
San Jose, California

| 1 pkg. Chicken Rice-a-Roni |
| 2 green onions (thinly sliced) |
| ½ green pepper (chopped) |
| 8 pimento olives (sliced) |
| 2 jars marinated artichoke hearts (drain, reserve marinade) |
| ½ tsp. curry powder or to taste |
| ⅓ cup mayonnaise |

6 servings

Cook rice according to directions, using oil instead of butter. Cool. Add onion, green peppers, olives, and artichoke hearts. Mix curry powder and mayonnaise together adding about half the artichoke marinade to make a dressing for the salad. Mix all ingredients well and toss with the dressing. Chill overnight.

San Jose, California's first capital and one of its oldest cities, has a rich history as the center of the agriculturally abundant Santa Clara County. Today, San Jose is California's fourth largest city, and its downtown is being recreated as the transportation, cultural, and economic center of what is now known as Silicon Valley—birthplace of high technology.

Herb Rice

Mayor Sheila Lodge
Santa Barbara, California

| 1½ tbsp. lightly flavored olive oil, other cooking oil, or butter |
| 1½ cups raw white rice |
| ½ tsp. dried basil leaves (crumbled) |
| ½ tsp. dried oregano leaves (crumbled) |
| ½ tsp. salt |
| 2¾ cups water |

4-5 servings

Heat oil or butter in 6-cup pot over medium heat. Add rice, herbs, and salt; stir until rice begins to turn opaquely white. Add water, bring to a boil, and cover. Reduce heat to low and simmer for 18 minutes (don't overcook). Stir rice to fluff.

Both rice and fish recipes (see Main Dish section) are easy to prepare, an essential requirement for a mayor's schedule!

Santa Barbara lies between mountains rising to 4,000 feet on one side and over 6 miles of public beaches on the other. For further information on Santa Barbara, turn to page 203.

Pesto-Cheese Torta

Mayor Barbara J. Doerr
Redondo Beach, California

| 1½ lb. cream cheese (softened) |
| 1½ lb. butter (softened) |
| sprig of basil |
| French bread baguettes (thinly sliced) |
| PESTO: |
| 3¼ cups fresh basil leaves and fresh spinach (half of each, firmly packed) |

1½ cups Parmesan or Romano cheese (freshly grated)

½ cup olive oil

6 tbsp. pine nuts

1 clove garlic (pressed)

Makes about 6 cups

With an electic mixer beat cream cheese and butter until smooth, scraping mixture down from sides of bowl as needed.

Prepare pesto: in blender or processor mix basil and spinach leaves, cheese, olive oil; stir in pine nuts and garlic. Season with salt and pepper. Set aside.

Cut 2 18″ squares of cheesecloth, moisten with water, wring dry, and lay flat one on top of the other. Use cloth to line mold smoothly—can use a 6″ flower pot. With fingers or rubber spatula, spread 1/8 of the cheese mixture in the prepared mold. Cover with 1/7 of the pesto filling, extending it to sides of mold. Repeat layering until mold is filled, ending with cheese.

Fold ends of cloth over top and press down lightly with your hands to compact. Refrigerate until torta feels firm when pressed, about 1-1½ hours. Invert onto serving dish and gently pull off cheesecloth. (If allowed to stand longer, cloth will act as a wick and cause color to bleed onto cheese.)

If made ahead of time, cover with plastic wrap and refrigerate up to 5 days. Garnish with basil sprig and serve with French bread slices.

Redondo Beach, California—a beautiful, urban coastal community located at the southern end of the Santa Monica Bay. Incorporated in 1892, today Redondo Beach is a pleasant mixture of old and new. Our 60,000 residents are attracted to Redondo's scenic waterfront, beaches, Veterans Park with our beautiful historic public library, and King Harbor, which consists of 1600 boat slips, restaurants, hotels, and the Seaside Lagoon. Our historic piers, modernized for the enjoyment of local residents and visitors, draw fishermen, shoppers, and diners alike. Our desirable coastal climate, with year-round warm air and cool breezes, and coastal recreational opportunities, bring millions of visitors each year.

Round Loaf Soda Bread

Mayor Christine E. Reed
Santa Monica, California

4 cups flour

1 cup sugar

1 tsp. baking powder

1 tsp. salt

1½ cubes butter or margarine

1⅓ cups buttermilk or sour milk

1 cup currants or raisins

12 servings

Coarsely mix butter with dry ingredients. Add milk and currants. Turn dough on lightly floured board; knead 30 seconds. Shape into 2 round loaves on greased cookie sheet; slash tops of loaves. Bake at 350⁰ for 1 hour. When done brush the tops with melted butter. Sprinkle top with caraway seed if desired. To serve, cut in wedges. It should be served warm—may be reheated in damp brown paper bag.

This bread has been enjoyed by everyone who has tasted it and it disappears quickly.

Santa Monica is located in the western portion of Los Angeles County at the Pacific Ocean. The city has an extensive recreational coastline and enjoys an ideal climate. Population is more than 90,000 and the city covers about 8.3 square miles. Educational, medical, shopping, religious, cultural, and business facilities are in abundance.

Sourdough Bread

Mayor Tony Knowles
Anchorage, Alaska

STARTER:	
2½ cups lukewarm water	1 tbsp. yeast
3 cups all purpose flour	
DAY 1:	
1 cup sourdough starter	2½ cups flour
2 cups lukewarm water	
DAY 2:	
4 cups all purpose flour	2 tbsp. sugar
½ tsp. baking soda	3 tbsp. oil
2 tbsp. salt	

Makes 2 loaves

For Starter: Pour water into a large bowl. (It is very important that water is lukewarm; too hot or cold will kill yeast.) Add yeast and wait a few minutes until dissolved. Add flour and beat mixture vigorously until blended. Pour into a jar or crock and cover. Set in a warm place for 24 hours. When you use the starter, take what you need, but leave at least 1 cup of starter in the jar. Add a cup of flour and ¾ cup water to the jar and mix. Put the covered jar in the refrigerator. It will store for several weeks. You can continue to add to this starter for years if you're careful with it. Some Alaskans *claim* their starters are 100 years old.

Day 1: In a large bowl, add ingredients to sourdough starter, cover with a tea towel, and put in a warm place for 24 hours.

Day 2: Mix ingredients into prepared batter. (At this point you should be able to work dough into a ball, if not, add more flour until dough is firm.) Knead dough for 10 minutes on a well floured surface. Coat with oil and drop into a large bowl. Cover and let rise until double (about 2 hours). Punch dough down, divide in two and form into long loaves on a well greased cookie sheet. Cover with a tea towel and let rise until doubled. Bake at 375⁰ for about 1 hour. Serve warm with butter.

This recipe takes a lot of time, especially if you're beginning with a new starter. It requires a lot of patience and a pioneering spirit, but is well worth the waiting.

Anchorage has over 220 miles of bike trails stretching throughout the municipality. For additional information on Anchorage, see page 197.

Spinach Salad

Mayor Tom Bradley
Los Angeles, California

spinach greens (amount depends on personal preference)
3-4 slices bacon (cooked crisp)
1 hard-cooked egg (grated)
oil and vinegar dressing

1-2 servings

Select tender spinach greens from the produce market, wash thoroughly, cut off stems. Refrigerate in a plastic bag for crispness. Cook 3-4 slices of bacon until very crisp (no fat should remain). Break chilled spinach greens into bite-size pieces in salad bowl. Add cool, crumbled bacon bits. Add dressing to taste and mix. Sprinkle top with grated hard-cooked egg. Serve immediately.

Ideal with beef, or fish main dishes.

Los Angeles is the second largest city in the United States. For further information on Los Angeles, turn to pages 198 and 199.

Stockton Salad

Mayor Barbara Fass
Stockton, California

2 pkgs. frozen mixed vegetables
½ cup green onions (sliced)
½ cup green olives (sliced)
½ cup asparagus (blanched)
⅓ cup olive oil
3 tbsp. wine vinegar
2 cloves garlic (crushed)
1 tbsp. capers
1½ tsp. salt
1/8 tsp. pepper

6-8 servings

Cook mixed vegetables until just crisp. Drain and chill. Mix with olives, onions, and asparagus. Combine oil, vinegar, capers, garlic, salt, and pepper. Dress salad and allow to marinate in refrigerator about 1 hour before serving. Put in crisp lettuce leaves and serve.

This salad recipe, submitted by Janet Clark, was judged a winner.

Stockton, a modern city in the lush agricultural lands of the San Joaquin Valley has been called the "food basket of the nation." For further information on Stockton, turn to pages 183.

CITY TRIVIA QUESTION #60

The 1904 World's Fair held in this city was known for a number of firsts—first hot dog, first ice cream cone and first glass of iced tea.

Answer on page 127.

Zucchini Bread

Mayor Philip R. Maurer
Newport Beach, California

3 eggs
1 cup oil
1 cup brown sugar
1 cup sugar
2 tsp. vanilla
3 cups flour
2 tsp. baking soda
½ tsp. baking powder
1 tsp. salt
1½ tsp. cinnamon
¾ tsp. nutmeg
1 cup raisins
1 cup crushed pineapple (well drained)
2 cups zucchini (coarsely grated)
1 cup walnuts (chopped)

Makes 2 loaves

Preheat oven to 350°. Beat eggs, sugars, oil, and vanilla. Stir in dry ingredients. Fold in zucchini, pineapple, raisins, and nuts until mixed. Pour into 2 lightly greased loaf pans. Bake 55 minutes.

Newport Beach is a quaint community made up of five small villages bound together by the beautiful Newport Harbor. The harbor is about two square miles in size and is home for some 10,000 yachts. The assessed valuation makes it the boating capital of the West. Newport Beach has a constant population of 67,800, which grows to more than 100,000 on weekends and during the summer. The harbor and beaches have become the playground for all of Orange County.

DESSERTS

Tucked away on a little peninsula, 130 miles south of San Francisco and 350 miles north of Los Angeles, lies the most elegant of America's beach towns—**Carmel-by-the-Sea**. The history of Carmel has been entwined with the birth of California some 50 years after Columbus discovered the new world. Cabrillo, on an exploratory voyage for Spain, first sited the white sand beaches and pine forests that eventually were to lie within the Carmel city limits. Today Carmel is a quaint little beach town filled with interesting shops and eateries. It is also the home of the Carmel Mission and is part of the 17-mile Highway 1 scenic drive from Pebble Beach.

Apple Pie

Mayor Clint Eastwood
Carmel-by-the-Sea, California

PIE SHELL:
1½ cups flour
2 tsp. sugar
1 tsp. salt
½ cup vegetable oil
2 tbsp. milk
FILLING:
⅔ cup sugar
¼ cup flour
1 tsp. cinnamon
3-4 cups apples (sliced)
½ cup sour cream
TOPPING:
⅓ cup flour
⅓ cup brown sugar (firmly packed)
½ tsp. cinnamon
¼ cup butter

6-8 servings

Heat oven to 375°. Combine pie shell ingredients; mix well. Pat into ungreased 9" pie pan and flute edges.

Combine filling ingredients; mix well and fill pie shell. Combine topping ingredients; sprinkle over pie and bake 45 minutes.

Arcadian Apple Cake

Mayor Mary B. Young
Arcadia, California

1 cup shortening
1 cup sugar
¾ cup brown sugar
2 eggs
1 cup buttermilk
2½ cups flour
½ tsp. salt
1 tsp. baking powder
1 tsp baking soda
2½ tsp. cinnamon
2 cups apples (pared and cubed)
TOPPING:
½ cup brown sugar
1 tsp. cinnamon
¾ cup nuts (chopped)

8 servings

Put cake ingredients (except apples) in large mixing bowl. Mix at medium speed 2 minutes. Fold in apples by hand. Pour into greased and floured 9"x13" pan.

Mix topping ingredients and cover cake with mixture. Bake at 350⁰ for 45 minutes.

Delicious served warm with sweetened, flavored whipped cream. Also good plain.

Arcadia, at the foot of the San Gabriel Mountains, is a true suburban "Community of Homes" boasting gardens and landscaping unrivaled anywhere. Rich in California history, the city is the home of the L.A. State and County Arboretum, located on the famous Lucky Baldwin Rancho, and the beautiful Santa Anita Racetrack. The cultural heritage is balanced with diversified light industry and business and a fine unified school system.

Baked Alaska

Mayor Tony Knowles
Anchorage, Alaska

GENOISE:

¼ cup melted butter

6 eggs

1 cup sugar

1 tsp. vanilla

1 cup sifted cake flour

FILLING:

1 qt. vanilla ice cream (softened)

1 cup fresh raspberries

½ cup Grand Marnier (optional)

MERINGUE:

5 egg whites (at room temperature)

½ tsp. cream of tartar

¼ cup sugar

½ tsp. vanilla

8-10 servings

Genoise: Preheat oven to 350⁰. Melt butter and set aside. In a double boiler (do not allow top pot to touch water in lower pot), break eggs, add ⅔ cup sugar, and beat at medium speed for 7 minutes. Add ⅓ cup sugar and beat on high speed for 3 minutes until mixture stands in soft peaks. Gently fold in vanilla and cake flour. Fold in melted butter. Do not overwork.

Pour batter into 2 9" greased and floured cake pans. Bake at 350⁰ for 35 minutes. Remove from pan and place onto cake rack to cool completely. (For this recipe you will only need one cake. You may freeze the other for another time.)

Filling: Mix Grand Marnier, raspberries, and softened ice cream. Freeze long enough that the ice cream can be shaped into a mound on the chilled genoise.

Meringue: Beat egg whites gradually; add cream of tartar and beat until foamy. Beat sugar in a little at a time; add the vanilla and continue beating until mixture is very stiff and glossy. Do not make ahead.

Assembly: Place genoise on an ovenproof serving dish. Mound ice cream mixture on top. Put in freezer for 1 hour. Make meringue. Take cake and ice cream from freezer and cover completely with meringue (in peaks). Bake 3-5 minutes in preheated 500⁰ oven until peaks are golden brown. Serve immediately.

This is a delicious and impressive dessert for entertaining.

Anchorage, Alaska's largest community is America's choice for hosting the 1992 Winter Olympic Games. For further information on Anchorage, turn to pages 197

Blintz Souffle

Mayor Dave Karp
San Leandro, California

12 uncooked or frozen cheese blintzes

7 eggs (beaten)

1½ cups sour cream

¼ cup orange juice

¼ cup sugar

¼ lb. butter or margarine (melted)

1 tsp. almond extract

1 tsp. vanilla

¼ tsp. salt

12 servings

Arrange blintzes in 9"x13" Pyrex dish. Mix remaining ingredients and pour mixture over blintzes. Bake at 350⁰ for 45 minutes or until knife comes out clean. Serve with sour cream and/or cherry preserves.

San Leandro is nestled between the Oakland foothills and the world famous San Francisco Bay. Long known for its mild climate, fashionable residences, and as "The Cherry City," San Leandro today is recognized as having one of the most stable economies in the west. Possessing the right proportion of residential, commercial, and light industry, combined with a modern shoreline and marina development second to none, San Leandro is truly a delightful place to live and raise a family and has earned this beautiful bay city unquestioned acclaim as a "model municipality" of the 20th century.

Buttery Lemon Squares
Mayor Anne B. Diament
Alameda, California

1 cup butter or margarine
½ cup powdered sugar (unsifted)
2⅓ cups all purpose flour (unsifted)
4 eggs
2 cups sugar
1 tsp. lemon peel (grated)
6 tbsp. lemon juice

1 tsp. baking powder
3 tbsp. powdered sugar

Makes 20 pieces

In large bowl, cream butter and ½ cup powdered sugar until fluffy. Add 2 cups flour; mix until blended. Spread over bottom of well greased 9"x13" pan. Bake at 350⁰ for 20 minutes.

Meanwhile, in small mixing bowl, beat eggs until light. Gradually add granulated sugar. Beat until thick and blended. Add lemon peel and juice, remaining ½ cup flour and baking powder; beat until blended. Pour lemon mixture over baked crust and return to oven. Bake 15-20 minutes more or until pale gold. Remove from oven and sprinkle evenly with powdered sugar; let cool. To serve, cut in small squares or bars.

Rich, and very good!

Alameda, a city of 74,000, sits in San Francisco Bay between San Francisco and Oakland. A third of its main island is a naval installation. A smaller island contains a Coast Guard Support Center. Alameda has been likened to a "midwest town set down in a major metropolitan area." It retains much of a small town atmosphere but has the advantage of easy access to larger cities. Alameda is committed to the preservation of its heritage while welcoming new "state of the art" business development.

California Fudge Cake
Mayor Thomas A. Payne
Bakersfield, California

2 squares unsweetened chocolate
1 cube butter or margarine
2 cups flour
1½ tsp. baking soda
¾ tsp. salt

2 cups granulated sugar

½ cup buttermilk

1 tsp. vanilla

1 cup boiling water

2 eggs

FROSTING:

1 square unsweetened chocolate

1 cube butter or margarine

½ cup brown sugar

2 tbsp. white Karo syrup

¼ cup sour cream

¼ tsp. vanilla

1 cup nuts (optional)

1 box powdered sugar

12 servings

Melt chocolate and butter in double boiler. Sift together flour, baking soda, and salt; set aside. In large mixing bowl beat sugar, buttermilk, and vanilla, at low speed; add hot butter and chocolate mixture, mix a few seconds, add boiling water, mix well. Add flour mixture to liquid; mix until blended, add eggs, and mix well. Pour into 9"x13" pan; put into oven and turn it to 350⁰. Bake 35-45 minutes.

Frosting: Melt chocolate and butter in double boiler. In mixing bowl put brown sugar, pour hot butter and chocolate mixture over sugar while mixing; add syrup, sour cream, vanilla, nuts, and powdered sugar and beat until blended.

Bakersfield—California's Golden Empire—is located at the southern tip of the San Joaquin Valley. Rich in oil, agriculture, and minerals, the city is within two hours of major commerce centers, mountains, and beaches. Bountiful, Beautiful, and Beckoning, we produce in abundance the needs of the nation. Bakersfield—where the past meets the future—a great place to call home.

Chocolate Angel Pie

Mayor Kile Morgan
National City, California

MERINGUE CRUST:

3 egg whites

1/8 tsp. salt

¼ tsp. cream of tartar

½ tsp. vanilla

¾ cup sugar

⅓ cup pecans or walnuts (chopped)

CHOCOLATE FILLING:

¾ cup semisweet chocolate pieces

¼ cup hot water

1 tsp. vanilla

1/8 tsp. salt

1 cup heavy cream (whipped)

6 servings

Combine egg whites, salt, cream of tartar, and vanilla; beat. Add sugar gradually, beating until very stiff and sugar is dissolved. Spread in well greased 9" pie pan. Build up sides. (Use cake decorator for fancy edge.) Sprinkle bottom with nuts. Bake in very slow oven (275⁰) 1 hour. Cool, fill with Chocolate Filling.

Chocolate Filling: Melt chocolate pieces in top of double boiler over boiling water. Add hot water, vanilla, and salt. Stir until completely smooth; cool. Fold in whipped cream. Fill shell and chill 4 hours or overnight. Serve with layer of whipped cream spread over top.

National City was part of the 26,000 acre Rancho de la Nacion during the period of Mexican rule in California. Incorporated September 17, 1887, National City will be celebrating its centennial next year. It is one of the San Diego region's major centers of retail trade—particularly automobile sales.

Cream Cheese Pie Modesto

Mayor Peggy Mensinger
Modesto, California

12 oz. cream cheese	½ tsp. lemon juice
2 eggs (beaten)	¾ cup sugar
2 tsp. vanilla	9" graham cracker pie crust
TOPPING:	
1 cup sour cream	1 tsp. vanilla
3½ tbsp. sugar	

8-12 servings

Combine cream cheese, eggs, vanilla, lemon juice, and sugar; beat with electric mixer until light and creamy. Pour into pie crust and bake at 350⁰ 15-20 minutes. Remove from oven and allow to cool 5 minutes.

Blend topping ingredients by hand; then pour over pie. Return to oven and bake 10 minutes longer. Remove and cool. Place in refrigerator at least 5 hours before serving. Just before serving, spoon fresh or frozen berries (slightly thawed) over each piece.

Our area produces a great variety of dairy products as well as eggs and berries. This recipe combines them in a very successful way. It came originally from a Knudsen Dairy publication (this firm has a large plant in Modesto), and I have used it for years with excellent results. It is quick and easy and very good.

While **Modesto's** name is Spanish for modest, we are proud of this community of 135,000 as a place to live and work. Located in the heart of the rich agricultural San Joaquin Valley, Modesto is headquarters of the world's largest winery (E & J Gallo) and has the country's biggest cannery (Tri Valley/S&W Growers). Our motto "Water, Wealth, Contentment, Health" dates from 1912 and refers to our publicly-owned irrigation district, which brings water from the mountains to make possible our diverse crops. Within 100 miles we can be

in San Francisco, on the Monterey Bay coast, or in the gold country of the Sierras, but there is much to do at home too with fine parks and recreation programs, cultural activities, and a variety of organizations and facilities. We think we have the best of all worlds.

Favorite Brownies

Mayor C. David Baker
Irvine, California

2 cups flour	½ cup buttermilk
2 cups sugar	2 eggs (slightly beaten)
1 stick margarine	1 tsp. cinnamon
½ cup Crisco	1 tsp. baking soda
4 tbsp. cocoa (¼ cup)	1 tsp. vanilla
FROSTING:	
1 stick margarine	1 box powdered sugar
¼ cup cocoa	1 tsp. vanilla
6 tbsp. milk	1 cup pecans

48 servings

Mix flour and sugar; set aside. Bring to boil margarine, Crisco, cocoa, and water and pour over dry mixture. Add buttermilk, eggs, cinnamon, soda, and vanilla. Mix all ingredients together and pour into wax paper-lined baking sheet with sides. Bake 20 minutes at 400⁰.

Frosting: Melt and bring to boil margarine, cocoa, and milk. Add powdered sugar, vanilla, and pecans. Beat with mixer and have ready to spread when brownies have begun to cool.

Irvine is a young community incorporated in 1981. It is located 35 miles southeast of downtown Los Angeles and six miles inland from the Pacific Ocean. The Irvine Business Complex, covering 4,000 acres and including more than 1,000 firms, is the largest master-planned industrial park in the nation. Engineering, high technology, and bioscience firms are the largest employers, along with the University of California.

Ginger Cookies

Mayor Edward Vincent
Inglewood, California

¾ cup shortening
¼ cup molasses
2 tsp. baking soda
½ tsp. cloves
½ tsp. salt
1 cup sugar
1 egg
2 cups flour
½ tsp. cinnamon
½ tsp. ginger

48 cookies

Melt shortening; cool, add sugar, molasses, and egg. Beat well. Add dry ingredients. Chill 1-2 hours. Roll into 1" balls and roll in sugar. Bake at 375⁰ for approximately 8-10 minutes.

Always a favorite, easy to prepare, and they travel well.

Inglewood is a city of 100,000 located immediately adjacent to Los Angeles International Airport in the South Bay section of Los Angeles County. Its proximity to the airport, California's major entertainment attractions, the mountains, and the sea, makes Inglewood ideally suited to those who wish to enjoy the southern California lifestyle. Known as the "City of Champions," Inglewood is the site of The Forum, home of basketball's Lakers, and beautiful Hollywood Park Racetrack, featuring the finest of horses and jockeys in thoroughbred racing.

Grape Tarts

Mayor Barbara Fass
Stockton, California

¾ cup butter (melted)
1 pkg. phyllo dough (available in frozen food section of most stores)
1 egg white (slightly beaten)
4 cups green seedless grapes (halved)
1 cup sugar
1 cup walnuts (chopped)
¼ cup tapioca
2 tbsp. butter
dried beans

8-10 servings

Preheat oven to 425⁰. Combine grapes, nuts, sugar, and tapioca. Set aside while preparing phyllo dough.

Generously butter 9"x12" fluted tart pan with removable bottom. Stack 10 sheets of phyllo on work surface. (Cover the rest with a slightly damp towel to prevent drying out.) Fold over pastry to form a book. Unfold 1 "page" at a time; brush with butter and sprinkle lightly with sugar. Repeat until the "book" is open and start on other side. (Don't worry if sheets tear, just keep them close together.) Take completed phyllo and lay into pan, fitting around the bottom and edges. Take a rolling pin and run it over the top to cut off excess.

Place pan on cookie sheet, line with foil, and weight with dried beans. Bake 5 minutes. Remove foil and beans, brush with egg white and bake until light brown. (Don't worry if phyllo rises, it will deflate when you put fruit in it.) Spoon grapes and nuts into dough and dot with butter.

Take 4 more sheets of dough and repeat process of brushing with butter and sprinkling with sugar. Place sheets on top of pan. Cut off excess leaving about 1" and then fold under. Place on cookie sheet and bake 35-40 minutes until golden brown. If top darkens too quickly, lay foil loosely

continued

over the top. Allow to cool. (Delicious served with vanilla ice cream.)

Janice Buente won the dessert category with this recipe.

Stockton, a modern city in the lush agricultural lands of the San Joaquin Valley, has been called the "food basket of the nation."

Harvard Beet Cake

Mayor Kay Calas
Carson, California

1 15 oz. can Harvard beets (drain, reserving ⅓ cup liquid)
2 tbsp. sugar
1 tbsp. cornstarch
¼ tsp. salt
¼ cup white vinegar
2 tbsp. butter or margarine
1½ cups vegetable oil
3 eggs
2 cups sugar
2 tbsp. vanilla
1 cup crushed pineapple (well drained)
1 cup small curd cottage cheese
½ cup coconut
2½ cups flour
2 tsp. cinnamon
2 tsp. baking soda
1 tsp. salt
1 cup walnuts (chopped)

12 servings

In saucepan, combine sugar, cornstarch, and salt; stir in beet liquid, vinegar, and butter. Cook until thickened. Add beets and let cool. Do not refrigerate.

Beat together oil, eggs, sugar, vanilla, pineapple, cottage cheese, and coconut. Sift flour, cinnamon, baking soda, and salt; add to pineapple/cottage cheese mixture. Fold in the beet mixture and chopped walnuts and pour into a greased and floured 9"x13" pan. Bake at 350⁰ for 1 hour.

A whole lot of ingredients have to be mixed together to come up with a high quality of life. **Carson**, California, has all those ingredients! A diversified job base, an abundance of well maintained neighborhoods, great shopping, a parks and recreation system the envy of all, innovative schools and an 11,000 student campus of Cal State University, and excellent proximity to freeways and airports. The ingredients are there...all blending together to realize Carson's motto of a "Future Unlimited."

Irish Brownies

Mayor Maureen O'Connor
San Diego, California

2 cups flour (sifted)
2 cups sugar
2 sticks margarine
9 tbsp. Ghirardelli's cocoa
1 cup water
½ cup buttermilk
2 eggs
1 tsp. vanilla
1 tsp. baking soda
ICING:
1 stick margarine
4 tbsp. cocoa
6 tbsp. milk
1 box confectioner's sugar
1 tsp. vanilla
1 cup walnuts (chopped)

Makes 30

Mix sugar and flour; set aside. Bring to boil cocoa, margarine, and water. Pour over sugar and flour; mix well. Add buttermilk, eggs, baking soda, and vanilla; mix well. Bake at 400⁰ for 20 minutes in a cookie sheet 16"x11"x1" deep.

Icing: Bring to boil margarine, cocoa, and milk. Remove from heat, add confectioner's sugar, vanilla, and walnuts. Beat well; spread on cooled brownies.

The reason **San Diego** is a special place to live has nothing to do with our beaches, mountains, parks, or fantastic climate. It is special because of the creative energy of our citizens. That "can do" spirit makes whatever we imagine possible.

San Diego is the site of Father Junipero Serra's first mission and is the home of one of the world's most famous zoos, and home of Orky, the whale, the largest mammal in captivity.

Modesto Brandy Peaches

Mayor Peggy Mensinger
Modesto, California

2 17 oz. cans yellow cling peach halves
1 tsp. lemon juice
¼ cup E & J Gallo brandy
nutmeg
¼ cup margarine or butter
¾ cup brown sugar (firmly packed)
heavy cream (whipped)

6 servings

Drain peaches and reserve ⅓ cup syrup. In a large saucepan, melt margarine or butter; stir in peach syrup, lemon juice, and sugar. Bring to boil. Add peaches and simmer 10 minutes, basting frequently. Add brandy and simmer 5 more minutes. Serve peaches warm with whipping cream and dash of nutmeg.

Modesto, headquarters of the world's largest winery—E & J Gallo. For further information on Modesto, turn to page 214.

Oktoberfest Streusel Coffee Cake

Mayor Fred Nagel
La Mesa, California

3 cups flour
6 tsp. baking powder
1 tsp. salt
1½ cups sugar
½ cup shortening
2 eggs (well beaten)
1 cup milk
2 tsp. vanilla
FILLING:
1 cup brown sugar (firmly packed)
4 tbsp. flour
4 tsp. cinnamon
4 tbsp. butter (melted)
1 cup walnuts (chopped)

12-16 servings

Sift flour together with baking powder, salt, and sugar. Cut in shortening until mixture is like fine cornmeal. Blend in well beaten eggs with milk. Stir in vanilla and mix just until well blended. Spread half of batter into greased 9"x12" pan. Sprinkle with half the streusel filling. Spread remaining batter over filling and sprinkle remaining streusel on top. Bake at 375⁰ for 45 minutes or until cake tests done with toothpick.

Filling: Mix sugar, flour, and cinnamon together and blend in melted butter. Stir in chopped nuts.

La Mesa, known as the "Jewel of the Hills" of San Diego County communities, is situated at the edge of San Diego's foothills, which provides beautiful views of the Eastern mountains. Long considered one of the most desirable places to settle and raise one's family, La Mesa is known for its superb access to the region's commercial and recreational areas. Important also as a regional shopping are, it nevertheless has retained a village atmosphere in its downtown area, where each fall its four-day Oktoberfest celebraton draws tourists from all over the region.

Old Fashioned Chocolate Fudge

Mayor George S. Hobbs, Jr.
Santa Maria, California

2 cups granulated sugar
2 oz. unsweetened chocolate
½ cup whole milk
⅓ cup corn syrup
2 tbsp. butter
½ tsp. vanilla
½ cup walnuts (chopped)

8-12 servings

In saucepan, mix sugar and chocolate together; stir in milk and syrup. Bring quickly to boil; turn down heat and allow to cook slowly. Stir in butter while cooking. After 7 minutes, test frequently, and when substance forms soft ball in cup of cold water, remove from fire. After mixture has cooled add vanilla and nuts and stir until it starts to harden. Pour out on buttered platter and cut into 1½" squares for serving.

This fudge recipe has been used in the mayor's family for over sixty years. The creamy fudges offered today do not measure up to this in his estimation.

Santa Maria started as a farming community in the latter half of the 19th century. Oil was discovered in the early 1900s, and the space industry started to contribute heavily to the economy about 1958 when Vandenberg Air Force Base began to develop twenty miles from the heart of the city. Nearly 90,000 people now live within an eight-mile radius of city hall.

Pecan Tarts

Mayor Charlotte Spadaro
Beverly Hills, California

½ cup butter
1 cup flour
3 oz. cream cheese
FILLING:
1 egg
¾ cup brown sugar
dash of salt
1 tbsp. butter (softened)
1 tsp. vanilla
⅔ cup pecans

24 servings

Old Method: Have butter and cream cheese at room temperature. Blend them with pastry blender; add flour and blend until smooth. Chill 1 hour.

New Method: Put cold butter and cream cheese into processor bowl. Add flour; blend until pastry forms a ball in bowl.

Shape dough into 24 1" balls. Press dough into tiny muffin pans.

Filling: Beat egg, brown sugar, salt, butter, and vanilla just until blended (don't overbeat or filling will run over edge of pastry). Put half the pecans in the bottom of pastry-lined muffin pans, then filling, then top with remaining pecans. Bake at 350° for 25 minutes. Cool in pans for 10 minutes; remove and cool on racks.

Few cities of comparable size are better known than **Beverly Hills**. As a city, it is very young—it was incorporated in 1914. Its history however, can be traced back to 1769 when the title of all land in California became vested in the King of Spain. Beverly Hills is justifiably known the world over for the quality of its merchandise and the imaginative flare in which it's displayed on Rodeo Drive. The world's leading designers (both men and women's apparel), jewelers, leather specialists, shoe stylists, and furriers have all found a niche in the unique shopping experience that is Beverly Hills. Its location, midway between downtown Los Angeles and the Pacific Ocean, makes Beverly Hills a vital part of the Los Angeles region urbanized area. Beverly Hills serves as an important retail, financial, and professional center.

Pineapple Carrot Cake

Mayor Lionel J. Wilson
Oakland, California

2 cups flour	½ cup coconut (grated)
2 cups sugar	1½ cups oil
1 tsp. soda	4 eggs
1½ tsp. cinnamon	1 cup nuts
1 tsp. salt	2 cups carrots (grated)
1 can crushed pineapple (undrained)	
FROSTING:	
8 oz. pkg. cream cheese	1½ tsp. vanilla
1 stick butter	½ tsp. salt
1 box powdered sugar	milk

8 servings

Place all ingredients in bowl, except carrots, nuts, pineapple, and coconut. Mix thoroughly. Add remaining ingredients. Bake at 300⁰ for about 1 hour in an oblong glass pan.

Frosting: Mix ingredients, adding enough milk to bring it to spreading consistency.

Oakland is proud of its designation as the "most integrated U.S. city" because of its diverse ethnic population and rich variety of cultural attractions. See page 188 for additional information on the city.

Poppy Seed Cake

Mayor Ronald K. Mullin
Concord, California

1 pkg. yellow cake mix
4 eggs
2 pkgs. instant butterscotch pudding
1 box poppy seeds
1 cup water
¾ cup cooking oil
powdered sugar

8-10 servings

Mix all ingredients until well blended. Bake in well-greased bundt pan 50-55 minutes at 350⁰. Remove from pan while still hot and sprinkle with powdered sugar.

Concord is in the San Francisco Bay Area, but is slightly inland so that we enjoy more sun year-round. We are very close to the Napa Valley where premium California wines are produced. Concord is a beautiful city and is changing from a sleepy, suburban community to a major employment center and the largest city in Contra Costa County.

CITY TRIVIA QUESTION #61

This Texas city is known for its towering "moonlights" which keep the city "awash in moonlight" every night.

Answer on page 149.

Raisin Oatmeal Cookies

Mayor Dale Doig
Fresno, California

1 cup butter or margarine (softened)
1 cup sugar
3 cups quick oats (uncooked)
¾ cup flour
1 tbsp. baking soda
½ tsp. cloves
½ tsp. cinnamon
1 cup raisins
¼ cup milk

Makes about 4 dozen

In large mixing bowl, blend together butter and sugar; add oats. Sift together flour, baking soda, cloves, and cinnamon. Add to oats mixture, blending well. Stir in raisins and milk; mix thoroughly. Roll dough into 1" balls. Place 3" apart on greased baking sheets. Bake at 350º 12-15 minutes, or until golden brown.

Fresno is the raisin capital of the nation. For further information on Fresno, turn to page 184.

CITY TRIVIA QUESTION #62

Only southern city saved on General Sherman's march to the sea and given by Sherman as a Christmas present to President Lincoln.

Answer on page 84.

Spanish Coffee Cake

Mayor Mary E. Kelsey
Burbank, California

2½ cups flour
1 cup brown sugar
¾ cup white sugar
1 tsp. nutmeg
1 tsp. salt
¾ cup salad oil
1 tsp. cinnamon
½ cup nuts (chopped)
1 cup sour milk or buttermilk
1 tsp. baking soda
1 egg (beaten)

8 servings

Mix flour, 2 sugars, nutmeg, salt, and oil. Remove ¾ cup of mixture; add to it cinnamon and chopped nuts. Mix well and set aside to sprinkle on top of cake. Combine sour milk or buttermilk, baking soda, and egg. Add to flour, sugar, and oil mixture. Stir slightly. Pour into shallow, well-greased pan and sprinkle crumbs on top. Bake at 350º for 35 minutes.

Burbank, the city of "People, Pride and Progress," is in the midst of celebrating its 75th birthday. Founded July 8, 1911, Burbank has everything—beautiful parks, wonderful residential areas, a vast array of recreational opportunities for residents, and a sound business foundation that boasts Lockheed California Co., Disney Studios, NBC, Warner Brothers, Columbia Studios, and The Burbank Studios, and includes a famous media district. Located a few miles from the busy city of Los Angeles, Burbank has retained, and closely guards, its "small town" atmosphere, with a population that is friendly and involved.

Strawberry Meringue Pie

Mayor Nao Takasugi
Oxnard, California

6 egg whites
¼ tsp. salt
2 cups sugar
1 tsp. vanilla
1 tsp. vinegar
1 cup whipping cream or Cool Whip
strawberries

6-8 servings

Grease 9″ pie plate generously; dust with flour. Beat egg whites at room temperature with ¼ tsp. salt, until stiff but not dry. Gradually add 1 cup of sugar 1 tablespoon at a time. Continue beating, adding 1 teaspoon vanilla, then the other cup of sugar 1 tablespoon at a time, and the vinegar. Pile meringue onto a pie plate, smoothing out to the edge. Bake 1½ hours at 275⁰, then at 300⁰ for 30 minutes. It will puff, crack, and settle. Turn off oven and let baked meringue cool before removing. Sweeten whipped cream to taste, add cut up strawberries, saving some whole ones. Pile sweetened whipped cream or Cool Whip on meringue and decorate with whole berries. Do not refrigerate this pie.

This recipe was judged the winner of the 1985 Berry-Oft Sweepstakes and is from Laura Lowry of Oxnard.

Oxnard, the Strawberry Capital of California, hosts the annual Strawberry Festival. For further information on Oxnard, turn to pages 187 and 188.

Wheat Germ Zucchini Cake

Mayor Dave Rosenberg
Davis, California

2 cups zucchini (shredded)
2 eggs
1 tsp. vanilla
¾ cup oil
½ cup milk
1 cup sugar
½ cup semisweet chocolate pieces
¾ cup wheat germ
2 cups flour
¼ cup cocoa
3 tsp. baking powder
¾ tsp. salt
½ tsp. cinnamon
¼ tsp. cloves

8-10 servings

Beat milk, eggs, sugar, vanilla, and oil together in one bowl. In another bowl, combine wheat germ, flour, cocoa, baking powder, salt, and spices. Stir wheat germ mixture into milk mixture. Fold in zucchini and chocolate pieces. Pour into greased and floured 9-cup or fluted pan. Bake in 350⁰ oven 60-70 minutes, or until done. Cool 15 minutes and invert onto a wire rack.

Davis, home of a major campus of the University of California, is the site of the first modern bike lane system in the U.S.; the 30-mile network of lanes is a working part of the city and university transportation system. Davis is situated in the Sacramento Valley near the California State Capitol and San Francisco, and is surrounded by some of the richest agricultural land in the world. Davis is a slow-growth community, attempting to retain its small-town character, and is a city of trees, parks, greenbelts, cooperatives—including the nation's

continued

first cooperative cable TV system—innovative housing concepts, energy conservation, and the use of alternate energy.

Pomona is named for the Roman goddess of fruit and bounty. Pomona developed over the last century from its origins as a small citrus town to a major financial and industrial center today with a population of more than 107,000. It is a city with character that has achieved an exciting mix of old and new, historic and contemporary, with planning and vision. It has the right mix of people, places, progress, and promise for the future.

Pomona Punch ("The Right Mix")

Mayor G. Stanton Selby
Pomona, California

4 cups sugar
6 cups water
1 46 oz. can pineapple juice
2 12 oz. cans frozen orange juice concentrate (thawed)
1 12 oz. can frozen lemonade concentrate (thawed)
5 bananas
7 28 oz. bottles lemon-lime carbonated beverage

60 servings

Dissolve sugar in water. Add juices. Peel and mash bananas (use food processor or blend); stir into juice. Ladle into wide-topped freezer containers, leaving 1" head space. Cover tightly; freeze. Makes 6 quarts.

To serve: Thaw fruit crush to mushy consistency, add carbonated beverage. Freeze maraschino cherries or fresh berries in ice cubes to float on top of punch bowl.

CITY TRIVIA QUIZ

Scoring System

Throughout *The Mayors Cookbook* there are 62 City Trivia questions with 130 answers. Answer each question, follow the instructions to the page with the answer, and tally your results.

Correct Answers	Level of Knowledge
0—25	Municipal Rookie
26—50	City Gazer
51—75	Metropolitan Marvel
76—100	City Slicker
101 and up	Urbanologist

MAYORS PARTICIPATION LIST

Abramson, Jerry—*Louisville, KY*—93
Adams, IV, T. Patton—*Columbia, SC*—64
Addison, Arnold—*State College, PA*—50
Alfred, Stephen J.—*Shaker Heights, OH*—135
Alkateeb, Joe—*Farmington Hills, MI*—105
Allison, Tomilea—*Bloomington, IN*—140
Anderson, Gary K.—*Decatur, IL*—103
Anstine, Robert—*Macomb, IL*—110
Anthony, Calvin—*Stillwater, OK*—156
Arrington, Jr., Richard—*Birmingham, AL*—81
Bailey, Bob—*Bolingbrook, IL*—121
Baker, C. David—*Irving, CA*—214
Baldelli, Charles C.—*Woonsocket, RI*—24
Barry, Jr., Marion—*Washington, DC*—45
Barthelemy, Sidney—*New Orleans, LA*—72
Berkley, Richard L.—*Kansas City, MO*—122
Beswick Carol—*Redlands, CA*—183
Bilotti, John D.—*Kenosha, WI*—121
Blackwell, Robert B.—*Highland Park, MI*—111, 119
Blessey, Gerald—*Biloxi, MS*—67
Bloomberg, Kathryn C.—*Brookfield, WI*—124, 130
Boeckel, Olga—*Middletown, NJ*—58
Bolen, Bob—*Fort Worth, TX*—166
Bonkowski, Ronald L.—*Warren, MI*—131
Bonner, Mary—*Dunedin, FL*—94
Boyle, Michael—*Omaha, NE*—165
Bradbury, Cecil W.—*Pinellas Park, FL*—99
Bradley, Tom—*Los Angeles, CA*—198, 208
Branca, Frank R.—*Miramar, FL*—85
Brooks, Al—*Mesa, AZ*—179
Broussard, Aaron F.—*Kenner, LA*—73
Brown, A.B.—*Riverside, CA*—184, 186
Buhai, Robert—*Highland Park, IL*—124
Bullard, John K.—*New Bedford, MA*—33
Busch, Gerald E.—*Kettering, OH*—128
Calas, Kay—*Carson, CA*—216
Caliguiri, Richard S.—*Pittsburgh, PA*—55
Callahan, Dennis M.—*Annapolis, MD*—39
Campbell, Thomas V.—*Idaho Falls, ID*—178
Canney, Donald J.—*Cedar Rapids, IA*—134, 139
Cannon, Jonathan H.—*Garden Grove, CA*—185
Carlson, Steven B.—*Jamestown, NY*—54
Casado, Tony—*Wichita, KS*—151
Chalos, Pete—*Terre Haute, IN*—103
Champine, Dennis—*Aurora, CO*—171
Chastain, Vicki—*Marietta, GA*—80
Cisneros, Henry G.—*San Antonio, TX*—163, 165
Clark, J.E.—*Portland, OR*—196
Coats, Andy—*Oklahoma City, OK*—153, 159
Coggeshall, Janice—*Galveston, TX*—150, 160
Cole, Benjamin—*Mayaguez, PR*—76
Cole, Jr., Edward L.—*St. Petersburg, FL*—87
Collins, William A.—*Norwalk, CT*—30
Connor, Harry A.—*Gastonia, NC*—65
Cooksey, Frank C.—*Austin, TX*—149
Corpening, Wayne A.—*Winston-Salem, NC*—96
Corrada-del Rio, Baltasar—*San Juan, PR*—76, 92
Cox, Gregory R.—*Chula Vista, CA*—189
Crabb, Juanita M.—*Binghamton, NY*—56
Crawford, Richard C.—*Tulsa, OK*—154

Crivaro, Peter—*Des Moines, IA*—127
Crozier, Ted—*Clarksville, TN*—71
Cvetko, Joseph A.—*Bellflower, CA*—202
Czarnecki, John V.—*East Lansing, MI*—123
Daddona, Joseph S.—*Allentown, PA*—43
Daily, Stephen J.—*Kokomo, IN*—115
Danks, Jr., Dale—*Jackson, MS*—99
Daoud, Alex—*Miami Beach, FL*—69
De LaRosa, Gil—*Pico Rivera, CA*—203
DePaulis, Palmer A.—*Salt Lake City, UT*—178
Dear, Donald L.—*Gardena, CA*—191
Debo, III, Jerry V.—*Grand Prairie, TX*—162
Del Vecchio, Alfred—*White Plains, NY*—49
DiVirgilio, Albert V.—*Lynn, MA*—17
Diament, Anne B.—*Alameda, CA*—212
Dodd, John D.—*Farmers Branch, TX*—150
Doerr, Barbara J.—*Redondo Beach, CA*—206
Doig, Dale—*Fresno, CA*—184
Dorler, Ronald J.—*Portland, ME*—25
Dressler, Robert A.—*Fort Lauderdale, FL*—77
Drinkwater, Herbert—*Scottsdale, AZ*—173
Dufek, Anthony V.—*Manitowoc, WI*—130
Dukes, Bill J.—*Decatur, AL*—98
Durrence, J. Larry—*Lakeland, FL*—100
Dyer, James E.—*Danbury, CT*—16, 25
Eason, James L.—*Hampton, VA*—64
Eastwood, Clint—*Carmel, CA*—210
Eilenberg, Carl—*Rome, NY*—39, 51
Erickson, Don—*Cheyenne, WY*—172
Fasi, Frank F.—*Honolulu, HI*—190
Fass, Barbara—*Stockton, CA*—183, 190, 194, 209, 215
Fedo, John A.—*Duluth, MN*—146
Feighner, J.W.—*Columbus, GA*—80
Feinstein, Dianne—*San Francisco, CA*—191
Flaherty, Francis—*Warwick, RI*—14
Flammer, Dan—*Carson City, NV*—175
Flippen, Martha—*Sandusky, OH*—114
Flynn, Raymond L.—*Boston, MA*—18
Fraser, Donald M.—*Minneapolis, MN*—125
Frawley, Daniel S.—*Wilmington, DE*—37
Frederick, Bill—*Orlando, FL*—88
Freedman, Sandra—*Tampa, FL*—73
Freeman, George—*Grosse Pointe Woods, MI*—108
Fulton, Richard H.—*Nashville, TN*—71
Galasy, Lou—*Longview, TX*—160
Gantt, Harvey B.—*Charlotte, NC*—87
Garner, Leslie H.—*Greenville, NC*—88
Giammona, Anthony A.—*Daly City, CA*—204
Giuliani, Alex—*Hayward, CA*—204
Giunta, Anthony J.—*Euclid, OH*—139
Gloyd, Betty—*Hoffman Estates, IL*—103
Godbold, Jake M.—*Jacksonville, FL*—93
Goddard, Terry—*Phoenix, AZ*—172
Goode, W. Wilson—*Philadelphia, PA*—58
Greenwald, Maria B.—*Cherry Hill, NJ*—40
Griffin, James D.—*Buffalo, NY*—50
Griset, Daniel E.—*Santa Ana, CA*—185
Guerra, Azelio M.—*West Haven, CT*—19, 33
Guido, Michael A.—*Dearborn, MI*—122
Guilianti, Mary—*Hollywood, FL*—62
Gulley, Wilbur—*Durham, NC*—89
Haakenson, Marlan—*Bismarck, ND*—156
Hackett, Richard C.—*Memphis, TN*—86
Hagstrom, Verne—*Quincy, IL*—112
Hardcastle, Charles—*Bowling Green, KY*—96
Harper, Charles—*Wichita Falls, TX*—158
Harrison, John Ray—*Pasadena, TX*—162
Hart, Thomas W.—*Davenport, IA*—113
Hartwick, Terry—*North Little Rock, AR*—86
Harvard, Jack—*Plano, TX*—151
Hatcher, Jr., John C.—*East Orange, NJ*—41

Hatcher, Richard G.—125
Hazama, Chuck—*Rochester, MN*—112
Hennes, Jr., Herb A.—*Huntington Park, CA*—194
Hobbs, Jr., George S.—*Santa Maria, CA*—218
Hoffman, Elizabeth C.—*North Tonawanda, NY*—44
Holland, Arthur J.—*Trenton, NJ*—37
Holley, III, James A.—*Portsmouth, VA*—78
Holt, Carlton B.—*Albemarle, NC*—66
Houston, J. Michael—*Springfield, IL*—104
Hudnut, III, William H.—*Indianapolis, IN*—109, 133
Huhn, Philip D.—*Long Branch, NJ*—55
Hussey, John B.—*Shreveport, LA*—94
Hutto, Emmett O.—*Baytown, TX*—158
James, Jr., Sharpe A.—*Newark, NJ*—49
Johnson, Clyde F.—*Clinton, IA*—104
Johnson, Karen B.—*Schenectady, NY*—42
Jones, Luther J.—*Corpus Christi, TX*—155
Jones, Robert—*Virginia Beach, VA*—65
Jourgensen, Linda S.—*Boulder, CO*—171
Kaminsky, David—*Lauderhill, FL*—91
Kannenberg, John—*Wausau, WI*—145
Kanzler, Carmelina Como—*New London, CT*—26, 28, 32
Karp, Dave—*San Leandro, CA*—211
Kell, Ernie—*Long Beach, CA*—205
Kelly, Kathy—*Clearwater, FL*—90
Kelsey, Mary E.—*Burbank, CA*—220
Kemp, Jimmy—*Meridian, MS*—91
Kempthorne, Dirk—*Boise, ID*—170
Keys, Michael B.—*Elyria, OH*—126
Kirschner, Kerry G.—*Sarasota, FL*—61
Klein, R.P. Rick—*Amarillo, TX*—159
Knowles, Tony—*Anchorage, AK*—197, 208, 211
Koch, Edward—*New York City, NY*—42
Kunk, Eugene B.—*Springfield, OH*—129
Lak, Richard S.—*Chicopee, MA*—20, 29
Latimer, George—*St. Paul, MN*—114
Leafe, Joseph A.—*Norfolk, VA*—70
Leon-Martinez, Angel—*Juana Diaz, PR*—74, 83
Leonard, Paul R.—*Dayton, OH*—106
Leone, Jr., John L.—*Bristol, CT*—24
Lindgren, Jon G.—*Fargo, ND*—154
Lodge, Sheila—*Santa Barbara, CA*—203, 206
Longo, Thomas J.—*Garfield Heights, OH*—142
Lowry, Emmett F.—*Texas City, TX*—161
Luedtke, Roland A.—*Lincoln, NE*—163
Lynch, Michael P.—*Monroeville, PA*—35
Maier, Henry W.—*Milwaukee, WI*—115
Majerus, Janet—*University City, MO*—138
Malone, Ronald L.—*Marion, OH*—144
Maloof, James A.—*Peoria, IL*—128
Manibog, G. Monty—*Monterey Park, CA*—201
Mann, Theodore D.—*Newton, MA*—27
Martinez, Raul L.—*Hialeah, FL*—69
Maurer, Philip R.—*Newport Beach, CA*—209
McCauley, Francis X.—*Quincy, MA*—21
McDermott, Thomas M.—*Hammond, IN*—137
McEnery, Thomas—*San Jose, CA*—206
McKane, Terry J.—*Lansing, MI*—131
McKinley, Bernard—*Waterloo, IA*—141
McNamara, John F.—*Rockford, IL*—140
McNamara, William J.—*New Britain, CT*—22
McNulty, Robert F.—*East Hartford, CT*—23
Meehan, Edward T.—*Mansfield, OH*—137
Menendez, Robert—*Union City, NJ*—56
Mensinger, Peggy—*Modesto, CA*—214, 217
Meyers, Maurice—*Beaumont, TX*—157
Milano, James E.—*Melrose, MA*—15
Milner, Thirman L.—*Hartford, CT*—22
Mitchell, Harry E.—*Tempe, AZ*—179
Mizelle, Johnnie—*Suffolk, VA*—100
Mocol, Herbert—*Mankato, MN*—143

PHOTO CREDITS

Stamford, CT—Mayor's Office

New London, CT—John Bucknavage

Springfield, MA—Michael Gordon

New Haven, CT—Stephanie Gay, *New Haven Register*

Binghamton, NY—Mike Fiur

New York, NY—Holland Wemple

Trenton, NJ—Steve Mervish, *The Trentonian*

Philadelphia, PA—Office of City Representative

Portsmouth, VA—Dennis Mook

Baton Rouge, LA—David Worley and Alan Lively

New Orleans, LA—Joseph Davi

Savannah, GA—Bob Morris, *Savannah News Press*

Kokomo, IN—John Bittner

Milwaukee, WI—Mayor's Office

Chicago, IL—Michelle Agins

Indianapolis, IN—Greg Persell

San Antonio, TX—Mayor's Office

Houston, TX—Owen Johnson

Omaha, NE—James Burnett, *Omaha World Herald*

Cheyenne, WY—M.E. Riley

Phoenix, AZ—Bob Rink

Denver, CO—Joan Schapley

Modesto, CA—Cathy Gorhan

Seattle, WA—Mayor's Office

Oxnard, CA—Mayor's Office

Anchorage, AK—Clark Mischler

INDEX